HERE'S WHAT THE REVIEWERS SAID ABOUT
FILM & VIDEO BUDGETS
(First Edition)

"Invaluable..." **VIDEOGRAM**

"Enjoyable reading even for those that really hate budget but like profits!" **IFPA**

"Effective advice...plus valuable money-saving tips." **VIDEO**

"A factual, detailed guide." **AMERICAN CINEMATOGRAPHER**

"Down-to-earth...valuable for both beginners and experienced independent producers. One comes away using the terminology and budgetary awareness of a professional." **CMJ NEW MUSIC REPORT**

"Shows how to design and compute budgets that will neutralize a financial officer's deepest frown." **CONCISE BOOK REVIEWS**

"Offers many money-saving ideas." **CINEMA CANADA**

"Comprehensive and completely practical." **PHOTOGRAPHER'S MARKET NEWSLETTER**

"Should prove indispensable in an area of research where so little information is available." **SIGHTLINES**

"Anyone contemplating an independent film or video career would do well to read this book." **YOUNG VIEWERS**

"Doesn't overlook even the smallest detail..." **BOOKPAPER**

"Useful advice." **FILM QUARTERLY**

FILM

&

VIDEO

BUDGETS

2ND EDITION

MICHAEL WIESE AND DEKE SIMON

Published by Michael Wiese Productions, 4354 Laurel Canyon Blvd., Suite 234, Studio City, CA 91604 (818) 379-8799 Fax (818) 986-3408.

Cover design by Art Hotel, Los Angeles
Copyediting by Bernice Balfour
Indexing by Ken Lee

Printed by Braun-Brumfield, Inc., Ann Arbor, Michigan
Manufactured in the United States of America

Library of Congress Cataloging in Publication Data

Wiese, Michael, 1947-

    Film & video budgets / by Michael Wiese and Deke Simon. — 2nd ed.
      p.   cm.
   ISBN 0-941188-22-1 : $26.95
    1. Motion picture industry—United States—Finance. 2. Video recordings—United States—Finance. I. Simon, Deke, 1945 - II. Title, III. Title: Film and video budgets.
   PN1993.5.U6W4915   1995
   338.4'779143'0973—dc20   94-48308

CIP   AC

Books by
MICHAEL WIESE

Producer to Producer
Film & Video Financing
Film & Video Marketing
Film & Video Budgets
The Independent Film & Videomaker's Guide
The American Film Institute Seminar: Financing & Producing Video
(audiotapes)

Books from
MICHAEL WIESE PRODUCTIONS

The Digital Videomaker's Guide
Shaking the Money Tree
Film Directing: Shot by Shot
Film Directing: Cinematic Motion
Fade In: The Screenwriting Process
The Writer's Journey

For Geraldine Overton & Julia Bronwyn Wiese,
my loving wife and two-year old daughter,
(who already knows the magical power of pennies)

To my wife Esther, and my daughters Sarah and Lena Simon.
This took a long time, didn't it?
Thanks for hanging in there with me.
I love you all very much.

TABLE OF CONTENTS

Acknowledgments

Many professionals contributed time and advice to make the information in *Film & Video Budgets* as accurate as possible. To them, we say, "Thank you! We owe you one."

- All-Payments Payroll Service, Burbank, CA.
- ASC Video Corp. Burbank, CA. Off-line video editing systems.
- Axium Payroll Services in Los Angeles and New York.
- Michael W. Barnard, filmmaker, Los Angeles, CA.
- Laurie Beale at Gonek Insurance Services, Inc., Woodland Hills, CA.
- Breakdown Services Ltd., Los Angeles, CA - for information about casting.
- Toni Casala, Casala Ltd. Beverly Hills, CA. Teachers/Welfare Workers
- Ron Clark, Pres. of Art/FX, Inc. Hollywood, CA. Graphic Design.
- Bob Dunn of Animal Services of Sylmar, CA.
- Lin Ephraim of Percenterprises Completion Bonds, Inc. L.A., CA. 310/551-0371
- Tom Fineman of the law firm Myman, Abell, Fineman, Greenspan, and Rowan, Brentwood, CA.
- Georgette Green an accountant at Ness Moadeb an Accountancy Corp., Santa Monica, CA.
- Barbara Gregson at Miller-Gregson Prods., Toluca Lake, CA. Clearances for feature film clips, stock shots, and archive footage.
- David Grober, Motion Picture Marine, Marina del Rey, CA. Underwater and topside photography and production.
- Dorain Grusman, LA, CA. Choreographer.
- Rick Hassen, Pacific Ocean Post, Santa Monica, CA.
- Stephen D. Hubbert, Instructional Support Tech., Calif. State Univ. at Long Beach, Long Beach, CA.

- Loni Kaufman, Publisher of <u>The Industry Labor Guide</u> which contains the most requested rates, rules and practices of all the major union agreements.
- Charles Kelly, Sound Mixer, L.A., CA.
- Robert Lakstigala, Designer/Producer and Dragon, Director of Digital Effects, Title House, Hollywood, CA.
- Howard Lavick, Department of Communications Arts, Loyola Marymount University, Westchester, CA.
- Mark Leemkuil, filmmaker.
- Media Services (union and non-union payroll service), in New York, Los Angeles, Vancouver and Toronto.
- Matt Miller and Anita LeGalt of AICP.
- Mike Minkow, Cinema Research Corp., L.A., CA.
- David Pauker, Santa Monica, CA. Post Production Supervisor.
- Brick Price of WonderWorks in Canoga Park, CA. Miniatures.
- Mark Rains, Associate Producer, Van Nuys, CA.
- Judy Santi at Halfnote Music Payroll, L.A., CA.
- Gabrielle Schary, Casting Director, Venice, CA.
- Nancy Severinsen, Film and TV Music Supervisor.
- Title House, Hollywood, CA. Titles and Opticals.
- Juerg Walthers, Director of Photography, L.A., CA.
- Merrill Ward, commercial and music video Producer/Production Mgr. and Assistant Director, world-wide. L.A., CA.
- Tam Warner, Van Nuys, CA. Choreographer.
- Dave Weathers, Supervising Sound Editor for features and TV movies, and Brian Murray at Pacific Ocean Post Sound, Santa Monica, CA.
- West Coast Helicopters, Van Nuys, CA. Aerial photography.
- Wexler Video, Inc., Burbank, CA. Video camera packages.
- Arthur Williams of AICE.
- Dick Ziker of Stunts Unlimited, Hollywood, CA.

INTRODUCTION

INTRODUCTION

The book you hold in your hands may be one of the most powerful tools you will ever encounter to help you produce your films and videos. Understanding budgets is the key to production. Without a road map you'll never make it to your destination on time or on budget.

This book was originally written in 1984 to supplement my first book, *THE INDEPENDENT FILM & VIDEOMAKER'S GUIDE*, which is devoted to the financing and distribution of documentaries and short films. A detailed exploration of budgets was beyond its scope and an area neglected by most books and courses.

Remarkably enough, you can't find another budget book that covers non-feature production. This book has sold more than 30,000 copies and is selling faster today than it did when it first came out. Numerous college film, video, and television classes use this book as a text. I am very proud that the book has been put into service in this way.

But production technologies and processes have changed since 1984 and it was time to completely rewrite, revise, and update every aspect of the first edition. So I turned to my friend and accomplished producer Deke Simon to wrestle with every rate, every line item, and every nuance of production budgeting.

This is not, however, a book about what things cost. The purpose of this book is to get you to seriously think about the production you are budgeting. If you are doing a documentary you might study the documentary budget and hopefully it will remind you of areas you may have overlooked. If you live in New York the budget will probably be higher than if you live in Phoenix or Seattle but not necessarily. It will depend on how well you research your budget, negotiate with crew and facilities, and design your actual budget. This book is a friendly and easy-to-use guide and will give you many ideas about how to approach budgeting, how to look for savings, how to negotiate, and so forth. Sorry, there is no magic formula. **Do not use the rates in this book for your own budgeting.** In the end, you're going to have to do the budget yourself.

Almost every film or video begins with a budget. Whether you are presenting a proposal to a client, a foundation, a government agency, or a department within your corporation, someone will want to see a budget. Budgets are shopping lists with which you determine what you'll need (and what you can afford). Budgets are determined by examining the script, storyboard or breakdown in great detail. Once the budget is defined, it becomes a blueprint for bringing your ideas into reality. Budgeting should excite you by this fact alone: you are moving closer and closer to making your ideas real.

Unfortunately, film and video projects do not allow for too many mistakes. Reputations are made and lost on the answer to the question *"Did you come in on budget?"* The cost of making an image on celluloid or magnetic tape can be significant. So it's best to prepare an accurate and detailed budget and know what you can and cannot afford.

For many people the idea of writing a budget brings on a cold sweat, chills, or the hives. But sooner or later, if you pursue the film or video production business, you will be called upon to account for costs, to prepare a budget. The purpose of this book is to assist you in overcoming your anxieties.

For 25 years, we have been actively involved in producing or overseeing the production of hundreds of hours of film and video programming. It has been our responsibility to negotiate rates with agents, crews, actors, narrators, composers, film labs, film and video equipment houses, post-production and special effect houses, and shipping companies. We've produced pay TV segments, documentaries, features, political television commercials, marketing reels, television spots, promos, shorts, educational films, television programs, infomercials, and all kinds of home videos. Each and every project had a budget.

This book represents our accumulated knowledge and experience. The budget formats in this book use the "standard" methods of production and equipment that most producers will use today. Study them, because besides being a list of necessary expenses, they are also a very well thought-out production process.

On some projects we've saved tens and even hundreds of thousands of dollars. On a few occasions we've blown it and made some expensive mistakes. What we will do in this book is share a career full of insights so you can avoid costly errors and even find savings in your budgets.

Study this book. Challenge it. Make it your own. You may discover many items you would otherwise have overlooked which will be worth the price of the book. Hopefully, our budgets will spark your imagination so that you will find innovative ways to bring more value onto the screen.

When you've completed your budget, your anxiety most likely will be replaced by a calm confidence. You'll know what you are doing. You'll know what you can do and what you can't. You'll know how to maximize whatever budget you have, make it go further, and make a real contribution to the production. We hope that what follows increases your ability to successfully produce your films and videos. Now go get 'em.

Best wishes,

Michael Wiese and Deke Simon
Studio City, California
April 1995

HOW TO USE THIS BOOK

Don't read the whole thing! (Feel better already don't you?!)

However, you will need to understand every line item in your budget and therefore we highly recommend that you first read the **line items** section in this book to familiarize yourself with the precise meaning of the budget items we use in these budgets.

Next, flip directly to the budget that is closest to the project that you are doing. Our budgets should get you 80% or more of the way to determining your own budgets.

If your type of production is not listed then go through our line items **(master template)**, selecting those items that do make up your budget items. Most producers get into trouble with their budgets because they forget something! That's where the information in this book will help immensely. It is very thorough and should give you the confidence that you are covered.

Another thing. Do not take the numbers that we use as the gospel. These numbers only approximate what things cost today in Los Angeles. You can't just take these numbers and plug them into your own budgets. Instead, you will have to research your own production facilities in your own towns and cities. You may readily find that your line items may be lower. In addition, you must negotiate (more on this later) to get the best budget possible. **<u>Do not copy the rates in these budgets.</u>** Sorry folks, there are no shortcuts when it comes to budgeting. You may grumble now, but thank us when you finish your production and still have some money left!

SETTING
UP
A
PRODUCTION
COMPANY

Chapter 1

SETTING UP A PRODUCTION COMPANY

He has half the deed done, who has made a beginning.
Horace, 65 - 8 B.C.

Horace had that right. So did Confucius who coined a similar encouragement five hundred years earlier—*"A journey of a thousand miles begins with the first step."* So let's get started.

Everyone has had to begin at the beginning. If you carefully follow the advice in this book these activities will help you get your own production company up and running. Think of that warm satisfaction that will come over you every morning, when you read your company's name on the door as you enter your office. Hey, we did it!! We're a real company!

For many, starting your own production company may seem daunting. This chapter will help dissolve that feeling of being overwhelmed. Take things one step at a time and you'll get there. Once it's done, you'll have a foundation to build on, dreams to achieve, and a snazzy new business card to flash around.

Incorporation

To incorporate...or not to incorporate? Most lawyers will suggest that you incorporate in order to protect your personal assets from liability.

If you are a United States resident, and plan to have 35 or fewer stockholders, (or maybe just one stockholder, you) most accountants will recommend a Sub-S Corporation. With a Sub-S, your company

11

owes no Federal income tax on profit. The profit passes through the company directly to stockholders (that includes you!). The company will still pay state income tax which, if you pay out or reinvest all your profits at year end, may only be the minimum.

How much does it cost to incorporate? It depends on the state, and on the fees of the attorney or accountant in charge. In California, the Secretary of State gets $900, plus $275 for a seal and stock certificates, plus fees. Shop around for an accountant or lawyer and compare fees. If you already have an accountant, maybe he or she will do it for you inexpensively.

If you choose not to incorporate, then it's probably a good idea to name your company and apply for a "dba", (Doing-Business-As). Your accountant can handle this for you, or you might have a local newspaper that will send you the forms and charge $50 or so for the required announcement in its pages.

Federal ID

Whether you are a dba or incorporated, you still must apply for a Federal ID number, which you need if you plan to pay the people who work on your projects. The ID number exists to help the IRS with its accounting. You can get a File SS4 form from the IRS or go through your accountant. Remember, if you are a sole owner, you are not on the payroll. You take your salary from company profit, and yes, you do owe Federal tax on your salary.

Every payment you receive will be written now to the corporation and not to you personally.

Business License

If you operate your business out of your house you can probably avoid a city business license, but strictly speaking, you should have one if you are a dba or incorporated. It's a city's way of keeping track of commerce, and making a little money—actually a lot of money! In Los Angeles, the minimum fee for motion picture producers whose productions cost less than $50,000 in a given year is $158.89. It goes up from there on a scale. If you are in the maximum production range of $4 million and up, the fee is $13,665.29, but by then you're so rich you don't care. Be sure to check locally for any special allowances for production companies or small businesses—anything for a break. For the first year you usually pay a standard fee, then you pay on the preceding year's gross income. The City Hall Clerk can get you an application form. They will love to help you because this is more money for the city's coffers.

Bank Account

You cannot open a corporate bank account until you have your articles of incorporation (that you prepare before filing for a corporation) and your Federal ID number. The bank will require copies of these documents.

For smaller companies, one business checking account should suffice. Ask if it can be an interest bearing account, which might help offset fees banks charge for business accounts.

If you have a sizable payroll, you may want to set up a separate payroll account and have a payroll service do the paperwork and actual payments. For small payrolls, most businesses do it themselves.

Be sure to go to the bank yourself, introduce yourself to the bank manager, president, or vice president. Get to know them. The day will come when you'll want to borrow money, set up an escrow account, or employ other services. All this will come much easier if they feel they know you.

Corporate Taxes

Surprise — your new business owes the state! Your accountant prepares the state income tax return and calculates what you owe. Happily, there's no Federal corporate income tax if you are a Sub-S Corporation.

Accounting Software

We've heard good things about the Quicken accounting program from Intuit. In most small companies, people do their own book-keeping, or hire a bookkeeper who may come in once a week or more.

Accountant

Your accountant can help you incorporate, give business planning advice, project a business budget, supply you with W-2 and I-9 tax payroll forms, and file your corporate and personal tax returns.

Your accountant will become one of your greatest allies. First, he or she will help you set up your business, making sure you don't miss any filing or tax deadlines. This is their business. What may be hard for you is extremely easy for them. They will enjoy their relationship with a film or video producer because in the same way that numbers baffle you, movies baffle them!

Attorney

Your attorney should be an *entertainment* attorney, as distinct from the garden variety corporate type. Entertainment attorneys know things the rest of us don't but should—like production contracts, options and rights acquisition, licensing, releases of every stripe, and where to have power lunches.

Your attorney should be someone whom you know and respect. Someone who can get things done in the entertainment community. Even if this costs more (on an hourly basis) you will be way ahead of the game when you want to do something whether it's closing an investment deal or getting a distribution contract. In addition, as you work with your attorney you will gain a great deal of knowledge your-self that will be of immeasurable benefit over the years.

Employees

Even in Hollywood, many incorporated production companies are made up of no more than one or two people. When you are in production you have many people on salary. When you are develop-ing your projects you want to have few employees to keep your over-head costs down.

In the beginning you will probably hire a full-time secretary or assistant to help with the administrative chores, which will be many. As your business grows, others will be brought on. Here's where you want to hire the right people for the job. You want people that supplement—no, complement—your skills. If you are not extremely well organized, then look for this quality in those you hire. If you are well organized, then you may want more creative types for those aspects of your business. Do not hire someone just like you, because your aim is to balance your company.

Create a fun atmosphere for people to work in and your productivity will soar. Make sure they are free to make contributions to the projects and credit them appropriately. Giving credit is one of the easiest (and cheapest) things you can do. It's a way of saying thanks that goes a long way.

Becoming a Signatory to Guilds and Unions

You may or may not have to deal with guilds, but in case you do, these are the main guilds (see Appendix for addresses): the Writers Guild of America (WGA), Directors Guild of America (DGA), Screen Actors Guild (SAG), and the American Federation of Radio and Television Artists (AFTRA).

The prevailing wisdom is that by using guild members, you get more experienced actors, writers, and directors, and that's mainly true. On the other hand, it all boils down to who you want to work with. Guild membership doesn't instantly qualify anyone for anything. You have to meet your prospective collaborators and decide for yourself.

Technically, guild members are not supposed to work with a production company that has not signed an agreement with their guild. A writer, actor or director may do it anyway, and sometimes use another name in the credits. Some work non-guild jobs happily, others do it grudgingly. Still others choose not to work with non-signatory companies at all. When guild members choose to work on a non-guild project, make it clear that they do so at their own risk, not the production company's.

15

One producer we know has three different companies: one signatory to SAG and AFTRA, one signatory to SAG, AFTRA, and the DGA, and one that is not signatory to anything. Why go through that paperwork nightmare? He wants to avoid dealing with residual payments for certain projects, and avoid paying the extra expense of pension and health (P&H) that guilds demand—usually around 10% to 13% of the member's gross salary. (For really high salaries, like stars, there is a cut-off beyond which the company does not have to pay P&H. Check with each guild for what it is.)

<u>WGA—Writers Guild of America</u> - To become signatory and hire WGA writers, your company must be legally structured, as in a Sub-S corporation (not a dba). Simply call and request the application forms. There is no fee to become signatory. Your company cannot disengage from signatory status until the current WGA agreement expires, and these agreements run for about five-year terms. You get a copy of the agreement when you join, or you can buy one in advance for around $15 to check it out.

<u>AFTRA– American Federation of Radio and Television Artists and SAG - Screen Actors Guild</u> – The company must be legally structured (not a dba, although there may be exceptions). There are a number of contracts companies can sign, depending on what type of programming they produce (i.e., free TV, cable, public TV, interactive, etc.). There is no fee, but a new company may have to provide a bond to cover payment of actors. Bonds can be in the form of a certified check, or a letter from a payroll service attesting that money is on account.

<u>DGA - Directors Guild of America</u> – The company could be a dba or incorporated or a partnership. The application requests information about stockholders and ownership. It asks for documentation, like a copy of the fictitious name statement or articles of incorporation. In most cases, the company must have a project lined up in order to become signatory. They want to know what the project is, what DGA member functions you'll be hiring, where the financing comes from, and if you have a distributor. Basically, they want to make sure members will be paid. If the financing looks shaky, they

may ask to put the DGA money in escrow. For TV movies and features, they may demand a security agreement that puts a lien on the film in case you go bankrupt. That way they can better collect any residuals. There is no fee to sign up.

IATSE - The crafts people and technicians who work in television and movies are represented by the International Alliance of Theatrical and Stage Employees (IATSE), and a host of other locals, including the Teamsters (the people who drive all the studio trucks and vans). Because it is such a complicated web, it can be extremely frustrating to get signatory information. You may end up gabbing with the secretary at the Plasterers and Cement Finishers local.

First of all, if you're a small production company doing low budget projects, you probably won't want to become signatory to the IA. The problem for little guys is that the sometimes restrictive practices and benefits packages make it too expensive. But just in case you need to know, here is some information.

Why become signatory to IATSE? The theory goes that union crews (camera operators, sound mixers, grips, electrics, etc.) are more experienced, hence more efficient. This is usually true—although there are plenty of excellent people who are not union members.

When you hire union crews, there's no negotiating; you pay whatever the going rate is for that job, plus the usual payroll taxes anyway. Plus you'll pay union fringes: Current Health/Retiree Health and Pension at approximately $2.40 per hour for every hour worked or guaranteed. Employees hired by the day get an additional 7.7% of their day's pay (paid at straight time rate) for Vacation/ Holiday. Employees hired by the week already have the 7.7% factored into the weekly rate.

To become signatory, write a letter expressing interest in becoming signatory. The address for the Los Angeles office is in the Resources section, but there are offices in most major cities. They send back a three-page questionnaire. If you are approved, you're in. For production companies, there's no fee. If you can't find the right office, call a payroll service (a company that handles union and non-union payroll for production companies), since these people seem to know the most about unions.

Bon Voyage

It may take you a week or two or several months to do all the paperwork required to set up your production company and become signatory to some or all of the unions.

If you are just getting started and want to get your feet wet on a production or two, then you probably won't go through this step. When you do set up your first corporation you'll find that it isn't as intimidating as you thought, and you'll feel empowered because now you are just like the big guys with all the same rights and privileges. Not only that, as president of your own corporation your parents will have something new to brag about around the neighborhood!

What follows is the nuts and bolts of budgeting; a potpourri of ideas that will help you think through and prepare your own production budgets.

If you come in under budget you'll be a hero. If you go over budget, the reputation will come to haunt you. This book is designed to help you become remembered for your remarkable foresight and ability to deliver a project on time and on budget. That's what clients, backers, and employees expect.

By careful planning and researching you can create a very accurate budget before the cameras roll.

PRE-PRODUCTION

Chapter 2

PRE-PRODUCTION

I know...why don't we put on a show!!

Ask any production veteran — Pre-Production will make you or break you. This is where you make the plans you live with in Production and Post. It's a grand scheme made up of a dizzying number of details. One production manager we know made big points with the executive producer by handing him a cup of espresso while on location in the middle of nowhere. Of course, that wouldn't have amounted to a hill of coffee beans if the production manager had forgotten to order lunch for the crew, and there was no food for a hundred miles, or a shortage of film stock.

Pre-Production is made easier by having a checklist that contains practically every personnel function, every service, and every piece of equipment you might use. For our purposes, that's the Budget Line Items section in this book. Use it to help you think through every phase of Pre-Production, Production, and Post. What you don't need from the list, discard.

We find it helpful when doing a budget to actually visualize a shoot, day by day, hour by hour, imagining what everyone is doing at any given time. This kind of detailed thinking also helps to work out the daily schedules.

It's important to think about contingencies during this phase. What if the weather turns bad? Do we have an alternate location? Is there something else we can shoot so we don't waste the day? What if we need something we don't have? Where are the nearest hardware stores, gas stations, restaurants, groceries, rental cars, and so on. If a crew member gets sick, do we have a list of people we can call? (For more tips and wise thoughts from old-timers, see the Money-Saving Ideas section.)

While the Budget Line Items is the ultimate Pre-Production checklist, here are some other goods and services you'll need during this stage.

Legal

If you don't have one, find an entertainment lawyer you can work with. Don't be afraid to call several. You will find them in or around the larger entertainment cities like New York and Los Angeles. Explain that you are interviewing prospective lawyers and you'd like to meet and talk about your project. Our experience has been that they are nice people who won't eat you for lunch—they may even take you to lunch. If you're not familiar with things legal, don't be afraid to ask all the questions people are too afraid to ask, like "Are you charging us for this meeting?"

In the meeting, explain the project, and ask about what services your lawyer will perform, and how much it will cost. For budgeting, you'll need to know how much to allot for the entire project. Some lawyers charge by the hour, but many accept a flat fee for a project, or a percentage of the budget. An average TV movie, for example, might have a budget of $2.5 million, of which 1% to 1.5% might go for legal fees. Once you've interviewed a few attorneys, you'll have a good sense of the range of prices for your project.

Your lawyer will probably generate various deal memos, contracts, personal release forms/materials releases/location releases, rights options, and the like. Tons of carefully worded paper will cross your desk and make you cross-eyed. Eventually you'll get used to it. Then it'll actually start to make sense.

One way to save money in the future is to enter these documents into your computer. On your next project, you may need to merely alter some details. Discuss this with your lawyer first, because laws change, and you may waste time generating your own document only to have your lawyer recommend a new one. In any case, you'll still want him or her to review documents before they go out for signature.

Some specialized stationers and bookstores, like Enterprise Stationers and Samuel French Books (see Resources section), have sample contract books for sale. These can often get you started, but the safest tack is to have your attorney examine any proposed contract.

Rights Acquisition

Is your project based on a book, article, stage play, screenplay, radio play, or someone's life story? If so, you'll need to get the rights to produce it. If it's published, call the publisher, and ask who owns the rights. If that doesn't work, try a large copyright search firm like Thomson and Thomson (800) 692-8833. If you're really desperate, try calling the U.S. Copyright Office, Washington, DC, (202) 707-3000. (There's a research fee of $20 per hour, and you can talk to the research people there for an estimate of how long it will take.) When you've tracked down who actually owns the rights you can negotiate to buy the rights or buy an option. You'll probably want your lawyer to advise you, since rights acquisition can be tricky.

An option gives you the exclusive right to later acquire the rights to a book or some other property. Here's how it works. An option allows you to tie up the property for a specified period of time (usually a year or two). This means no one else can take the project from you. During the option period, you will look for financing, write script drafts, and attract stars. The option agreement usually states that if the term ends with no production agreement, and if the option is not renewed, then the rights revert back to the original owner. If, however, the project goes forward, the option will spell out the terms for actually buying the rights, including how much money and profit participation (if any) the owner will get. Option agreements can be simple or complex, depending on the property and who is involved. We've bought options for a dollar. We argue that our time trying to get the property into production is worth something and refuse to pay for an option. Other times, when it's clear the property has immediate value, you must pay for an option. If it's Liz Taylor's life story, expect to pay a few hundred thousand.

On the other hand, if the property you want to produce has been published in another form, then you must acquire the rights. Having control of a property is the first element you need to begin to leverage your project into reality. If you don't write a script yourself then you'll have to option or buy the rights to one.

Staff Contracts

If your company has become a signatory to one or more of the guilds, you may want to use standard deal-memo forms for personnel such as writers (WGA), directors, stage managers, associate directors, unit production managers (DGA), and actors, dancers, narrators (SAG and AFTRA).

Call the guilds (see Appendix) and ask for copies of the standard forms appropriate to your project (i.e., feature film, videotape music concert, etc.). Have your lawyer review the forms just in case they need to be customized. If a guild doesn't have forms, it's up to your lawyer to create the contract, which, in most cases, is fairly simple.

The deal memos state that you agree not to pay less than the guild minimum scale. To find out how much that scale is, as well as basic guild rules, you need to refer to the appropriate rate cards and Basic Agreement books, which you get from the guilds. (Also see Resources section for The Labor Guide.) We advise getting the books and cards, even though you may wind up calling back several times to confirm the rates, residuals, and other matters for your specific project. It's now a running joke in our office that whoever gets to confirm rates with a certain guild (which shall remain nameless) also gets a free hour of psychotherapy and a group hug. That's because the rates seem to change overnight depending on whom you talk to. We usually go back and forth a few times until it's finally settled. (Also see "Negotiating with Crews" later in this chapter.)

Music Clearance

If copyrighted music is an important part of your project, start the clearance process as soon as the script is "locked," that is, approved. Why start early? Some music may be too expensive, or perhaps the owner won't give permission for its use. Until you know what you can use, and how much it will cost, your budget will be incomplete.

When you clear a piece of music, you pay a license fee to the copyright owner in exchange for the right to use that music in your show. The price depends on what medium you use (i.e., feature film, television, home video, CD-ROM, etc.), what territories you'll distribute to (U.S., North American, European, etc.), and what term you want, or can afford (three years, five years, perpetuity) .

Many producers use a music clearing service to track down copyright owners and negotiate prices. If your needs are at all complex, this is the way to go, since it is a specialized business. If clearances are not obtained correctly, and if you're caught, owners can get nasty and throw injunctions at you, forcing you to re-edit or even destroy release prints or dubs.

Music clearance services do charge different fees for their work, so call a few to compare. If you're in New York or Los Angeles (or at your public library), check the Business to Business phone directory for either city to get a listing. Clearance services are also listed in such production guides as *The LA 411*, *The NYPG* (New York Production Guide), and *The Hollywood Reporter Blu Book*, available at many bookstores.

It is prudent to contact a clearance service or your attorney, even if you believe your music to be in the public domain, or if you intend to claim "fair use." Public domain music must be verified as such, and "fair use," while it may apply to limited use of music in news, criticism or scholarship, may or may not be appropriate for your project. And one last little tip. Somebody started the rumor that producers can use up to eight bars of a song without paying for it. Sorry—no can do.

Feature Film Clips

If you want to use clips from Hollywood feature films in your project, you may be in for a trip on a long and winding road. With patience and perseverance you will prevail. The cost per clip depends on the rights you or your distributor needs. So the first step is to call your distributor and find out. If you don't have one yet, then anticipate what rights you'll need by talking to a few producers of similar projects who have been through the distribution wars.

What rights are there to be had? The big banana is "worldwide (or as they sometimes say, 'throughout the universe'), in all media, in perpetuity," which means you can use the clip in any territory (or on any planet), in films, television, interactive, and home video for all eternity. Ask for these rights first, because you never know, you just might get them. On the other hand, if you really don't need these rights (they will cost more), go for what you do need. Most major studios, for example, won't grant rights in perpetuity—the usual term is three years or so. (This is usually not long enough for home video distribution which generally requires seven years.)

Rights are broken down by territory and by media/distribution format. For example you could ask for:

U.S. & Territories TV rights
North American TV rights
World TV rights/ World TV
All Rights (includes free TV/pay TV/cable TV/satellite-delivered
  TV)/HomeVideo/Airline/Non-Theatrical
  (educational)/Interactive, and so forth.

Be clear about what rights and clips you need from the outset; otherwise, the conversation gets confusing very fast. After you know what rights you want and what clips you want, how do you find out who owns the feature film so you can start negotiating?

First, try calling the studio directly. Remember that over the years, many film libraries have been sold, and you need to find the current owner. If you've rented the video, check the front or tail credits for the distribution company's logo.

Or, you can try a number of reference books:

- The BIB Books is a four volume series from the Broadcast Information Bureau in Philadelphia (215) 238-5300. The books are a compilation of all films, TV films, series, specials, etc., appearing on television. Distributor information is provided. The cost is a mere $725 for all four volumes, or you can buy last year's set at half price. If you live in L.A., try the poor man's way with a visit to the Academy of Motion Picture Arts and Sciences Library. If you live elsewhere, try charming your way into a local television station that may have a copy.

- Footage '91: North American Film and Video Sources. The book describes 1,750 sources of archival and stock footage of every kind. Cost is $115 plus shipping. Also available on CD-ROM for Mac ($199.95 plus shipping). Call 800-633-2033.

- There is also an international group called Focal (Federation of Commercial Audio Visual Libraries Ltd.) in London. From the U.S., call 44-81-423-5853. Their publication lists many sources for footage around the world.

- The U.S. Copyright Office, Washington, DC, (202) 707-3000 will do a search to determine ownership or whether a film is in the public domain. There is a charge of $20 per hour.

Finally, you can hire a research and clearance service to locate the owners, and negotiate the rights. Services charge by the hour, or anywhere from $1,000 to $2,000 per week, depending on the show, its length, the nature of the clips etc. Finding a research and clearance person can be tough, since they aren't listed in the yellow pages. Some of the above clip reference books may have lists. Or ask for a recommendation from a studio's clip licensing department. Even if you've used a service, have your own attorney review the license agreements from the studios before you sign.

So now you've located the owner and negotiated the rights for the license fee. Are you done? Nope. Many producers forget the next step, and pay dearly when they go over budget.

The use of many clips requires the producer to get permission from, and pay residuals to "third parties" like actors, writers, and directors. (On many pre-1960 features, you don't need to do this, but ask the studio if there are any outstanding items to clear with third parties, regardless of the year of release. Fred Astaire, for example, had a permission clause put into his contracts as early as the 1940s, and now producers must go through his estate!)

All actors <u>recognizable in a scene</u> must give their permission, and be paid at least SAG/AFTRA scale (call the respective guild for clip rates). Stunt people get more money and may even ask for what they originally got for the stunt! You are excused from crowd scenes with extras, but crowd scenes with recognizable credited actors must be cleared. For the writers and directors of the film with your desired clip, call the respective guild for clip rates.

Somehow, producers can get the idea that since they worked so hard and paid so much to license a film clip, the musical score ought to be part of the deal. Sometimes it is, but most of the time it's not. If not, add that to the list for the music clearance (see above).

Archive Film Clips and Stock Footage

Need clips from old movies, newsreels, old cartoons, educational films and the like? Need a stock shot of a 1977 Mustang cruising Hollywood Boulevard?

Studios have a <u>stock footage department</u> where standard fees average $50 per foot (on 35 mm) with a 10-foot minimum cut ($500). Or go to a <u>stock footage library</u>. Some have both stock and archival footage, while some specialize in one or the other. Also see the *Footage '91* book as mentioned above.

Here's the way archive footage works by way of a recent example.

We needed a series of "impact" shots for an athletic shoe commercial—funny shots of old cars, planes, people, and cartoon characters crashing into things or getting creamed in imaginative ways. We called five different stock footage companies, and each happily supplied us with a 3/4 inch or VHS preview reel of shots they thought we'd like. The charges for researching and assembling these reels varied from zero (we went there and screened stuff for an afternoon) to around $150 for about an hour's worth of clips. We then picked the clips we liked, and edited them into the off-line version of the spot. We sent the spot back to the stock footage library with a list of the clips so they could see for themselves how many seconds of each clip we used. We paid for each clip by the second (rates ranged from $25 to $45 in this case). The library sent us a clean master on BetaSP, which we edited into the spot in our On-Line session.

Michael says, "I executive-produced a feature documentary, THE BEACH BOYS: AN AMERICAN BAND. The rights clearances filled two books larger than two New York City phone books. For every clip we used, even if it was only a few feet long, we had to get something like nine underlying rights; the master recording license, the sync license, the footage rights, celebrity appearances, background actors, plus guild payments to writers, directors, and musicians (other than the Beach Boys). It was horrendous and consumed an extraordinary amount of time. I believe a paralegal worked on the project for a year and a half just clearing rights. When all was said and done we learned that we had missed a few that almost resulted in major litigation and required an additional $60,000 to make the suit 'go away'. You've got to really make sure the bases are covered when you do programs that use so much of other people's source materials."

The Script

Once a feature script has been approved by whoever green-lights the project, it is ready for <u>script breakdown</u>, to be analyzed for its production elements. The same applies to any script, from student film to industrial to commercial.

How many actors does it have, how many locations, props, stunts, special effects, and so forth? Script breakdown is beyond the scope of this book, but two good references are <u>Film Scheduling</u> by Ralph Singleton. and <u>The Hollywood Guide to Film Budgeting and Script Breakdown for Low Budget Features</u> by Danford Chamness. (There are also software programs for script breakdowns and scheduling that tie in to budget programs.) In the sequence of things, once a script has been broken down, it is ready for budgeting and scheduling.

The Script / Budget Connection

A budget is not realistic unless it is based on a final shooting script. A shooting script will help determine the number of days, number of locations, setups per day, and crew size that will be necessary. Travel and location expenses can be accurately calculated. Actors, props, costumes—every detail will have a direct cost associated with it. Without a shooting script you are reduced to guesswork.

Some filmmakers would rather get a lump sum (say $100,000) and assume this will certainly be enough to produce their film. They lack the willingness to work out in advance what they will need for each and every item. An investor will, on the other hand, look for a film or videomaker with a professional attitude—one who can submit a complete and accurate budget. Film and tape production is far too complex to "guess" or "feel" what it will cost.

If you are making a documentary film, do not use the standard rule-of-thumb so often quoted that says 16mm documentaries cost $2,000 per minute. If you make this assumption, a 10-minute documentary would cost $20,000. It might. It might not. The "guestimate" is meaningless because it may not take into account costs such as animation, titles, special effects, talent, locations, sets, and so forth. Whenever possible get a finished script (better yet, a finished script plus storyboards) and then begin budgeting. Scenes are easy and cheap to change on paper, but once you're shooting, it can be like turning around the Queen Mary in a bathtub.

The Summary Budget

A "detailed" budget lists each and every line item. A multimillion dollar feature budget could run a hundred pages. A "summary" budget, also called a "topsheet," is just that—a summary. It groups the line items into categories so that an investor or client need only look at one short page to see how the money is allocated. The categories might be grouped like this:

01-00 Story Rights
02-00 Script
03-00 Producer's Unit
04-00 Direction
05-00 Cast
06-00 Travel and Living—Producers/Director
07-00 Travel and Living—Cast
08-00 Residuals
09-00 Above-the-Line Fringe

10-00 Production Staff
11-00 Extra Talent
12-00 Sound Stage
13-00 Production Design
14-00 Set Construction
15-00 Set Operations
16-00 Special Effects
17-00 Set Dressing
18-00 Property
19-00 Wardrobe
20-00 Make-Up and Hair
21-00 Electrical
22-00 Camera
23-00 Sound
24-00 Transportation
25-00 Location Expenses
26-00 Picture Vehicles/Animals
27-00 Film and Lab
28-00 Travel and Living—Crew

29-00 Below-the-Line Fringe
30-00 Editorial
31-00 Post-Production Videotape/Film and Lab
32-00 Optical Effects
33-00 Music
34-00 Post-Production Sound
35-00 Titles and Graphics
36-00 Stock Footage
37-00 Insurance
38-00 General and Administrative Expenses

This sequence of categories is fairly standard, but different producers and studios often create their own versions. Once you have assessed all your categories and line items, feel free to group them in any way you (and your accountant) like. (You will be assigning each category code numbers for tracking purposes, as above, but more on that later.)

There are standardized budget formats, like those used by the AICP (Association of Independent Commercial Producers—see Appendix), that are used for commercial bidding. With this format, an ad agency or client can quickly review competitive bids from different producers and compare costs on a line-by-line basis before awarding a contract. Other producers who like the AICP format simply borrow it for their own use.

The budgets in this book are arranged according to the Summary Budget above. It is a format that has been useful for us, but feel free to adapt it to your own needs. Use whatever format works for you. All the budgets in this book are available from MWP as an Excel document for the Macintosh. (See back of book for the order form.)

Negotiations

Negotiating is a fundamental skill in producing. Actually, it is just clear communication. If you are good at it, you can reduce your costs 10%, 20%, 30%, or more. Webster's definition of *negotiation* is "to confer, bargain, or discuss with a view of reaching agreement, to succeed in crossing, surmounting, moving through." For our purposes, it is when two or more people settle on the specific terms of the exchange. This could take the form of cash payment, deferred payment, title credits, profit sharing, or any number of other elements. (We believe there should always be some form of an exchange even if you are getting something for free—such as a thank you note or flowers.)

An agreement is only an agreement when both parties agree upon the terms of the exchange. If this is not the case, you are still negotiating. You're going to have to negotiate. There's no way around it. This skill allows you to do "more with less." It gives you the opportunity to clearly define the exchange with the people with whom you'll work.

Too often, wages and prices are not fully discussed. Each person has only a partial understanding of the arrangement. Assumptions are made and it's not until the bill comes and all hell breaks loose that the differences are apparent. Then it's too late. Feelings are hurt. Trust and confidence are broken. Friends are lost. And to top it all off, more money is spent than planned—all because the terms of the agreement were not clear. This just cannot happen if you want to produce films. Life is too short. It's better to learn how to negotiate, come to an honorable agreement, and get on with it.

In America and most Western countries people somehow feel funny about negotiating. They pay the full price rather than face the embarrassment of negotiating. But in the Far East, Southeast Asia, India and Africa, negotiating is considered polite. If you negotiate, you get involved with people, you learn something about each other. It's extremely rude in Java to pay the first price asked. It's expected that one will banter back and forth two or three times before settling on a price. It's part of the accepted social exchange.

(An interesting note: in Indonesia it's not buyer beware but seller beware. If you charge an unfair price you will be ostracized. It's considered very poor manners to charge too high a price.)

In the Western world—where the attitude is there's a sucker born every minute—remarkably, people are still embarrassed to question a price tag or a rate card even when it seems too high. But when they do, more often than not the price will be reduced. You <u>can</u> get a discount on a refrigerator at Sears or an Eclair at Camera Mart, but first you've got to ask.

<u>Question every price.</u>

Could the price be lower? Assume it can. Don't accept the first quote offered. Write it down. Don't worry, it'll still be there when you come back. In film and tape production, prices are more flexible than you might assume. Freelancers' rates are flexible. So are rates at labs, equipment rental houses, and video editing facilities. You simply have to ask! It's not unusual to receive anywhere from 5% to 50%.

<u>Shop around.</u>

Check at least three sources for the same job or piece or equipment—prices can vary tremendously. Once when we needed a special effect, we were quoted three prices: $4,500, $2,000, $600. Through these discussions we studied the effect and found a way to do it for $300. It finally cost 15 times less than the first estimate!

<u>Give yourself time.</u>

Do the necessary research to find the best price and the best quality. If you are forced to do something right away (for example, typeset titles on a Sunday), you will spend two or three times the normal price for "rush charges." Furthermore, with added pressure the job may not come out as well as you hoped. Rush shipping is usually an unnecessary waste. The difference between a next-day delivery ($17) and same-day delivery ($150) is significant. Leave enough time to do the job well. Plan ahead and save money.

<u>Collect information.</u>

Give yourself time to collect information, and you'll be ahead of the game. Most information is free. If you are too busy, hire a research assistant. The more you learn, the more options you'll discover. You'll find new technical processes, locate facilities, and be less willing to pay the first price quoted. The more "mystical" or complex a job seems to you, the more it will cost. Once understood, these things lose their mystique. With enough time and information, and the willingness to negotiate rates, you'll gain that necessary edge to make the best deal possible and save money. You'll also find better ways of doing the job.

Negotiating with Crews

Take time to talk with the person you want to hire. Describe the shoot, what you want to accomplish, the working conditions, who else will be in the crew and cast. Learning about the project will increase his or her interest in joining you. The person will get an image of what the shoot will be like and all its intangible benefits. Perhaps the shoot includes locations in Taiwan and he's always wanted to go there. Perhaps she'll be working with a favorite actor or personality. Maybe the cause of the film is close to his heart. Or maybe none of the above counts and it's strictly business, but at least you tried.

Michael says, "I recently spent two weeks in Sydney , Australia, interviewing directors of photography, production managers, and art directors for a feature I'd like to do in Bali. I chose Australia because the strong dollars' exchange rate immediately gives me a 25% edge. But more important, I found out that Australians have worked throughout the South Pacific so they are accustomed to the weather, working conditions, and accommodations. Many had even worked in Bali before. Each person had his own strengths and weaknesses but overall of the twenty some people I interviewed I only found two with whom I wouldn't want to work. Now that's the kind of situation you want to be in when looking for department heads and crews.

"I was also able to place these people (by asking their colleagues) into A, B, and C categories in regard to their experience and fees. This gave me a financial and experience palette with which to work."

What follows may get a little thick. For many readers, this is more information than you will need to know. For others, as your production budgets increase your knowledge of negotiations will necessarily have to increase as well. We decided we'd lay out the details for you so you'd know what you will one day have to face. Hang in there, take it a chunk at a time, and you'll see it's not as intimidating as it seems at first glance.

Flat Rates vs. Hourly Rates

There is great confusion in the industry about hiring a crew member for a flat rate of say $300 for a day's work, a "day" being anything the producer says it is. Producers love this approach because they can work crews until they drop from exhaustion and not pay any overtime. Crew people hate these kinds of flats, for obvious reasons.

The fact is, except for some positions (see <u>Exceptions to the overtime rule</u> below), the labor law (1994) says people must be paid at regular, straight time wages for the first 8 hours of work per day, or for the first 40 hours of work per week. For non-union workers the wages are negotiable, for union workers they are set. Any hours worked over those must be paid at 1.5 times the regular rate (time and a half) up to 12 hours in a day. In some states, after 12 hours, the employer must pay double time. Other states do not have such a rule, and the worker continues to be paid at time and a half. Call a payroll service to find out the rules that apply to the state in which you are shooting.

Exceptions to the overtime rule.

Such positions as Production Designer, Director of Photography, Art, Director, Set Decorator, Production Accountant, or a Costume Designer are "on call." These people are regarded as "management" of a sort, since they head their departments. This means that in non-union situations, the person can be hired by the week, at a flat rate, with no allowance for overtime. In union cases, there are limits, and overtime pay, that vary by the job and by state.

Here's an example of how the wage structure can work for regular employees:

Key Grip (non-union)

Let's say you offer the Key Grip the hourly rate of $20. This means you'll pay him $20 per hour for 8 hours of work. That's a minimum guarantee. If you let him go after 7 hours, he still gets $160. (A half-hour for lunch is not counted as work time.) Every hour after 8, and up to 12, he gets time and a half, in this case $30. If he works 12 hours (a typical day), he gets $280. Any time after 12 hours may be double time (some states have it, others do not), in this case $40, and the second meal is counted as work time (i.e., do not deduct it). If he works for eleven and three quarter hours, you prorate the hourly wage to the nearest quarter hour. Because he is non-union, he gets no benefits for pension, health, vacation and holiday. You do apply normal employer contributions for Social Security, etc., in the form of an approximately 18% payroll tax.

Key Grip (union)

With the union worker, in this case IATSE, the minimum straight time wage is set. For First Company Grips in Los Angeles, it's $26.98 for the first 8 hours. If you are budgeting for a 12-hour day, that's $215.84 for 8 hours, and $40.47 for 4 hours, or $161.88. (After 12 hours, it's double time.) The total for 12 hours is $377.72.

Because he is an IATSE member, he also gets Pension and Health benefits to the tune of $2.46 for every hour worked ($2.46 x 12 = $29.52). Plus 7.719%, based on straight time pay for Vacation and Holiday ($26.98 x 8 hrs. x .07719% = $16.66). The grand total (without payroll tax) is $377.72 + $29.52 + $16.66 = $423.90 for 12 hours of work. The payroll tax is figured on the gross wages not including benefits, in this case $377.72.

Let's say you're doing a non-union show, you're fat on script and lean on money. You anticipate going 12-hour days. So calculate your hourly rates for crew by working backward.

For example, you figure the show can afford to pay a Key Grip $300 for a day's work of 12 hours, with no double time. If you break that out, it becomes $21.42 per hour for 8 hours, and $32.13 per hour (time and a half) for 4 hours.

When you call the Key Grip, explain that you're paying $21.42 per hour for 8, and time and a half after that. Now there's no potential for confusion.

Work Hours and Pay Hours

For budgeting purposes, there's an easy way to figure your total gross wages, and that is to distinguish between *work hours* and *pay hours*. Work hours are the total hours worked, in the case of our Key Grip that's 12 hours. Of his 12 hours, 8 hours are on straight time, and 4 hours are at time and a half. Those 4 hours of time and a half equals 6 *pay hours*. How do we get that? Multiply the number of overtime hours worked (4) times the pay rate (time and a half or 1.5). 4 x 1.5 = 6, so the *total pay hours* are 8 + 6 = 14.

When you do your budget, instead of spending time calculating the time and a half pay for all your different hourly employees, do it the quick way. If you know you're budgeting for a 12-hour day (12 *work* hours), you simply multiply the person's hourly rate times 14 *pay* hours. In the Key Grip's case, that's $26.98 x 14 = $377.72.

In states with <u>no</u> double time, a 13-hour work day is 15.5 pay hours. A 14 hour work day is 17 pay hours.

In states <u>with</u> double time after 12 hours, a 13-hour day is 16 pay hours. A 14-hour day is 18 pay hours.

When you negotiate with your crew people, be straightforward and honest, so everyone knows what the deal is. By starting with an hourly rate, and knowing it goes to time and a half between the 8th and 12th hours worked, maybe double time after that, you've made it crystal clear.

Most people will not work for less than an 8-hour minimum (for unions it's standard). The exceptions are when you are hiring someone for a longer project and they'll throw in a few half-days. If it's a union shoot, review what the P&H and Vacation and Holiday rates are, and how they are applied.

Another note on double time.

In states like California that mandate double time after 12 hours, there is a common but technically illegal practice you should be aware of. When booking crew, some producers try to wangle the double time out of the equation. They'll say, "Oh, by the way, we may go over 12 hours on this day or that, do you think you could waive the double time, and count extra hours as time and a half?" The crew member, wanting the gig, will often comply. Whether you use this ploy is your business, but if you do, make sure the same rules apply to everyone.

Finally, you or the Production Coordinator should prepare a deal memo for each crew member, reiterating the hourly wages, and the formula for paying them. The crew member signs it, then the Producer signs it. No confusion. Standard deal memo forms are available by mail from Enterprise Stationers (see Appendix).

Budget for at least 12 hours of work per day, and try to allow an extra 10% of the person's gross wages for an "overtime" contingency. Some producers reduce the overtime contingency to 5% and just routinely budget for 13- or 14-hour days. It really depends on the demands of the script or the shooting situation.

Work out what you will offer for hourly rates in the budget before you make your calls to crew, and <u>be consistent in your rates across the various departments</u>. This is important, because if you are inconsistent you'll have unhappy people on the set, or spend valuable time renegotiating rates. For example, the Gaffer's rate should be the same as the Key Grip's rate. The Best Boy Electric and Best Boy Grip rates should be the same. All Grips and Electrics should get the same. And so on. People know what the show is paying, and they can take it or not.

What do you do if you really want a particular crew person, a Key Grip for example, but your hourly rate is too low? Try sweetening the deal with a little more money on the "kit rental" (the box of supplies he brings to the job). That way, you've kept his rate the same as those on a comparable level, but he's making a bit more money for his tools and equipment. Do this only if this is someone you cannot live without, otherwise, you'll be making side deals on kit rentals all over the place and leaking money for no good reason. Generally, if you can't make suitable deals within your budget, look elsewhere.

If you have negotiated your deals honestly and fairly with the above formula, you eliminate the jealousies that can occur when people in the same job level make different amounts of money. There are no secrets on the set. If there are inequities they'll be exposed before the first roll of film.

Sometimes you'll be doing a non-union shoot, and calling union members to work on it. You need to say it's non-union, because union crews are used to getting whatever the minimum rate is for that job, plus union fringes.

IATSE's fringes are current Health/Retiree Health and Pension at approximately $2.46 per hour for every hour worked or guaranteed. Members hired by the day get an additional 7.7% of their day's pay (paid at straight time rate) for vacation/holiday. Employees hired by the week already have the 7.7% factored into the weekly rate.

Invoice Fees

This brings up the "invoice fee." Some crew people who usually work on big budget productions like concerts and awards shows will work non-union only if they are given an "invoice fee," which is extra money comparable to the union fringes. It is paid as a percentage (usually 20% - 25%) of their gross wages. If this is the case, and you are not a union signatory, you may as well go through a union payroll service and pay the union fringes that way. Or look elsewhere for your crew. Documentary crew people do not usually ask for invoice fees.

Union vs. Non-union — a Note of Caution

Let's say you're doing a non-union show for a large production company, and it's time to staff up. (The following situation is unlikely to happen with a smaller company or a low-budget project.) If you hire union people for your non-union show, and if the union discovers this, it can picket, and you can be pretty sure that union members will not cross the line. The union wants to become the bargaining agent for the crew, and if a certain percentage of the crew votes to have the union represent them, the producer has two choices: either sign a deal with the union, or do not sign. If the producer does not sign, all union members must leave the show (if they want to stay in the union). If you have hired union people in key positions (Gaffer, Key Grip, Sound, Camera, etc.) you'll probably be down for a day or so while you restaff.

What to do? Try to hire non-union people, especially in key positions. How do you know if they are non-union? This part is tricky. It's actually illegal to ask a person if he or she is in the union. Why? Because in the eyes of the law it is deemed discriminatory. You can say, "This is a non-union show, do you have a problem with that?" If you're lucky, the person will volunteer that he is non-union or otherwise available. Otherwise, ask for a resume and then check to see if he works union shows.

Remember, this is unlikely to happen unless you are with a large production company doing a lot of business that the union would like to staff with its people. And please don't take the foregoing as a diatribe against unions. In fact, unions really do provide people with a decent wage and pension/health benefits, and that's to the good.

Your ability to negotiate rates that are affordable and fair have to do with your own relationships with crew members, the attraction of your project, and your production budget. If you have a multimillion dollar budget, it's out of line to ask people to work long days for low pay. If you have a shoestring budget, you'll have to ask for favors.

<u>Here's a checklist to have in front of you when negotiating crew rates</u>.

1. Schedule. The number of prep and wrap days. The number of shoot days. Anticipated number of hours per day.

2. Hourly or weekly rates. Formula for overtime rates consistent with the same level jobs in other departments. No guaranteed minimum hours.

3. Kit Rentals.

4. Meals. Provided or a per diem.

5. Pre-production/technical survey days. Rates.

6. Travel days. Rates.

7. Per diems, lodging, etc.

8. Pay day(s).

9. Payroll taxes for non-union crew.
Pension/health/vacation/holiday fringes for union members.

10. Credits.

11. Profit sharing (if appropriate).

12. Deferments (if appropriate).

Let's take these points one by one:

Schedule
Discuss all "prep," "shoot," and "wrap" days as well as any holi-days, breaks in the schedule, and time off. (Union crews are paid for holidays; non-union generally are not.)

Rates
Hourly or weekly rates as discussed above.

Kit Rentals
Kits contain special tools of the trade, and the production is better off renting them than buying them. Make-Up, Hair, Key Grip, Gaffer, Construction Coordinator, and many other positions have kit rentals (also called "box" rentals). Most people have standard kit fees, but if you need to sweeten the pot for someone while keeping his or her daily wage on a par with others in the same position, upping the kit rental is a way to do it.

Meals
There is a standard practice when it comes to figuring meal time. If the producer caters lunch, the minimum time is one half-hour, and it's off the work clock. If you have a "walk-away" meal, meaning that people are on their own, you must allow one-hour, and only a half-

hour is off the clock. We do not recommend "walk-away's" because that's exactly what happens. An hour and a half later your crew wanders back mumbling about the long lines at Taco Jack's. Generally, breakfasts are offered before the call time, or as "walking meals," meaning people munch as they work. "Second meals," meaning dinners, are counted as work time.

Catering is usually the best bet, since the crew is kept close at hand, and more focused on the shoot. For large crews, hire a catering service, and they can advise you about menus. For small crews of 5 to 15, pass around a menu from a local restaurant that delivers. Don't do what one well-known (but un-named) producer did. The crew had been working hard for 6 hours (the usual maximum span between meals) and there was no lunch in sight. When someone finally brought this to the producer's attention, he sent an assistant out for a bag of candy bars! The crew did not revolt that day, but a lot called in "sick" the next day. We can't stress enough the value of feeding your crew well. It's well worth it.

Pre-Production/Technical Survey Days
Pre-production meetings and technical surveys (also called "tech scouts") can be anything from a minimum 8-hour call with overtime (union) to a negotiated half day rate (non-union). These meetings and surveys prepare people for the job, and are usually well worth the expense.

Travel Days
Again, there are no set rules. Travel days can be 50% of the daily straight time rate (non-union) to an 8-hour minimum with overtime (union). The producer pays for all transportation, including taxis, limousines, air fares, and extra baggage related to the show.

Lodging/Per Diem
Lodging is arranged and paid by the producer. On overnight trips, a per diem ($40 to $50 per day) is usually paid to each crew member to cover meals and incidentals. When lunches on the set are provided by the producer, you can either deduct the cost of lunch from the per diem, or let it slide and create some good will. By choos-

ing to eat breakfasts and dinners at McDonald's, the crew will take home more cash. On low budget productions, the per diem may be miniscule or non-existent, as long as the producer provides all meals.

Pay Day
Be specific on the pay schedule and stick to it. Paying people on time will quickly gain you a favorable reputation. Slow or non-payment will also earn you a reputation!

Payroll Taxes—Pension and Health
(Also see Chapter 4, *Above-The-Line Fringe*, and *Below-The-Line Fringe*)

To hire union employees on an official union shoot, either the production company or the payroll service must be a signatory. Consult the union rate card or the payroll service for the appropriate fringes in your state.

As an employer, you'll be paying the usual FICA, FUI, SUI, and Workers' Compensation on any employee's payroll, union or not. Check with your accountant and your union local or payroll service for up-to-date figures.

If you hire non-union people, we suggest you deduct taxes per the W-2 IRS Form completed by the employee. You can only pay on a 1099 Form (and not withhold taxes) if the employee is a true Independent Contractor, which is to say he has a company and a Federal ID number. If you've hired someone as an independent contractor and he doesn't have a Federal ID number and he doesn't pay his taxes, the IRS can and will go after the production company for an employee's delinquent taxes. Life is too short for that mess.

Credits
Commercials, music videos, and sometimes industrials give no on-screen credit. Features and documentaries do. With above-the-line credits, and a few below-the-line, like Director of Photography, Production Designer, Composer, Line Producer, and Editor, discuss the size and placement of the credit. With crew, once the credit is

determined, and included in the deal memo, its size and placement is left to the producer's discretion. If credits are a puzzlement, rent a few videos that are like your project and write down the sequence and placement.

Profit Sharing
On most projects there probably will not be profit sharing, but if you feel someone has made a major contribution to the film, or worked for low or no wages, compensation can be enhanced by a percentage of the profits. (In order to give away percentages you must be sure your project is structured so that you can do so. Ask your lawyer.)

Deferments
Deferments are salaries which are paid later. Deferments are almost unheard of on large projects, but smaller projects that are labors of love are another story. If you are paying someone on deferment, you both should have a clear, written understanding of when the deferment is paid. Before the investors receive their money? Before the actors? After any over-budget expenses are paid first? Exactly when?

Anyone taking a deferment will appreciate this demonstration of integrity and responsibility.

Michael says, "We recently did an infomercial that made a lot of money for the sponsor. I decided to put together the financing for our own infomercial. I went back to everyone who'd worked on the previous job and said that I'd be willing to pay their full fee (as before) or they could defer some or all of their fee for some equity in the profits from the infomercial. Everyone either deferred all or part of their fee even though they knew it was a risky proposition. This way I hoped to be able to provide more compensation for the people I work with. In addition, being able to go to investors and tell them that I already had a large part of the project paid for (from deferments) they more readily invested. The crew's deferment was treated exactly like a cash investment with crew and investors receiving their monies at the same time. I also deferred my fee figuring I couldn't ask others to do what I wouldn't do myself."

That ends the checklist for negotiating with crews. We suggest completing your budget before you do your crew deals. This way, you know what you are paying for each position, you know how much lee-way you have on kit rentals, and you've considered all the other items on the checklist. Now make your calls, and you'll find it's not really negotiating at all; it's more like staffing up with those who agree to the terms you offer. If your terms are fair, and your passion for your project high, you'll have no problem getting a crew.

Unions

Why hire union crews? Sometimes there are certain people whom you know and whose work is first rate, and you just want them. Perhaps they will not work non-union. Whether you are producing a commercial, a telefilm, or a feature, if your company is not signato-ry to IATSE, you can still work with union people by going through a payroll service that is a signatory (see Payroll Services below).

It's worth noting that IATSE and Teamsters both have special agreements for telefilms and some other projects. The easiest way to contact the appropriate local (there are tons of them) is through a payroll service. The DGA also has some special deals for low budget projects which allow the production company to defer partial salaries.

For readers who wish to prepare a union budget and include all the additional rates and fringes, the names and addresses of the major unions and guilds are in the Appendix. You may also obtain current rates and the major rules and practices governing work by buying a copy of The Labor Guide (see Resources), which saves a lot of leg-work by compiling it in one volume.

Taken as a group, the rules of the various guilds and unions are complex and overwhelming. Studied one at a time, they begin to make sense. You can understand the concerns, needs, philosophies, and restrictions inherent in each union.

For many producers, especially those with limited budgets, unions rules and regulations make working with them prohibitively expen-sive. And the truth is, most union people will work non-union projects.

Payroll Services

A Payroll Service is a wonderful thing. The service takes your employee's completed and signed time card showing hours worked, and hourly rate, and calculates what is owed. Then they add on the requisite union fringes, if any, such as Current Health, Retirement Health, Pension, Vacation and Holiday. Finally, they issue the check, and you are free of the hassle!

Since the service also acts as the employer of record, Workers' Compensation and unemployment go through them, not you. Plus, they complete and send W-2 forms to all your employees at year's end. Fees are usually 2%-4% of your total employees' gross wages or on the entire invoice of gross wages plus fringes, depending on the company. If you can afford it, it's great headache relief.

Payroll services can act as your signatory to SAG or AFTRA for industrial/ educational programs, but not for TV, features, commercials, home video, or interactive. That means if you're shooting an industrial/educational project, you can use the payroll service to pay SAG or AFTRA members without being a signatory company yourself. If you are shooting any of the other kinds of projects, your company must become signatory to legally hire those members (for a further discussion of signatory status, see Chapter 1).

To legally hire members of the DGA, WGA, and AFM (American Federation of Musicians), the production company must be a signatory. You can then hire a payroll service to handle the payroll chores, if you want.

For IATSE (which includes Teamsters) a payroll service can act as your signatory, and your non-signatory company can now use union crews. Call a payroll service for details, since there are many if's, and's and but's and you need to customize the service to your project and your company.

Productions for Large Companies

Large companies have accounting departments with layers of approvals. And, they like to hold onto their money as long as possible to earn interest. This can add up to slow payments that drive people crazy.

It's bad business when a crew has to wait more than 10 or 15 days to get paid—especially if they were promised prompt payments. Try to make accounting departments stick to a pre-agreed schedule, and even make it a contractual point with the company.

Below-the-Line Rates

The below-the-line rates in this book are non-union. By definition then, there are no set rates, it's all open to negotiation and industry standards. That's why we usually cite a range rather than a specific figure. The rates are loosely based on a 12-hour day, which is average for most shoots, meaning some will be 10 hours and some 14. None of the rates take into account payroll taxes or union fringes (pension, health, vacation and holiday).

Negotiating for Equipment and Services

Film labs, video post houses, equipment rental houses, catering companies and the like are all open to negotiation. If you have a lot of work for them, if you contact them during one of their slow periods, if you can offer lots of future work, or even if none of the above apply, you can ask for discounts. Be brazen—in a nice way—and you'll be surprised.

If you are not familiar with the service or equipment you seek, call around to several companies and ask for bids. Talk through the situation, and ask dumb questions—the good companies will be happy to answer them because they want your business, both now and in the future, when you know the ropes.

After you've been educated by several places and have their bids, you can compare apples to apples and start your negotiating. There's no harm in saying you have a bid for twelve dollars per person from Brown Bag Catering, and, asking if the Tastee Treat Company can do better for the same menu.

Sometimes companies will say yes to your request, but only if you pay when service is completed. Try to establish a credit line wherever you go so that you don't have to pay bills for 30 to 120 days. This way you may be able to make a little interest on the money in your bank account boosting your assets. Weigh the costs versus the benefits.

Production Schedule

Studios or others who are financing your project will want to see a Production Schedule. Use the budget and breakdown to help forecast how long each phase will take. Again, the above-mentioned books can help.

Cash Flow Schedule

A Cash Flow Schedule projects expenses across the production schedule, and helps both the producer and the financing entity plan for the major cash transfers.

When you are producing a film or video or television show for a distributor or broadcaster you generally receive your payments on a payment schedule, never all at once. This means that you will have to know exactly how much cash is needed when. You prepare a cash flow schedule so that you can meet your needs.

Here's a tip. The usual pattern for cash transfer is one third on signature of contract, one third on start of principal photography, and one third on delivery of the master. Try to get most of the last payment at the start of post-production. With cash on hand, you can cut a much better deal with your editing facility. Otherwise, you pay them whenever the last transfer arrives, which can be 30 or even 60 days after delivery of the master (see Cash Flow Chart in Appendix).

Casting

The way features and larger productions find actors is to hire a Casting Director. These people have extensive contacts with agents, and take your script and/or character descriptions and arrange for the appropriate actors.

Casting Directors cost, but they do everything for you except make the decision. You show up at the appointed day, take a seat, sip your coffee, and watch as actor after actor performs. You can direct the actor if you want, or leave it up to the Casting Director. They'll also videotape each actor for an extra charge. At the end of the session, they'll arrange for any callbacks. They also negotiate the agreements with actors and agents, and handle SAG or AFTRA paperwork.

Casting Directors for movies and TV shows usually work by the project, and get a flat fee which is based on how much talent there is to cast, and and how long it will take. Usually the producer has allotted a fixed amount in the budget— $20,000 to $40,000 is typical for a low- to mid-level feature.

For commercials, they usually hold the first session without you, and send you a video. You view the tape and sit in for the callbacks only. Commercial Casting Directors charge anywhere from $400 to $600 per day. If a Casting Director is outside your budget, however, there are some other routes.

Many scripts are written with specific professional actors, hosts, or narrators in mind. If you know who you want, simply call the Screen Actors Guild (in Los Angeles 213/954-1600) or AFTRA (in Los Angeles 213/461-8111) and ask for agency listings. From there you get the actor's agent, and you can make your offer. If you know you want a union actor, try going through the Academy Players Directory, a multivolume set of books with photos of known and not-so-known actors with their agency listed. It's a trip into fantasyland just looking through the books. You can buy the books, or visit the library at the Academy of Motion Picture Arts and Sciences in Beverly Hills.

If you don't know who you want, you can call talent agencies cold and talk to the agents, asking them to send pictures and resumes. Or you can place ads for open auditions (the infamous "cattle calls" actors despise) in local trade papers read by actors (available at any good newsstand).

Or, you can join the modern age and use Breakdown Services, Ltd. With offices in New York, Los Angeles, and Vancouver, this casting service can get tons of actors eager to audition for your project no matter where you live. Here's how they operate.

You send them a script, and they do character breakdowns from it (or you prepare your own character descriptions and FAX them in). They release the breakdowns to agents and personal managers wherever you indicate. If, for example, you are in Miami, and you only want local actors, then that's what you get. If, however, you're willing to audition out-of-town actors, then your breakdowns go to agents and managers everywhere.

Within days (sometimes hours) you'll receive 8x10 glossies and resumes. Tons of them. You then call the agents of the actors you want to see and arrange for appointments. The best news is there's no charge to producers for the service. (For non-union feature projects, you'll have to pay a $200 refundable deposit—sincerity money that your project is financed and truly ready to cast.) Call Breakdown Services in L.A. at (310) 276-9166.

In dealing with any agent, know in advance whether it's a guild or non-guild shoot, what the tentative shoot dates are, and how much you are prepared to offer. Agents always get 10% of their client's gross salary, but you can try to fold the agent's fee into the gross, instead of adding it on top.

If you are handling the auditions yourself, you'll need to be prepared. Have a waiting area for actors where they can be greeted and sign in. Have "sides" on hand-a few pages of script the actor prepares while waiting. In the audition room, which should be spacious

51

enough to allow movement, have a video camera and an operator. Chances are, you'll want to review some of the actors' auditions on tape. For most parts, allow about 10 to 15 minutes for each actor, and try to stay on schedule. You'll probably get exhausted saying the same thing to each actor, but keep your energy up and remember that they are there to help you achieve your vision.

<u>Actor Clearance</u>

One final note on working with union actors. At least 12 hours before start of shooting, you or the Casting Director, must call the actor's guild, and verify that they are members in good standing. If they are not, you cannot employ them legally until the matter is straightened out.

Post-Production

You haven't even started shooting yet and it's time to consider post. The reason is, there are several post-production processes to use, and you have to budget for one of them.

First question: Are you shooting on film or videotape?
Second question: Are you editing on film or videotape?
Third question: Is your finished product (Edited Master) on film or tape?

These are five possible combinations (simplified) for the picture path. (The audio path depends on the picture path you choose.)

A. Shoot on film. Edit on film. Master on film.

B. Shoot on film. Edit on videotape. Master on film.
(Some Off-Line editing systems use computer disks, gut for convenience, we'll continue to say "tape.")

C. Shoot on film. Edit on videotape. Master on videotape.

D. Shoot on film. Edit on film. Master on videotape.

E. Shoot on videotape. Edit on videotape. Master on videotape.

Let's take each one and follow its path from shooting to mastering.

A. Shoot on film. Edit on film. Master on film.
    1. Production.
    2. The negative is processed.
    3. The negative is sorted to select circled takes.
    4. Circled takes are printed (and the negative is stored in a vault).
    5. Dailies (Workprint) are synced with audio and screened/logged.
    6. Workprint is edited/approved/Negative Pull List.
    7. Negative is cut.
    8. Color timing and printing into Answer Print, Printing Elements, Release Prints.

B. Shoot on film. Edit on videotape. Master on film.
    1. Production.
    2. The negative is processed.
    3. The negative is sorted to select circled takes.
    4. Telecine (circled takes are transferred to tape).
    5. Off-Line Editing.
    6. Edit Decision List.
    7. Negative Pull List.
    8. Negative Cutting.
    9. Color Timing/Printing Lab/Printing Elements/Release Prints.

C. Shoot on film. Edit on videotape. Master on videotape.
    1. Production.
    2. The negative is processed.
    3. The negative is sorted to select circled takes.
    4. Telecine (circled takes transferred to tape).
    5. Off-Line Editing.
    6. Edit Decision List.
    7. On-Line Editing (with color correction).

D. Shoot on film. Edit on film. Master on videotape.
    1. Production.

2. The negative is processed.
3. The negative is sorted to select circled takes.
4. Circled takes are printed (and the negative is stored in a vault).
5. Dailies (Workprint) are synced with audio and screened/logged.
6. Workprint is edited/approved/Negative Pull List.
7. Negative is cut.

At this juncture, the path goes one of two ways:

A/8. Telecine (transfer to video).
A/9. On-Line Edit (assembly, titles, dissolves, etc.).
A/10. Video Master and Duplication.
   Or...
B/8. Film Opticals (dissolves, etc.).
B/9. Timing (color correction).
B/10. Lab Processing/Answer Print.
B/11. Telecine (transfer film master to tape master).

E. Shoot on videotape. Edit on videotape. Master on videotape.
1. Production.
2. Window Dubs and/or digitize masters into non-linear edit system.
3. Scenes selected from window dubs (paper editing).
4. Off-Line editing/Graphic effects from camera originals.
5. Edit Decision List.
6. On-Line Editing.

Why go through all this? Your distributor probably has definite feelings about what format your master should be, film or tape. You need to be very clear about what format the master should be created on and what the primary distribution mode will be before budgeting.

Booking Post-Production Facilities

A big part of your budget will be post-production, so if you're not familiar with this phase, call two or three editors, post houses, and audio post houses to talk through your project and get bids on the job.

Once you've identified the post houses you like, put your estimated editing days on hold. Even though the editing schedule will slip and slide, at least you are on their schedule books and won't be forgotten.

Completion Bond

Let's say you have what's known as a negative pick-up deal for your proposed feature film (or less frequently TV or other project) where your distributor agrees to pay you an agreed sum when you <u>deliver</u> your competed film master. You take that contract to a bank or group of investors, and you borrow the money you need for production against the contract.

The only hitch is, the investing group wants to be sure you'll make the film you say you'll make, on time and on budget. So they demand a completion bond (or completion guarantee).

If this is the case you must go to a completion bond company that will scrutinize you, your company, the project, your partners, and your family dog. If they agree to provide the completion bond, it gives them certain contractual rights, among them the right to monitor your production closely, and to step in if you even look like you're going over budget. "Stepping in" can mean giving you strong advice, or it can mean taking over the reins of production (which rarely happens). Should the worst occur, and the project goes belly up, the completion bond company gets stuck with repaying the investors. To protect themselves against that, they put themselves in a position of recoupment, second to the investors, just in case they can finish the film and get it to market.

The cost is usually 3-6% of the total budget, above- and below-the-line. Plus, they insist that the budget contain a 10% contingency. At present, there are only three American completion bond companies in existence, all in L.A. (See Acknowledgments.)

Insurance

Just about any project that's hiring people or renting gear needs to be insured. For one thing, most equipment vendors, film permit offices, and others need proof of insurance, so it's pretty hard to produce anything without the proper insurance.

There are many insurance brokers that specialize in film and television production insurance. Make sure they are accessible to you day or night in case of emergency. And make sure they can FAX certificates of insurance to whoever needs one promptly, like within an hour or so if necessary.

The type of insurance depends on what you're doing. If you are setting up a production company you may just need liability and clerical workers compensation insurance. When you get into pre-production, send a script and a copy of the budget to the broker. Be sure and point out any stunts, special effects, animals, boats or aircraft, or hazardous shooting.

You'll probably need some or all of the items in an "entertainment package" or "producer's blanket policy" such as:

Cast Insurance - covers delay due to death, injury, or sickness of principal cast members. The artist must pass a physical exam (paid for by the producer).

Negative Film and Videotape - covers loss or damage to raw and/or exposed or recorded stock.

Faulty Stock, Camera, Processing - covers loss or damage to stock caused by faulty materials or equipment.

Props, Sets, Wardrobe - covers loss or damage.

Extra Expense - covers delay due to damage of property or facilities.

Miscellaneous Equipment - covers loss or damage to equipment owned by or rented to production company.

Third Property Damage Liability - covers damage to property of others (with conditions).

Comprehensive General and Automobile Liability - required for filming on city or state roads, or any location requiring permits.

Non-Owned/Hired Car Liability - covers rented personal cars or production vehicles.

Umbrella Liability - usually a $1 million General Aggregate Limit.

Monies and Securities - covers loss of stolen cash.

Workers' Compensation - required by state law, this coverage applies to all permanent and temporary office and crew workers, and provides medical, disability or death benefits to anyone injured in the course of employment.

Guild/Union Travel Accident - necessary for any guild or union member on location.

Errors and Omissions (E&O) - covers legal liability and defense against lawsuits alleging unauthorized use of ideas, plagiarism, libel, slander and such. This coverage is usually required by distribution companies prior to release. Note that the insurance carrier (not the broker) must approve your application for this coverage. In order to do that, your attorney must have reviewed and approved the script. Allow at least a week for the insurance carrier to approve your E&O policy.

Michael says, "When I was at Vestron Video we hired many producers to do clip compilation programs. Sometimes the cost of the E&O insurance was as much as $15,000 on a show with a budget of $75,000! It's very expensive because, regardless of the budget of the program, the insurer is taking a chance that there will not be any claims."

The cost of insurance depends on many factors, such as the budget of your show, whether there are stunts, travel, big stars and so on.

Many producers allow 3% of the total budget as an allowance, but you can get an actual bid by calling an entertainment insurance broker and answering their questions about the show.

Locations

Scouting. Are you hiring a Location Manager to help you find locations and plan your shoot? If so, get an estimate on how much time he or she thinks it will take to do your job, and factor it into the budget. Be sure to ask about and include expenses like mileage, still film, processing, and video.

If you are scouting locations yourself, bring along someone familiar with production. There are lots of hidden traps here, and you need to consider things like electric power, weather, noise, neighborhood happenings (when school lets out), traffic, parking, rest rooms, eating places, light at various times of day, and so on. Once you have a location you think you like, show it to the Director and the Director of Photography so you can plan your shots.

State and City Film Commissions. Many producers and location managers use a film commission's library to view photos of possible locations. They narrow down the list, and visit those that look most promising. (In the very near future, many commissions' libraries will be on computer servers and accessed by modem.) Out-of-town producers can call and discuss their needs. The commission will then send or fax them information about what's available. Since your show represents dollars for city or state coffers, and a boost to the local economy, most commissions will fall all over themselves trying to help.

State film commissions are usually listed among official state offices, or through the state chamber of commerce. They may also have information about support services, such as housing, catering, transportation, and so forth.

Location Services can also help you. Most have listings of homes or other sites. You go to their office and review photos, find places you want to visit, and have a look for yourself. Most do not charge a fee to the producer, since they get a percentage from the home owner.

Location Fees. This is the money you pay to the owner of the place, and the price can be from $1 to many thousands of dollars per day. If you're hurting for money, charm your friends and their friends into loaning a location. But be advised, most professionals wouldn't even think of turning over their own house to a crew—they've seen what can happen! That means you have to be especially careful if you want to keep your friendships. We've often used "lay-out boards," 4 x 8 sheets of thin cardboard, to cover carpets and floors. We bring our own food, drinks, and toilet paper, and leave the place spotless. For larger shoots, especially through services, it's much more official. There's a contract, proof of insurance, and often strict rules about what can and cannot be done, and at what hours.

Location Permits. In many cities and counties, unless you are shooting in a bonafide studio, you need a permit—even if you are 2 miles up a private road in a basement. A lot of production happens without permits, because either producers don't know the rules or choose to ignore them. Call the city or county film permit office early on to get local fees, and all the rules and regulations. If you have to close streets, or have stunts or special effects to do, you may need police and fire personnel, which the permit office will tell you about.

Budgets from All Department Heads

For any large production, or where money is especially tight, ask all your department heads (Director of Photography, Key Grip, Gaffer, Art Director, Key Make-Up, etc.) to prepare department budgets. This helps everyone think through their jobs, and puts many heads together to troubleshoot. If their totals are too high, you've still got time to think up brilliant ways to do the same thing but cheaper. Some production companies insist on each department head signing off on the final department budgets.

Art Direction/Production and Set Design

This area covers anything from a stylist to help make your product shot look great to building huge sets. After you've done your script breakdown and know what you need, have conferences with your production designer to plan and budget everything from staff needs to materials and construction costs to strike crew and cartage. As mentioned above, ask the production designer to prepare a department budget. If it's too high, you'll need to collectively sharpen your pencils.

Credit Accounts with Vendors

Many vendors will rent you equipment only if you've completed a credit application and provided proof of insurance. Having accounts around town also allows you the convenience of paying bills at the end of the month instead of C.O.D. Typical vendors are for cameras and lighting equipment, dollies, trucks, film and tape stock, props, sets and greens, wardrobe, labs, and post-production.

Production Forms

Need to purchase order books, sample contracts, release forms, call sheets and the like? Call Enterprise Stationers in Hollywood (213-876-3530, or outside of California, 800-896-4444). For $3, which includes shipping, they'll send you their catalogue.

Purchase Orders

Vendors won't release equipment to be charged to account without a PO, so use a purchase order when booking jobs or ordering supplies. A PO corresponds to every invoice, and thus every expense is monitored. The system prevents unauthorized purchases. All invoices can be checked off in the PO book when they come in. You can buy a PO book in any stationery store.

Check Requests

When you have to pay cash and need a check, fill out a Check Request Form. This keeps a record of who wants what for how much. It's usually signed by the Production Manager if less than $500, and by the Producer if more.

Tracking Costs

On larger productions that boast an Accountant or Auditor, the Unit Production Manager completes a Daily Production Report which records how many hours crew and cast worked, how much raw stock was used, how many people were fed, location fees, equipment used, and so on. The Accountant reviews the Production Report and calculates the expenses in each category.

How do you know if you're over or under? Since you're a really smart Producer, you already know, for example, how much overtime you've allowed for cast and crew. You can easily prorate that amount over the number of shoot days. If, after a number of days, you are consistently over on your daily allowance of overtime, or raw stock, or whatever, you know you're getting into hot water. Unless you're saving comparable sums elsewhere, it's time to cut back, which may mean a heart to heart chat with the Director.

"Hot costs," as they are sometimes called, can (and should) also be tracked weekly in a Weekly Cost Report that shows costs for each category in the budget. (For forms, see Enterprise Stationers in the Resources section.)

Just because you have a Production Accountant don't think you can slack off. As the Producer, you are responsible for tracking costs, and it'll be your backside in a sling if you come in over budget. So check the checker, and carefully review the Accountant's calculations. You may have to look hard. For instance, one Accountant we *used to* know ignored the SAG cutoff on actor's fringes (if an actor makes more than X dollars on a project, the company only has to pay Health and Welfare on the X amount, but not on anything over that amount). The result was an overpaid movie star. Imagine that.

Contact Sheet

As you begin to build your personnel for your project, start and maintain a Contact Sheet. Most producers like to organize it by Department. The list should have each and every person's name, address, and phone numbers, beeper numbers, car phones, faxes, and so forth. The idea is to reach anyone on the show at a moment's notice. This list (or a shortened version of it) can be circulated among all production people.

Conclusion

If you're like most producers and production managers we know, when you're not on the phone, you'll spend a good part of pre-production off in a daze somewhere, mentally chewing through every aspect of the production. This is a good thing, because you will jot down all sorts of items you would have otherwise forgotten. Your friends and family will get used to this, and eventually stop talking to you altogether. Don't worry, you're only doing your job.

LINE ITEMS

Chapter 3

LINE ITEMS

Little strokes fell great oaks.
Benjamin Franklin in *Poor Richard's Almanac*

First there are the budget *categories*, then the *line items* —the nitty gritty details without which we have no budget at all. This chapter shakes the budget so that all the line items fall out into the daylight where we can study them.

The budget example that follows is a hybrid of film and videotape, loosely based on a TV movie or low-budget feature. For the scope of this book, a small feature is about as complex as we'll get. This will provide you with more than enough material for just about any project: student film, music video, industrial, concert, or documentary. This budget is therefore a master checklist to help you remember every production item in your project.

Feature film budgets distinguish between "above-the-line" and "below-the-line." "Above-the-line" refers to the producer, director, actors, script and writers, the so-called creative elements. These are also divided because "above-the-line" could vary tremendously since it is a function of expensive creative talent, where "below-the-line" figures are more stable and predictable. In many ways the word "creative" is a misnomer, since many jobs below-the-line call for equal creativity. Everything else—crew and equipment, and everything editorial—is "below-the-line."

The separation is made because above-the-line people often get salaries based on their current standing in the industry, and may also get "points" (percentages) in the film's profit. This above-the-line figure is therefore based more on market conditions and the all-important hype factor than on the hard rock reality of the below-the-line, which reflects what the actual production may cost and less inflated star salaries. Executives or investors can therefore readily see the differences in cost between above-the-line (talent) and below-the-line (production) costs and determine if they are getting their money's worth.

The budgets in this book for documentary, short, industrial, and so forth, retain the above/below the line format because it has now become standard. The exception is the commercial format, which is based on a design from the Association of Independent Commercial Producers (AICP).

One more note before we dive in. Occasionally, you'll see a sub-category called *Desperate Measures*. This was inspired by the line

Desperate cures must be to desperate ills applied
(John Dryden, English poet, c. 1687).

When you're so stone broke that you must resort to *Desperate Measures* to complete your project, we hope these little tips will be helpful.

Above-The-Line

01-00 Story Rights
Options
Rights Purchases

02-00 Script
Writer's Salaries
     First draft
     Second draft
     Polish
Research
Clearance/Title Registration
Copyright
Script copying

Script delivery service
Secretaries
Script timing
Storyboards
Development
Travel and Living

03-00 Producer's Unit
Executive Producer
Producer
Associate Producer
Assistants
Secretaries
Consultants
Producer's Miscellaneous Expenses
Car Expense

04-00 Direction
Director
Assistants
Car Expense
Agency Fee

05-00 Cast
Lead Actors
Supporting Cast
Day Players
Casting Director/Staff
Casting Expenses
Choreographer
Assistant Choreographer
Secretaries
Narrator
Agency Fees
Stunt Coordinator
Stunt Players
Stunt Costs/Adjustments
Stunt Equipment

Looping/Voice Over (Actors' fees)
Cast Overtime

06-00 Travel and Living—Producers/Director
Air Fares
Hotels
Taxi/Limo
Auto
Rail
Excess Baggage
Phone
Gratuities
Per Diem

07-00 Travel and Living—Cast
Air Fares
Hotels
Taxi/Limo
Auto
Rail
Excess Baggage
Phone
Per Diem

08-00 Residuals (e.g., 2nd run)
Writer
Director
Actors

09-00 Above-The-Line Fringe

Note: In the sample budgets, all fringes, both above- and below-the-line, are calculated <u>within each category</u> and indicated as Payroll, DGA, WGA, AFTRA, SAG, etc. We present the following laundry list so you can see all the Fringes in one place. For good measure, this list is repeated below-the-line as Line Item 29-00.

Payroll Taxes:
> FICA-SS (Social Security)
> FICA-HI (Medicare)
> FUI (Federal Unemployment Insurance)
> SUI (State Unemployment Insurance)
> CREW WKCOMP (Workers' Compensation)
> OFFICE WKCOMP
> HANDLING FEE (Payroll Service)

Guilds/Unions:
> DGA DIRECTOR
> SAG/AFTRA
> WGA WRITER
> SAG/AFTRA/DGA WK COMP
> VACATION/HOLIDAY (Union)
> AFM (American Federation of Musicians)

Below-The-Line

10-00 Production Staff
Unit Production Manager
Assistant Directors
Stage Manager
Production Coordinator
Script Supervisor
Production Auditor/Accountant
Technical Advisors
Production Assistants
Teachers/Welfare Workers
Secretaries

11-00 Extra Talent
Stand-ins
Extras
Extras Casting Fee

12-00 Sound Stage
Stage Rental
Power
Production Office

Telephone
Dressing Rooms/Shower
Make-Up
Wardrobe
Storage
Green Room
Parking

13-00 *Production Design*
Production Designer
Art Director
Assistants
Model Makers/Miniatures
Sketch Artists
Set Estimator
Purchases/Rentals
Research/Materials
Car Expense
Film

14-00 *Set Construction*
Construction Coordinator
Labor–Foreman and Crew
Scenic Painters
Scenic Backdrops
Greens
Purchases (Building Materials)
Rentals
Equipment
Set Strike

15-00 *Set Operations*
First Grip (Key Grip)
Second Grip (Best Boy)
Other Grips
Boom/Dolly/Crane Grips
      Grip Prep
      Grip Shoot

Grip Wrap
Grip Overtime
Craft Service
Purchases
Rentals
Crane/Dolly Rentals
Cartage
Grip Expendables
Box Rentals
Key Grip
Craft Service
Air Conditioning/Heating

16-00 Special Effects

Special Effects Person
Special Effects Assistant
Additional Labor
Special Effects - Pyrotechnical
Special Effects - Mechanical
Manufacturing Labor
Fabrication
Expendables
Rentals

17-00 Set Dressing

Set Decorator
Swing Gang—Lead
Swing Gang
Additional Labor
Expendables
Purchases
Rentals
Loss and Damage
Box Rentals
Set Decorator
Lead Person
Car Expense
Film

18-00 Property
Property Master
Assistant
Purchases
Rentals
Loss and Damage
Box Rentals
Car Expense
Film

19-00 Wardrobe
Costume Designer
Costumer
Additional Costumers
Expendables
Purchases
Rentals
Alteration and Repairs
Cleaning and Dyeing
Loss and Damage
Box Rentals
Car Expense
Film

20-00 Make-Up and Hair
Key Make-Up Artist
Additional Make-Up Artists
Hair Stylists
Special Make-Up Effects
Purchases
Rentals
Box Rentals
Film

21-00 Electrical
Gaffer
Best Boy
Electricians

Additional Labor
Purchases
Equipment Rentals
Additional Lighting and Equipment
Generator
    Driver
    Fuel
Loss and Damage
Box Rentals
    Gaffer

22-00 Camera

Director of Photography
Camera Operators
1st Assistant Camera
2nd Assistant Camera
Still Photographer
Expendables
Camera Package Rentals (Film and Video)
Video Truck
Video Studio or Truck Crew
Additional Equipment
Steadicam Operator and Equipment
Teleprompter/Operator
Video Assist/Operator
Helicopter/Airplane/Tyler Mounts
Motion Control/Animatics
Maintenance/Loss and Damage
Box Rentals

23-00 Sound

Mixer
Boom Operator
Expendables (Batteries, etc.)
Sound Package
Walkie Talkies
Radio Mics and Head Sets
Beepers

Cellular Phones
Sound Stock
Misc./Loss and Damage

24-00 *Transportation*
Transportation Coordinator
Drivers
    Captain
    Production Van Driver
    Camera Truck Driver
    Stakebed Driver (Construction)
    Set Dressing Driver
    Wardrobe Driver
    Props
    Cast Trailer Driver
    Cast Trailer Three Holer Driver
    Prod. Office Trailer Driver
    Honey Wagon Driver
    Maxi Van Driver
    Car Carrier
    Insert Car
    Water Truck Driver
    Caterer
    Caterer Assistant
    Additional Drivers

    Star Dressing Trailers
    Crew Cab
    Production Van
    Camera truck
    Stake Bed
    Set Dressing
    Props
    Wardrobe/Make-Up
    Cast Trailer (Mobile Home/Dressing Rooms)
    3 Room Cast Trailer
    Prod. Office Trailer
    Honey Wagon (Portable Toilets)

> > Water Truck
> > Gas Truck
> > Maxi Vans
> > Car Tow Trailer
> > Car Trailer
> > Camera Car
>
> Gas and Oil
> Repairs and Maintenance
> Honey Wagon Pumping
> Meal Money

25-00 Location Expenses
Location Manager
Assistant
First Aid
Fire Officers
Security
Police
Permits
Parking
Catering Service
> Crew Meals
> Extras
> Ice/Propane
> 2nd Meals
> Sales Tax
> Tent/Tables/Chairs

Location Office Drinks/Snacks
Location Office Supplies
Location Office Equipment
Location Office Space Rental
Location Office Telephone/Fax
Shipping and Overnight
Gratuities
Location Site Rental
Location Survey
Auto Rentals
> Location Manager

Assistants
Miscellaneous Expenses

26-00 Picture Vehicles/Animals
Animal Trainers
        Boss Wrangler
        Assistant Wrangler
        Wranglers
        Riders/Handlers, etc.
Animals
        Veterinary Expenses
        Feed/Shelter
        Transportation
Picture Cars
Other Picture Vehicles
Special Equipment

27-00 Film and Lab
Raw Stock (Film - Production)
        Second camera
        Sales Tax
Lab—Negative Prep and Processing
Videotape Stock (Production)

For Editing on Film:
Dailies/Workprints
Sound Transfers
Projection
Tests
For Editing on Videotape:
Telecine
Video Dailies Tape Stock

28-00 Travel and Living—Crew
Air Fares
Hotels
Taxi

Auto
Rail
Excess Baggage
Phone
Per Diem

29-00 Below-The-Line Fringe

Payroll Taxes:
        FICA-SS (Social Security)
        FICA-HI (Medicare)
        FUI (Federal Unemployment Insurance)
        SUI (State Unemployment Insurance)
        CREW WKCOMP (Workers' Compensation)
        OFFICE WKCOMP
        HANDLING FEE (Payroll Service)

Guilds/Unions:
        DGA (Assistant Directors, Stage Managers, UPM's)
        SAG/AFTRA
        SAG/AFTRA/DGA WK COMP
        VACATION/HOLIDAY (Union)
        IATSE/Teamsters

30-00 Editorial

Editors
Assistant Editors
Music Editor
Sound Editor

For Film Editing:
Cutting Room Rental
Purchases
Cutting Room Equipment Rental

For Videotape Editing:
Off-Line Editor
Off-Line Editing System

On-Line System and Editor
On-Line Effects
Videotape Dubs and Transfers
Screening Copies and Videotape Masters
Closed Captions

31- 00 Post-Production Videotape/Film and Lab
For Film Editing and Mastering on Film
Duplicate Work Prints
Negative Cutter
Develop Optical Negative
Timing (Color Correction)/Answer Prints
Inter-Positive/Inter-Negative
Check Prints
Release Prints
Master Tape/Film Film/Tape Transfers
Standards Conversion
Cassette Duplication

For Off-Line Videotape Editing /Negative Cutting /Mastering on Tape
Telecine Transfer to Videotape Master
Master Record Stock

32- 00 Optical Effects
Fades, Dissolves, etc.
Digital Visual Effects

33- 00 Music
Composer
(All-In Package includes: Arrangers, Copyists, Musicians, Instruments, Studio, Engineers, Stock, etc.)
Licenses and Buy Outs

34- 00 Post-Production Sound
Spotting for Music/Sound Effects
Music Scoring Stage
Music Mix Down
ADR and Foley
Narration Record

On Film
Laydown
Conforming to Mag Film
Pre-Lay (Digital Work Station)
Pre-Dub
Final Dub
Printmaster
Optical Sound Transfer
Stock/Dubs/Transfers (Film)

On Video
Laydown
Pre-Lay Music and Effects
Mix
Layback
Stock/Dubs/Transfers (Video)

35-00 Titles and Graphics
Graphic Designer and Workstation
Stock and Dubs
Motion Control
Computer Generated Graphics
Cel Animation

36-00 Stock Footage
Film and Tape Clips Licensing
Stills Rights
Artwork Rights

37-00 Insurance
Producer's Entertainment Package
       Negative
       Faulty Stock
       Equipment
       Props/Sets
       Extra Expense
       3rd Party Property Damage
       Office Contents
General Liability
Hired Auto
Cast Insurance
Workers' Comprehensive
Errors and Omissions

38-00 General and Administrative Expenses

Business License
Legal Expenses
Accounting Fees
Completion Bond
Telephone/FAX
Copying
Postage and Freight
Office Space Rental
Office Furniture
Office Equipment and Supplies
Computer Rental
Software
Transcription
Messenger/Overnight
Parking
Storage (Equipment/Supplies/Film/Tape)
Still Photographer
          (Equipment/Supplies/Film/Processing)
Publicity
Wrap Party
Hospitality
Production Fee

These are the basic costs which may be incurred in every budget in this book. They should cover 95% of all the items in your own budgets, so study this list to be sure you've included everything your project will require.

The next section provides a detailed description of these line items and associated costs. **Our numbers should only serve as guides.** **Your actual costs will vary depending on your geographic location, your skill in acquiring goods and services, and your inventiveness in solving production problems.**

01-00 Story Rights

If you base your project on copyrighted material like a novel, a song, or a magazine article, you not only need the owner's permission, but you'll have to pay the owner for the right to make the film version. The same applies if you are telling someone's life story, unless you are gathering material from public domain sources like court transcripts and newspaper stories, and even then, you must be careful about defamation of character.

To track down the owner of the copyright, call the publisher. If that doesn't work, try a large copyright search firm like Thomson and Thomson (800) 692-8833. Or, you can go through the U.S. Copyright Office, Washington, DC (202) 707-3000. For a $20/hour research fee, they'll track down the owner, or determine if a property is public domain.

Once you know who the owner is, negotiate to buy the rights or buy an option. You may want your lawyer to advise you— rights deals can be complex and you'll want to get it right the first time.

Desperate Measures

If you really can't afford a lawyer, you can buy Film Industry Contracts, written and published by John Cones ($89.95). It contains all kinds of contracts, including an option agreement. (We make no guarantees.) Mark Litwak will have a contracts book out soon as well and Samuel French Books in Los Angeles (213) 876-0570 will carry it. Or, since you're broke but willing to put in sweat equity, go to a university law library and take notes from among the volumes of entertainment industry contracts.

An **option** gives you the exclusive right to hold the property for a specified term (usually a year or two) while you look for financing, or write script drafts, and attract stars and a director. The option agreement usually states that if the term ends with no production agreement, and if the option is not renewed, then the rights revert back to the original owner. The option payment (if any) is non-refundable.

That's why a renewal clause is important. You don't want to have the project on the verge of a "green light" somewhere and then have the option expire with no renewal.

If the project goes forward, the option spells out how much money the copyright owner then gets for the rights. These agreements can be simple or complex, depending on the property and who is involved.

$$$

A TV movie option for someone's life story might cost the producer anywhere from $500 on the low end to $10,000 on the high end or more if it's a famous person. When the project is made, the rights payment may be anywhere from $50,000 to $75,000 for an average TV movie (unless you're dealing with a blockbuster personality, when the sky's the limit).

Desperate Measures

Use your native eloquence and passion to convince a rights owner that your earnest efforts to get the project sold constitute sufficient consideration. Then you buy the option for a dollar (some money must change hands to make it legal). It's a perfectly valid option agreement.

Michael tells one of his option stories:

In 1973, I optioned a 1958 best-selling Japanese book by a writer who was then Japan's leading novelist. It cost me nothing for the option itself. I held the rights for two years while I wrote several screenplay drafts, attracted some actors, and made the studio rounds with "my property." My option stated that if the film went into production (it never did) the author would receive $15,000 total and 5% of the producer's net profits. As it turned out, I was the third person to option the novel. The author had already received money through the various options even though a film was never made by any of us.

02-00 Script

02-01 Writer's Salaries

The writer is the unsung hero of production. When the show is a hit, audiences think the actors or narrator just made up the words on the spot. When a show flops—lousy script! In fact, dialogue is only one small part of a writer's job. Structure, theme, and overall creative treatment are even more important. Don't scrimp on the writer—get the best you can for your budget.

For budgeting, the script is the most important element in the entire production. The more work put into a detailed script, preferably a "shooting script," the more complete the budget and the greater the savings.

Our advice is to write the script unencumbered by thoughts of budgets. When you're happy with it (except you know it's too expensive), sharpen your pencil and see what you can do to save money. Can that night scene be just as effective if shot in daylight? (Saving extra lights.) Can those two scenes in the two bedrooms be shot in one bedroom? (Saving a camera setup.) Can the car chase become a foot race? If you find you've saved money but gutted the story, maybe you went too far. You be the judge.

The writer's fee will vary depending on the scale of the project and the overall budget. We give some figures below from the Writers Guild of America rate card, but don't use them without going through the WGA rate card yourself, as there are numerous if's, and's, and but's that make every project unique.

$$$
Program between 45 and 60 minutes in length.
Network prime time.
Writer's Fee: Story $8,860
                Teleplay $14,610

Program between 30 and 60 minutes in length.
Other than network prime time.

High budget ($300,000 and over).
Writer's Fee: Story $5,689
                Teleplay $9,853

Narration writing for television program between 45 and 60 minutes.
Writer's fee: $11,666

Documentary between 30 and 60 minutes in length.
High Budget ($200,000 and over)
Story and Telescript: $9,922

For a short, a documentary, an industrial or an independent feature using non-WGA writing talent, these are not necessarily the figures to use. You'll need to see how much you can afford for the script, and how much the writer is willing to take. For example, a 45-minute home video might budget anywhere from $1,000 to $6,000 for the writer.

Treatments and screenplays do not necessarily have to cost an arm and a leg. It will depend on your ability as a negotiator, the perceived value of the writer, and the timeliness of the subject matter.

Desperate Measures
When a writer (WGA or not) is eager to get his or her property produced, or just get some work, you can strike a "spec" deal. This means the writer:
a) becomes your partner and gets paid an agreed sum, plus a percentage of the "back end."
b) gets paid an agreed sum at an agreed time but no percentage. Or some combination of the above.

What about the WGA? If a guild member chooses to work non-guild, it's not your problem. Just be up front about it.

Clearances (included as part of Legal in 38-00 General and Administrative)

After the screenplay has been approved on the creative side, you'll need to pass it through a legal clearance procedure to make sure you haven't inadvertently named the maniacal serial killer after the chairman of an international conglomerate. The clearance people also check on other things, like titles and place names. Consult your attorney on this.

02-08 Script Timing

For features and TV movies, the Script Supervisor reads the script and estimates the time it will play on screen. Obviously, one has this done after the script has been approved for shooting, and not while it is still in the hands of the second of nine screenwriters who will eventually rewrite it.

02-09 Storyboards

These can be anything from a Director scrawling a succession of shots on a napkin to a full blown presentation by a professional storyboard artist. For complicated scenes (or nervous first-time Directors), a storyboard can really help visualize what action you want to happen when, and where to place the camera to get it on film. Many experienced Directors use storyboards for stunts, special effects, or any potential difficulty with continuity. (*Terminator 2* had 10 storyboard artists.)

Producers also use boards to jazz up a pitch meeting. (Ad agencies have been doing this for years.) The pictures help convey action and feeling, and may help you make your sale.

$$$

Storyboard artists earn $1,500 to $2,500 per week. Storyboards can cost $50 and up per frame depending on complexity and whether they are in color or not.

(You may also have a creative director and artist create key art for a poster which may also be used for financing presentations. These cost $1,000 to $30,000 or more.)

03-00 Producer's Unit

03-01 Executive Producer
For smaller projects it's quite likely there won't be an Executive Producer. But if there is one, it's likely he or she is key to getting the project financed. Executive Producers (the good ones) are people with a clear eye on the project's vision, and a hand on the phone. They have that most essential element: connections.

The Executive Producer often arranges financing for the project. It is his reputation for launching successful works that gets the project financed. The Executive Producer often hires the producer and director and oversees the project in the most fundamental way. He usually has acquired and/or developed the script or story as well.

$$$
The Executive Producer receives a flat fee or percentage of profits or both. For a TV movie or feature in the $3.5 million budget range, he or she could earn from $100,000 to $150,000. For a $150,000 home video budget, the Executive Producer can get from $10,000 to $20,000.

03-02 Producer
The Producer is the one person responsible for the entire production from soup to nuts. He or she is on the project longest and oversees all elements of the production, including preparing the budget, breaking down the script, hiring the director, camera operator, crew, and actors. Producers are often "hyphenated people," such as "producer-director" or "writer-producer."

$$$
Producers can be paid a flat fee and often participate in profit sharing. Or they may prefer a weekly salary. The rates are negotiable and vary widely. A student film Producer-Director probably gets zip. A Producer of an exercise video with a major star might get $1,500 to $2,500 a week. A TV movie "line producer" on location (actually a DGA job known as Unit Production Manager) gets about $4,400 a week.

If there is no Executive Producer, the Producer packages the project (script, director, major actors). The Producer handles the financing and the allotment of budget monies, negotiates the major contracts, and approves all expenditures. Sometimes a Producer is hired for just part of a project.

A Line Producer, for example, oversees the pre-production and principal photography. The job ends when shooting is wrapped, plus a week or so for office clean-up. On some projects the Producer also directs. Sometimes a Producer and a Director will work together on a project. The fees then can be fairly similar. but again, it greatly depends on the project, the reputation of the people involved, and the length of time each spends on the film.

Desperate Measures
Make the Producer your partner, and defer salary to "back end," or some future point. Or pay below rate and defer the balance. This approach can apply to anyone "above-the-line" on your project, if they're game. It can work for "below-the-line" people as well, but they are usually accustomed to being paid at the end of the day. Every person and situation is different.

03-03 Associate Producer
Unfortunately, there is a lot of confusion around the title and job description of associate producer (and producer, for that matter). The title loses some of its credibility when it is indiscriminately given to relatives, girl and boy friends, and investors.

The title can be as fictitious as a fairy tale, or it can be real. When it's real, it's often a title given to the Production Manager as a perk (see Production Staff 10-00). It's also real on TV series production, where the AP can also be the Post-Production Supervisor, shepherding the project through the labyrinth of post. Since we're not dealing with episodic TV production in this book, we can skip the category.

03-06 Consultants
Consultants is a line item that covers a great number of possible contributors to the project: financial consultants, distribution

consultants, historians, scientists, police experts, and medical advisors. He or she usually receives a flat fee or retainer. The consultant can be called upon at various times throughout scripting or production should the need arise.

04-00 Direction

04-01 Director

The Director is the person responsible for bringing the script into reality, the person with an artistic vision—an ability to work with people and images and bring a story, concept, or idea into fruition. The Director's ideas usually alter the script and its development, so if you know who the Director will be, get his or her input early on in the development process.

The Director is also involved in casting and often the selection of a Director of Photography. The Director is hired for artistic taste, ability to get the job done on budget, and to help determine the logistical approach to shooting the film or tape. He or she is a multitalented person, responsible for a wide range of responsibilities. Often the Director's work continues through the editing of the film.

On smaller projects and documentaries, the Director can also be the Camera Operator, or the Writer, or even the Producer. You may be able to make a flat deal with a Director, or bring the Director on for a specific number of days and pay on a daily basis.

Desperate Measures

If the Director really wants to see the project made, or if it's a personal project, salary could be deferred until profits start rolling in. When you are starting out and producing low budget projects, you cannot afford to pay thousands of dollars to a Director (even if that's you!). DGA? Again, if a Director wants to work non-guild (and plenty do!), it's not your problem.

$$$

Just for purposes of ballparking, the Directors Guild gives the following minimum rates in a few selected categories:

Freelance Live and Tape Television

> Dramatic non-network or network non-prime time (low budget):
> 16-30 minutes $2,414   4 days' work
> 31-60 minutes $3,009   5 days' work
>
> Network prime-time variety specials:
> 31-60 minutes $20,098   18 days' work
>
> Dramatic network prime time:
> 31-60 minutes $24,377   15 days' work

Film Basic Agreement—Theatrical Motion Pictures

> Shorts/Documentaries:
> Weekly salary $6,763
> Guaranteed Prep period   2 days
> Guaranteed Shoot days   1 week + 1 day
> Guaranteed Cutting days   0
>
> Low Budget Films (up to $500,000)
> Weekly salary $5,951
> Guaranteed Prep period   2 weeks
> Guaranteed Shoot days   8 weeks
> Guaranteed Cutting days   1 week
>
> High Budget Films (over $1,500,000)
> Weekly salary $9,469
> Guaranteed Prep period   2 weeks
> Guaranteed Shoot days   10 weeks
> Guaranteed Cutting days   1 week

If the Director is incorporated, with Federal ID number et al., he or she may want to do a "loan out" agreement, in which you pay his or her company directly, but not make his or her FICA, FUI, and SUI payments. Generally, however, you will pay DGA Pension and Health (currently 12.5%). If the Director is not incorporated, then he or she becomes your employee, and you must pay payroll tax and DGA Pension and Health (assuming it's a DGA project).

05-00 Cast

05-01 Lead Actors and 05-02 Supporting Cast
Leading Actors and Supporting Cast are as important to the success of a film or videotape as a good script. To cast actors, refer to the section on Casting in Chapter 2. Rates can vary tremendously based on the name, experience, and perceived value of the actor. If your project is not for broadcast or theatrical release, contact SAG or AFTRA about non-broadcast rates.

$$$
These are some samples of the minimum Screen Actors Guild rates:

Theatrical and Television $504 per day $1,752 per week

Low budget Theatrical Motion Picture
   (total cost not exceeding $1,750,000)
Day Player $448
Weekly Player $1,558

These are only a few of the various rates. See the Screen Actors Guild (SAG) or AFTRA rate books for other fees including meals, overtime, travel, night work, looping, rerun compensation, and so forth.

The better known an actor, the higher the rate. This could be double scale (two times the minimum) or much, much more. The more an agent can get for a client, the more he will try to charge each time, so it's worth negotiating. Because there are so many actors competing for the same jobs, you'll find prices may drop as the competition escalates.

Some agents take 10% of their actors' fees. If an actor is paid $1,000, the agent will get $100, the actor $900. Most agents will add 10% on top of the fee, so it will cost you $1,000 plus 10%, or a total of $1,100 (plus payroll taxes, and if it's a union job, the approximately 13% for Pension and Health). Be sure you understand this distinction when negotiating with agents.

The guilds also make pay distinctions for what an actor does in a scene. If an actor speaks it's one rate; if he speaks five lines or less it's a cheaper rate; if he walks through a scene it's another. Be sure you understand your needs when hiring guild actors, as it will affect the rates you will be charged.

If an actor is a "loan out" follow the same procedures as for Director, but apply the appropriate SAG or AFTRA Pension and Health.

Desperate Measures
- Student actors may be willing to work free.
- The American Film Institute (L.A.) has a deal with SAG, whereby its students' films can use willing SAG actors without charge.
- Use non-union actors and pay below scale (say $100/day).
- Use union actors and pay below scale (it's not your problem).
- Check with SAG to see if your project qualifies for their Experimental

Film Agreement. If your film is no longer than 35 minutes, and its budget is no more than $35,000, you may qualify. You may then use any willing SAG actors and defer their salaries until the film is sold.

05-04 Casting Director/Staff
If you can afford it, a good Casting Director takes much of the headache out of casting. (See the Casting section in Chapter 2.)

Casting Expenses

If you are handling all the casting chores yourself, you'll need a room to hold auditions, a waiting room for actors, copying of the "sides" (the script pages they'll audition with), a consumer video camera and operator, and music playback.

Dialect Coach

When an actor needs extra help with the spoken word, a Dialect Coach is hired. Maybe the actor speaks English with a heavy Chinese accent, and it's a problem, or maybe the actor needs to speak English with a Chinese accent. The Dialect Coach is the fixer.

Desperate Measures

The cheap way to get coached on dialects is to buy a booklet and audio cassette instruction packet. Samuel French Books in Los Angeles has them for about $18 (see Resources) in a variety of flavors, from Cockney accents to Australian, to French to New York. Now you can strip down to your undershirt, face yourself in the mirror, and say "You talkin' to me?" until you get it perfect.

05-06 Choreographer

If you are producing the remake of *Singin' in the Rain*, you already know what a Choreographer will do for you. For the rest of us, suffice to say that if people are going to move to music, also known as dancing, you'll probably want a Choreographer to bring it all together.

Some Directors are terrified of staging actors, either to music or not. Some situation comedy Directors even hire choreographers to help them block the action in imaginative ways. Sometimes a script will call for a character to do a "spontaneous dance," and the Director may want a Choreographer to make it special. Or you may have a beauty pageant that needs to be staged. So think of choreographers as more than dance designers—they can be movement designers too.

Desperate Measures

Music video producers on tight budgets often hire "choreographers" who are young people with great hip hop skills. If you can find one through a dancing school's hip hop or funk classes, you can probably get them for next to nothing. Be careful, however, since lack of experience with cameras can waste a lot of time.

$$$

Choreographers are not in any union. A reasonable pay range is $300 to $600 per 12-hour day, depending on experience. A major feature might pay $1,000 per day, and famous choreographers may command even more.

Deke's choreographer story...

Once I produced two musical comedies for kids that were so low budget we tried to squeak by without a Choreographer. We couldn't. On the first day of rehearsal, when the music played all the actors stood about like posts. We knew we were in trouble. As a favor, a Choreographer friend of the Director rescued us and even his simple moves, taught to the actors in one day, made all the difference. Lesson learned.

05-08 Narrator/Voice-Over Artist

The narrator is the voice-over used in documentaries, commercials, and sometimes features. Depending on the notoriety of the personality, the rates vary greatly from below scale to whatever the market will bear for well-known voices. We know one guy with a voice so deep and masculine he's always called for truck commercials. He gets $750 per hour. Commercial rates vary depending on whether the commercial is for local, regional, or national usage. Usually you must negotiate with the narrator's agent. The agent will find as many reasons as possible to ask for a high rate for his better known clients. When the commercial is aired the narrator also receives additional money through residuals (check with the actor's guild for rates).

$$$

Rates mostly depend on length of program. Here are some samples from the AFTRA rate card for Non-Dramatic Programs:

Announcers (10 lines or more)
Between 0 - 15 minutes	$295 (3 hours)
Between 15 - 30 minutes	$484 (7 hours)
Between 45 - 60 minutes	$616 (12 hours)

Audition narrators when possible, either in person, or get an audio cassette from them or their agent. Many voice-over agencies have compilation tapes they'll send you with dozens of voices.

Once in a while you can work "on spec" with narrators. For example, say you book a narrator to do three commercial spots. As it turns out, you also have another two spots to do but you are not sure whether the narrator will be right for the spots. To save everyone time, ask if he'll do another two spots on spec. If you or the client like and use the narration, he will get paid. If the client rejects the spot, then you're not responsible for paying for the unused reading. Agents. of course, hate this, but if you've developed a good relationship with a narrator he or she is likely to go along with it since it saves them a trip back to the studio. If the spec recording is used, call the agent and ask to be billed.

Desperate Measures
Narration for experimental films or "cause" projects has a cache to it. Actors often do it for love and recognition. If your project has that kind of appeal, go to the biggest actor you can think of and ask if he or she will do it for minimum scale. You may be pleasantly surprised.

Models
Models are covered under the AFTRA agreement, but not SAG. Rates vary according to whether you are hiring top talent or not. Modeling agencies have portfolios which you can go through when selecting models. They will also inform you of the various rates based on the model's experience and the type of modeling required.

05-10 Stunt Coordinator

Use top professionals to do stunts for the best, safest stunts. Getting people hurt or killed is just not acceptable.

The Coordinator is your source for everything stunt related: costs, personnel, equipment, safety. He or she breaks the script down into stunts and provides cost estimates. Stunt wisdom says to budget for at least two takes per stunt.

On the set, the Coordinator helps place cameras, and generally runs the set when cameras roll.

$$$

Good Stunt Coordinators (don't use any other kind) get paid $3,500 to $5,500 per week. When the Coordinator actually directs the 2nd unit, he stops being paid as the Coordinator and starts getting paid as a 2nd Unit Director, a DGA position that gets $10,000/week for high budget pictures.

05-11 Stunt Players

These are the foot soldiers of the stunt world: the men and women who leap from a helicopter over the Empire State Building and burst into a ball of falling flames.

$$$

They are covered under a SAG agreement that pays a minimum rate of $504 per day, plus what is called an *adjustment*. The adjustment is based on the degree of difficulty and danger in the stunt. For $50 you get a guy to take a fall as he runs along a rocky road. For $2,000 or so she'll turn over a flaming car, or plunge from a high rise. A fully enveloped fire burn, running, will cost you about $3,500. (If you are licensing a stunt clip from a feature film, you must negotiate with the stunt person. You may have to pay what he or she got for the original stunt.)

05-12 Stunt Costs/Adjustments

These are completely determined by the script. If you've got serious stunts, the only way to budget them is to ask a Stunt Coordinator to break it down. Just for example, let's say you want a guy to drive a car into a telephone pole. The player gets his daily 8-hour rate of $504. His adjustment might be $500. The two cars (remember, two takes) will run about $500 each. And the cost of the phone pole, its installation, and dressing with wires could easily run $1,000.

05-13 Stunt Equipment
Ditto.

05-14 Looping
SAG day players (actors hired by the day for original production) receive 100% of their day rate for looping sessions

SAG weekly players receive 50% of the pro rata day rate for a four-hour session. After four hours, they get 100% of the pro rata day rate.

06-00 Travel and Living—Producers/Director

If you are shooting with the whole company in some far away place, you need to transport your people and house them.

06-01 Air Fares
Since union actors, writers, directors, and certain crew (Directors of Photography, Production Designers) must travel first class, the Executive Producer and Producer will naturally want to travel first class as well. If you're doing a non-union show, then it's negotiable, but try and make the same deal for everyone to keep the grumbling down.

06-09 Per Diem
Per Diem for Producers and Directors on features can be in the $100 a day range. On low budget, non-union projects, if everyone is fed three squares a day, transported and sheltered, there may be no per diem at all.

07-00 Travel and Living—Cast
07-01 Air Fares
As we said above, all actors working a union show must travel first class, unless it isn't available.

07-08 Per Diem
Per Diem for a SAG actor on an overnight location is $53.00 per day for three meals. If the Producer provides lunch, you can deduct $15.00. If the Producer provides breakfast, you can deduct $10.50. Or you can be nice and not deduct anything. It's up to you and how close you have to shave it. For the same question with crew, see 28-00 Travel and Living—Crew.

08-00 Residuals
When commercials play, or when TV programs air after their initial run or are syndicated, or when a program enters a "Supplemental Market" (e.g., home video release or "in-flight") or a film goes to TV, extra monies, called residuals, may be owed to actors, directors, writers, and musicians. Residuals can either be factored into a production budget (as TV movies often do for its second run), or not. Check with the distributor or studio ahead of time. If included, check with the guilds for residual rates, or consult The Labor Guide (see Resources).

09-00 Above-the-Line Fringe
Anyone who works for you (who is not a "loan out" from his or her own corporation) is an official "employee" in the eyes of the law. "Fringes" are what your company must contribute to appropriate government agencies and union pension/health funds on behalf of your employees. The package is also called "payroll taxes." These include:

- Social Security and Medicare (FICA-SS and FICA-HI) 7.65% employer's portion, and 7.65% employee's portion deducted from salary.

- Federal Unemployment Insurance (FUI) .8% of first $7,000 in salary.

- State Unemployment Insurance (SUI) adjustable by state. In New York and California it's 5.4% on the first $7,000 in salary.

- <u>Workers' Compensation</u> rate is set annually by state and differs with each industry. Workers' Comp. is less for office people than for grips climbing poles to rig lights. Call your state agency to ask how much to average out for your project. Can be as low as 1.1% and as high as 7%. For purposes of illustration, let's say 4%.

- <u>Payroll Service.</u> If you are using a payroll service, add another 2%-4% to cover their charges.

The sum total of these adds up to 18% - 21% of a person's gross salary. Your accountant, or your payroll service, can keep you abreast of any changes in the individual percentages, and can handle actual payments from your company to the respective government agencies and union funds.

In addition to the payroll taxes, union employees receive pension and health benefits. These are some current rates as examples. Call each guild, or your payroll service, to get accurate rates for your project and your geographical area.

WGA	12.5%
SAG	12.8%
AFTRA	12%
DGA	12.5%

For example, adding together all of the above fringes, if an Associate Producer earns $1,850 per week, add another 21% ($388.50) in payroll taxes to get the actual cost to your company—$2238.50.

If you are paying someone from a guild, say a Director (and the person is not on a loan out from his or her own company), then you owe his or her salary, say $2,235 for four days of work, plus the payroll taxes at 21% ($469.35), plus the DGA Pension/Health at 12.5% of the salary ($279.38), for a grand total cost to you of $2983.73.

If the person is on a loan out, then you pay the base salary of $2,235, plus the DGA Pension/Health ($279.38), (but no payroll taxes) for a total cost to you of $ 2514.38.

Note: In the sample budgets in this book, all fringes are calculated as part of each category. The Above-The-Line (09-00) and Below-The-Line Fringes (29-00) are duplicated only as a laundry list to help remind you of what can be included.

10-00 Production Staff

10-01 Unit Production Manager

A good Production Manager, or UPM, is the glue between all the loose ends of the production and the Producer/production company. In many cases he creates the original budget, and then spends the next weeks or months sweating bullets so that the production sticks to it. He schedules the main blocks of production, books the crew, supervises location scouts and contracts, organizes the casting process, and works with the Director and Producer to keep everything running smoothly, on schedule and on budget. Some UPMs are released after shooting, while others stay on through editing, right up to delivery of the final master. On really small productions, the Producer may have to take on the work of the UPM, but if that's the case, be aware that it's difficult to split your mind between the creative parts of your shoot, and the logistical nuts and bolts that hold it together. One part or the other will probably suffer. A UPM can also be a "Line Producer."

$$$

The pay scale for Production Managers varies, like everything else. We know one excellent PM who works a network Saturday morning live action kid's series and makes about $1,400 per week. It helps, of course, that his job lasts for about five months.

The UPM is also in a DGA position. Minimum scale for a TV movie, for example, when shooting on location, is $3,786 per week, plus a production fee of $700 per week, plus severance allowance of one week's pay. Check the DGA rate card for appropriate minimums and production fees for your show.

For non-union home video productions in the $100,000 budget range, a Production Manager can earn $1,000 to $1,200 per week.

10-02 First Assistant Director

The "Velvet Fist" is an apt description of the First AD. This person keeps the set running smoothly and efficiently – always one step ahead of the next shot. He or she coordinates with all the department heads to make sure everything is ready and safe before each shot. The First AD also creates a shooting schedule for each day's work, coordinating cast and crew so that make-up, wardrobe, and rehearsal with the Director can go on while the crew is busy setting up. Every possible moment must be used to accomplish something. It helps to have a First AD with a strong voice and a commanding presence.

In television, with multicamera shoots, the Assistant Director often sits with the Director in the Control Room, and assists with show timing and getting camera people ready for upcoming shots.

$$$

First AD's in the DGA are paid a minimum of $2,569 per week on movies for studio shoots (plus a production fee of $475/week), and $3,595 on location (plus a production fee of $586/week).

For non-prime time dramatic programs on videotape, AD's (as they are called in television) earn $1,549 for a 40-hour week.

On any shoot where there is potential for chaos on the set—many actors, props, sets, crew, equipment, and so on, it's worth having someone function as a First AD.

On larger productions, like TV movies and theatrical features, there is also a **Second Assistant Director**, and even Second Second AD's. Since the First AD should not leave the set, the 2nd AD helps the First AD by carrying out orders off the set, like trying to pry the star out of her mobile home before panic grips the Producer and Director. The Second also handles the call sheets for the next day's cast and crew, and various other production reports. The Second Seconds are hired when there is even more potential for chaos. There must have been dozens for Ben Hur's chariot race.

$$$

The DGA scale for Key Second AD's is $1,722 per week in studio (plus production fee of $363/week), and $2,406 on location (plus production fee of $475/week).

10-03 Stage Manager

In television, when the Director and Assistant Director are in the Control Room, someone has to keep order on the set, cue performers to speak, get make-up in for touch up, make sure everything is ready for shooting, and so forth. That's the Stage Manager's job. It helps to have someone who can crack the whip pleasantly.

$$$

DGA scale for Stage Managers is $1,428 per 40-hour week for non-prime time programs.

10-04 Production Coordinator

The Coordinator runs the production office, and usually arrives on the first day carrying a large briefcase or box containing every production form, phone book, and restaurant guide in the city. The good ones are geniuses at knowing whom to call for anything from scenic backdrops of the Swiss Alps to iced cappuccino. They must be "buttoned up" people—very reliable, detail oriented, trustworthy, and calm under fire.

$$$

Production Coordinators are paid anywhere from $600 per week on low budget projects to $1,200 a week on movie locations.

10-05 Script Supervisor

On movies, the Script Supervisor handles timing, which is the estimating of how long a script will play on screen. If a script is long or short, it's best to know well before shooting begins, so you can make changes inexpensively. The Script Supervisor stays close to the Director on set, marking the takes the Director wants to keep, keeping notes on what goes wrong in a take, and watching for continuity.

If an actor wears an eye patch on his right eye before lunch, and on his left eye after lunch, you've got a break in continuity, and an unintentionally funny scene.

$$$
Script Supervisors make $1,200 to $1,400 per week on movies. Also allow for Polaroid camera and film for continuity shots.

Desperate Measures
On very simple, low budget, non-union projects, the position can be filled by an exceptionally bright Production Assistant at $500 or $600 per week.

10-06 Production Auditor
This person keeps track of your expenses, and produces daily and weekly cost reports. For movies, they are paid anywhere from $1,200 to $2,500 per week. Feature projects have an Assistant Auditor.

10-07 Technical Advisor
When you need a true expert on the set, bring in a Technical Advisor. If you're shooting a cop movie, have a cop who really knows the ins and outs of cop reality. Maybe you should have a crook also. Technical Advisors can also be brought on for safety expertise (when, for example, the script calls for underwater scenes or scenes with airplanes). Rates vary, of course, on who it is, but figure anywhere from $800 to $1,500 per week.

10-08 Production Assistants/Associates
All minor tasks not specifically assigned to other crew members are handled by the production assistants. They make petty cash purchases, are the primary "gofers" on shoots, and work on the shoot's logistical elements. This entry level position is the lowest rung on the ladder, so you often get people who think they want to work in movies but might be into serious self-delusion. You can always tell because they roll their eyes when asked to get you a cup of coffee, or worse, just stare blankly in slack-jawed stupidness. Top-flight PA's

are cheerful, think on their feet, and are self-motivated problem-solvers who are worth their weight in gold. Larger productions need several PA's who report to the First Assistant Director, Production Manager, and/or Producer.

$$$
Figure $50-$125 per 12-hour day for a PA, plus mileage if they drive their own cars.

Desperate Measures
When you're too broke to hire a PA, try the local college Film/TV Department and ask for volunteer "Interns," who work for the experience, and free lunch.

10-09 Studio Teacher/Welfare Worker
If you have minors on your set (under age 18), and if they are being paid, state law dictates that you hire a Teacher/Welfare worker "to care and attend to the health, safety, and morals of all minors." This is usually one person who wears the two hats of teacher and welfare worker.

There are various regulations that vary by state, but the general idea is that kids of various ages can only work specified hours, must have specific rest and recreation periods and mealtimes, must be with a parent or guardian, and, on school days, must spend specified hours being schooled. In California, for example, a baby under five months old can only "work" for twenty minutes a day, and can only be exposed to a maximum of 100 foot candles of light for 30 seconds at a time. On the other hand, a 16- or 17-year-old kid working on a non-school day does not require a teacher/welfare worker at all. In California, you need one teacher for every 10 kids on a school day, and one for every 20 kids on a non-school day. Check with a studio teacher service in your state for the local regulations.

Two other points about employing kids. Permits and permits.

• The production company needs a permit to employ minors. In California it is obtained through the Division of Labor Standards and

Enforcement (also called the Labor Commission). It is usually free, and they'll want proof that you have workers' compensation insurance.

• The child also needs a permit, and this is the #1 problem on the set. Parents somehow believe that all their kid needs is terminal cuteness, and they are terribly dismayed when the teacher bars them from the set and all hope of child stardom goes up in smoke. It's easy to avoid this—just tell the parents that a permit will be required from the Labor Commission.

Finally, when you are using kids in certain circumstances, in certain ways on non-school days or after school hours and they are unpaid, you may be able to avoid hiring a teacher. Check with a Studio Teaching agency to find out if your project qualifies. Be warned, however, that should an accident happen, your liability is probably less if there is a Teacher/Welfare Worker on the set.

$$$
Typical rates:

Non-union — $200 to $225 per 12-hour day.
Union (IATSE)—approximately $260 day for 8 hours.
(Book through the local.)

11-00 Extra Talent

Extras are also called "atmosphere" because they lend authenticity to a scene. "Stand-ins" are extras who resemble specific leading actors and "stand in" while lighting is customized for the star.

Extras in the Screen Actors Guild (SAG) require minimum payments. For example:

$$$
SAG West Coast Rates
General Extras $ 65 per day (8 hours)
Special Ability   75
Dancers, Skaters, Swimmers   275
Stand-ins   90

There is additional compensation when the extra also supplies an extra change of clothes ($9), period wardrobe ($18), hairpiece ($18), pets ($23), camera or luggage ($5.50), car ($27), motorcycle ($35), and so forth. See Screen Actors Guild rate card or The Labor Guide.

Desperate Measures

For non-union projects you could pay below scale rates, or even just coffee and doughnuts—well, maybe throw in a free lunch (some people just want to be in the movies!).

Michael says, *"that's exactly what we did for the 'Hardware Wars' bar scene. We handed out fliers asking people to show up for coffee and dough-nuts at a San Francisco bar at 10 A.M. on a Sunday morning. We gave costumes to everyone when they entered and had them sign a release. We even had a friendly policemen pull people in off the streets for us when we needed more extras."*

12-00 Sound Stage

Prices of studios and sound stages vary depending on the size, location, and equipment provided. They can be rented for months, days, or hours. Some include a complete television control room, videotape machines, audio room, video control, cameras, lights, and even crews. Others are just four lonely walls you fill with what you need.

When you do rent a stage, be sure to ask about the little charges that can sneak up and bite you, such as power usage,(some stages have no power, and you'll have to provide a generator; see 21-00 electrical), office space, dressing, make-up and hair-dressing rooms, wardrobe room, green room, school room, eating area, tables and chairs, prop and set storage, prop and set assembly area, parking, telephone and fax, security, keys, rehearsal stage, first aid, stage manager, 2nd heat-ing and air conditioning. *(Have you ever worked in a non-airconditioned soundstage in L.A. in August with dancing actors dressed up in Santa's rein-deer suits? Deke has. It's not pretty. Consider temperature and humidity and how it may affect your project.)*

$$$

Prices for Sound Stages vary depending on the setup.

- A fully equipped 2,400 square foot stage with video control room, three cameras, two machines, and full crew can cost from $9,000 to $14,000 for one day of shooting, depending on how many lights you use, and how much time you spend loading in your set (the day before), and striking it (the day after).
- A four-wall 4,700 square foot stage with three-wall hard cyc (a clean, painted background) air-conditioned, sound proofed, with limited parking, some production offices, make-up, dressing rooms and lounge can cost $525 per 10-hour prep and strike day, and $750 per 10-hour shoot day, plus power at $20 per hour, and other charges for phones, kitchen, stage manager, and whatever lights are used.
- A similar four-wall package for a larger stage, say 16,000 square feet, can cost $1,400 for prep and strike days, and $2,500 for pre-light and shoot days.

Desperate Measures

You can set up anywhere if all you need is a roof over your heads. Just run the studio checklist on your proposed location (adding items like toilets or honeywagons). Spend a minute standing silently— what you hear in the background is what you'll hear on your show. Is there an airport nearby? A kennel? A turkey farm?

13-00 Production Design

The "look" of your show is the domain of the Production Designer or Art Director. Big projects have both functions, the Art Director reporting to the Production Designer. Smaller ones have one or the other.

13-01 Production Designer/Art Director

He or she takes a script and, with the Director, interprets it visually, giving the set concrete detail, authenticity, and hopefully, inspiration. A Production Designer can be employed for a wide range of jobs during production. He or she can illustrate perspectives, scenes, set designs, and create scale models, attend to color schemes and textures, and have charge of all sets and the way they are dressed.

Depending on your budget, the Production Designer can work every day on the set, assuring that the look of the show has the greatest visual impact. He or she is that "third" eye only concerned with how things look. During the hustle and bustle of the shoot, they don't have to worry about anything else.

$$$
For non-union, small projects, figure $1,000 per week for someone starting out; in the range of $1,400 per week for journeyman level; and $2,500 per week and up for masters on larger projects.

Union scale for Art Directors is about $1,765 to $2,159 per week depending on experience.

Assistants' pay may range from $500 to $1,400 per week non-union, and about $1,615 per week union. Also allow for research, Polaroid, film, and car allowance, depending on the project.

13-04 Model Makers/Miniatures
Sometimes it helps everyone, especially the Director, to see a miniature of a set to visualize where to place actors and how best to shoot it. These are called Design/Study Models, they're made of foam core, and they can cost as little as $500 or as much as hundreds of thousands—if what you're studying is a scale model of Disneyland.

Shooting miniatures is another sort of job done by the same kind of company. If your script calls for futuristic space vehicles or submarines, or the destruction of Manhattan by a tidal wave, miniatures are one way to do it. Cost is by the project, as little as $150 for a single item or $350,000 for a space fleet.

13-05 Sketch Artist
Used by Directors and Art Directors to help visualize scenes and place cameras. Allow $1,000 to $1,500 per week.

13-06 Set Estimator
When there are so many sets and attendant costs that the
Production Designer is overwhelmed, a Set Estimator is brought in to
do his thing. Allow $800 to $1,100 per week.

14-00 Set Construction

There are two ways to go about Set Construction:

• Hire a Construction Coordinator who will supervise crew, purchases, rentals, equipment, cartage, strike and disposal. Everyone will
therefore be on your payroll.
• Retain a set construction company that will do it all for you, at
a mark-up, but save you the trouble and expense of putting more people through payroll.

There is no way to enter set costs. You may be building the inside
of Peter Rabbit's bunny hollow, or the entire length of Captain
Nemo's *Nautilus*. That's why coordinator's and construction companies exist—to give you bids.

14-01 Construction Coordinator
Allow $1,300 to $1,800 per week; plus tool rental ($750 - $850
week), and truck rental ($150 - $250 per week).

14-02 Labor
Carpenters, Painters, and Foremen are key areas for labor. Some
sample weekly rates:

Foreman	$1,700 - $2,000
Painters	$1,200 - $1,700
Scenic Painters	$1,800 - $2,200
Carpenters	$1,200 - $1,700

15-00 Set Operations

The Grips and the Electricians are like eggs and bacon. They need each other. Electricians actually handle the power to the set, and with the Grips, lights get hung or set up, and shaded properly for each scene. Grips do other things too, as described below. (Electricians are in 21-00 Electrical.)

15-01 First or Key Grip
The First or Key Grip is the head of the Grip Department. In addition to working on lighting with the Electric Department, Grips handle all other rigging and setting up necessary for a shoot—like hanging scenic backdrops, setting up dolly track, blacking out a window, and so on.

$$$
Key Grips (non-union) get $300 to $400 per 12 hour day.

15-02 Second or Best Boy Grip
$250 to $300 per 12-hour day non-union.

15-03 Grips
$200 to $250 per 12-hour day

15-04 Boom/Dolly /Crane Grips
The person who sets up booms, dollies, and cranes and works them smoothly. Sounds easy—it isn't!
$250 to $300 per 12-hour day

15-05 Craft Service
The "Craft" refers to the working people on a set—all the grips and electrics, camera people, props people, etc., who get real hungry and thirsty between meals and need a quick pick-me-up. So Craft Service means those who service the crafts people by having hot coffee, cold drinks, and munchies of all sorts. Even producers are welcome.

The job usually goes to a person or company for one package price that includes labor and food. Sometimes a "box rental fee" is added to cover the overhead on all the food gear like hotplates and coffee urns.

$$$

Figure $500 to $600 per week for the person, plus whatever budget for food you all agree on.

15-06 Grip Rentals

This line covers the miscellaneous grip and some electrical equipment that may be needed—power cables, spider boxes, stands, scrims, apple boxes, and more. It is often included in the grip truck/lighting package (see 21-00 Electrical).

<u>Dolly Rentals</u> (included under "Grip Rentals")

No, this isn't an order-to-go from Radio City Music Hall. A dolly is a four-wheeled moving camera platform. Not all shoots require moving camera shots, but for that extra bit of production value, movement can bring life to an otherwise static shot. Using a dolly will take more time to set up than tripod or hand-held shots, especially if plywood or tracks need to be laid for a smooth ride.

Cranes are in this category also. They usually adopt the names of Greek gods (Zeus, Nike, Apollo). Stage cranes go up to around 19 feet. Mobile cranes (mounted on cars or trucks and equipped with power cells and batteries) can get up to 29 feet and higher. Only in rare cases will a crane be rented for most small and low-budget projects. You can always dream.

There are different kinds of cranes and dollies from a few companies. Consult with the Director and the Director of Photography and agree on type of equipment, how much track, and whether you need any of the extras that come with them. Don't forget about cartage (if you do it) or delivery charge (if they do it).

$$$

Depending on what you rent, prices can go from $150 per day for a Western Dolly, to $250 a day for a Doorway Dolly.   Stage cranes go from $205 to $295 per day. Local pickup/delivery can be $125 to $200. Mobile cranes are $300 to $625 per day, not including accessories or per mile charges.

15-08 Box Rentals

Lots of craftspeople have boxes or kits that they will rent to you. Key Grips may have all sorts of goodies that may be cheaper to rent than put in the Grip Package. Make-up people have make-up stuff. Gaffers have lighting stuff.

Box Rentals can also serve another useful purpose. Say you really want a certain Key Grip, but his daily rate is higher than you can pay for other Key people. (As discussed earlier, it's important to keep rates equal between the same levels of personnel in each department.) Pay him the same daily rate as other Keys, but up his pay on the Box Rental. That way you're not lying when you say all Keys are getting the same day rate. It's sneaky, but it takes care of business.

15-09 Air Conditioning/Heating

In Los Angeles, there hasn't been a major sound stage built in 30 years, so most do not have air conditioning. On hot summer days, you'll need it. Air Conditioning/Heating companies size the unit to suit the need. Rarely will they be asked to cool a stage higher than 8 feet above the floor (although some big stars insist on cooling the whole building so everyone is comfortable).

These companies help out in other ways too. For example, if you need to see breath for winter scenes, they'll regulate the temperature and humidity for you. Temperature can be as high as the fifties and still get "breath" with proper lighting and humidity.

Air conditioning comes by the unit ton. Figure 100 sq. ft. per ton as a starting point, than add lighting load, and the number of people. The company will get you an estimate of tonnage needed.

$$$
Prices are based on the size of units plus time and labor. A 5 ton rents for $50 per day (500 sq. ft.) An average stage unit is 8 to 10 tons at $60 to 70 per day.

Heaters are less—one furnace for a 2,000-2,500 sq. ft. stage is $65 per day. These prices do not include power and fuel.

16-00 Special Effects

These effects are mechanical, or pyrotechnic, not computer-created—anything from a shot in which a baby pulls a car door off its hinges to small gags, like squeezing a sneaker and having green slime ooze out of its heel (we actually did that for a shoe commercial).

Obviously costs depend on whether you're blowing up a Las Vegas hotel (a friend of ours worked on that one) or doing something simple like the shoe gag.

16-01 Special Effects Person

The Key Special Effects Person works closely with the Stunt Coordinator to make the effects as terrific as possible, and safe for cast and crew.

$$$

Rates vary from $1,250 to $2,000 per week.

16-03 Additional Labor

If there's rigging to do before a special effect can be shot, you'll save time and money bringing in a rigging crew so all is ready by the time the rest of the company gets to the shot.

$$$

Allow $750 to $1,000 per week per person.

16-07 Fabrication

If you need just the right gizmo for your flotchet, and you're in the Mojave Desert, you'll be glad your Key Special Effects Person brought along his mobile workshop. In town, or out, give your Special Effects people enough time to fabricate what you need. Fabrication costs depend on script.

17-00 Set Dressing or Set Decoration
17-01 Set Decorator
The Set Dresser or Set Decorator works with the Production Designer to furnish the sets with all the stuff that makes a home a home, or an office, or a torture chamber...

$$$
Rates go from $1,250 to $1,800 per week.

17-02 Lead Man
He, or I guess she, why not...is the person in charge of the Swing Gang (see below).
Rates go from $1,000 to $1,300 per week

17-03 Swing Gang
Movers of furniture or whatever accoutrements accouter the set.
$600 to $1,000 per week

18-00 Property

Stuff actors pick up and use.

18-01 Property Master
The Property Master purchases and rents all necessary props. On smaller shoots, he may also handle the special effects props and design special riggings.

Michael's prop story:

Once I needed a specialty person who knew how to rig water props. The shot called for us to pour champagne into a three-glass pyramid, culminating in a champagne waterfall. I had tried this shot once without an experienced prop person, with disastrous results. In Manhattan, I found a guy known as "Mr. Water." ("Oh, yeah," they'd say, "that's a job for Mr. Water.") And sure enough, he knew everything there was to know about water—how to make it pour, how to light it, how to pump it, and how to suction it. He designed a special water rigging with complicated spouts, nozzles, and pumps that made the shot work. (He was paid a flat rate plus a rental charge for the riggings which he designed.)

$$$

IATSE lists numerous classifications of "prop people," such as Prop Maker Foreman, Prop Maker Gang Boss, Special Effects Foreman, Upholsterer, Draper Foreman, Greens Foreman, and many others. See IATSE rate card for the various costs and work rules involved.

Figure from $250—$350 per day for a Prop Master.

Box Rental might fetch $250 per week. (Get friendly with him so you can peek inside...it's a trip.)

If you use firearms or explosives you need what's called a Licensed Powder Man, who gets a 10% bonus if the explosive explodes—deliberately that is.

19-00 Wardrobe

19-01 Costume Designer

Sometimes these people are called upon to actually design clothing; other times they supervise the purchase and rental of wardrobe, and the assembly of custom clothing. In any case, you are relying on their aesthetic sense to work well with the Director and Production Designer. The clothes, after all, must fit the overall look of the show, like a hand in a glove.

Sometimes Costume Designers get stuck with odd jobs. Here's Deke's Costume Designer story from a low-budget children's show:

Humpty Dumpty had to fall off his wall, shatter into pieces, and get put together again. The Costume Designer was determined to make the gag work. She found a maker of fiberglass kayaks and had him fashion one complete egg suit, and one "shattered" egg suit. When Humpty fell, he fell out of frame...the camera "shook" with the impact...and then we cut to an overhead shot of poor Humpty on his back with big egg shell fragments all about. It wasn't exactly high tech, but when I saw the little kids' faces get all worried about Humpty, I knew it had worked like a charm.

$$$
Rates go from $1,400 to $2,200 per week – unless you're Edith Head.

19-02 Costumers
On shows with no Designer per se, the Costumer might head the department. When there are lots of costumes, you might have a men's and a women's Costumer, each of whom would head their own divisions, hire other wardrobe people, and so forth.

$$$
Rates go from $1,000 to $1,200 per week.

19-08 - 19-12 Alterations / Repairs / Cleaning / Loss and Damage / Film
These are really separate line items, but suffice to say they can sneak up on you. If, for example, you are shooting a fist fight at the OK Corral, you may need all of the above, plus duplicates for Take 2. Let your script be your guide.

20-00 Make-Up and Hair

Whether you've got actors who just have to stand there and look gorgeous, or monsters with blood oozing from eye sockets, the Make-Up Artists and Hair Stylists are the folks who do the job. They purchase, prepare, and apply all facial and body make-up, special effect transformations, prosthetics, wigs and hairpieces.

Since make-up is the first chore of the day for actors, get cheerful make-up artists who will send the actors out in a good mood. Seriously.

Also allow enough time. Men usually take about 15 minutes to a half-hour. Women can take an hour or more. And will. No matter how hard you rap on the door.

When you have a big star, he or she may insist on a personal make-up/hair person, who usually charges twice what your regular person charges. There's not much you can do about it either, except beg for a cheaper rate.

20-01 Key Make-Up Artist
Allow from $250 to $350 per day, plus Box Rental of $30/day.

20-03 Hair Stylist
Allow the same.

20-04 Special Make-Up Effects
This line item covers everything from prosthetics (fake body parts), appliances (extra body parts, like heads that fit over your own head), gaping wounds, blood, scraped faces or knees, extra long finger nails, and so on. You need to budget for purchases, design and manufacture, and the time to apply them.

20-05 - 06 - 07   Make-Up/Hair Supplies
Consult your key people and budget for them.

21-00 Electrical

You'll decide what you need for lighting with your Director, Director of Photography, and Gaffer. They will discuss the creative approach, ordering every light they may need. Then you call the lighting company and make your deal for your grip truck and lighting package.

Equipment houses can recommend gaffers and grips for your production, which may eliminate hiring additional people from the rental house to watch over equipment or drive the truck. It's worth asking these things when shopping for your equipment needs. Generally, however, the Director of Photography will have a list of favorite Gaffers and Key Grips.

21-01 Gaffer

This person heads the Electric Department, translating the requests of the Director of Photography into specific orders for renting grip and lighting equipment and setting up lights, light rigging, and all electrical functions for the set.

Consult regularly with your Gaffer (and indeed with all department heads) to troubleshoot for upcoming situations. They can alert you to potential delays, as well as the need for more or less manpower or equipment. In fact, we've found it helpful to have one or more small, informal production meetings in the course of a day, in which a few department heads gather for a few minutes to hash things out for the next few hours or the next day.

$$$
Rates for Gaffers are $300 to $400 per 10 hour day.

21-02 Best Boy

The Gaffer's first assistant. The Best Boy can also keep track of what instruments are used from a truck, so that when he returns the truck to the lighting equipment company, he makes sure you are not charged for instruments not used (if that was your deal), and not charged for any damage you did not cause. It may cost you an extra day to have him do this, but on large lighting orders it's probably worth it.

$$$
Rates go from $250 to $300 per 10-hour day.

21-03 Electricians

They rig, place, operate, and strike all the lighting gear. Rates go from $200 to $250 per day

21-04 Additional Labor

If you have a complicated electrical setup, consider bringing in a separate crew of electricians ahead of your shoot crew. That way you

117

virtually plug in and shoot when the time comes. The cost will more than offset what you'll pay your regular company to sit around for a few hours waiting—and losing momentum.

21-06 Equipment Rentals (Lighting /Grip Package)

Your lighting package may be a portable Omni kit for talking heads (usually comes with the camera package), a medium-size 2-ton grip truck with a full complement of small to large lights and grip gear, or a 40-foot trailer with enough candlepower to light a square dance in a cornfield.

Often you can strike a deal where a certain minimum is paid for the basic grip truck and lighting package. You are then charged an additional rate for any other equipment that you use. This way you are assured of having all the equipment you need, but you don't have to pay for it unless you use it. This does not apply to large items, like HMI lights, because an equipment house won't want to tie these up on spec. HMI's are usually charged out by the hour or by the day.

You will be asked for a certificate of insurance, which you get by calling your broker. Sometimes you can hire an "approved" free-lance gaffer known by the rental house and get better rates. (If the equipment houses know that competent people will be using their gear, they know it will receive less wear and tear.)

$$$

For a 2-ton grip truck figure $250 per day (plus mileage outside a given radius); larger trucks go up to $800 or more. Then you add a per instrument charge for bigger lights. A complete lighting package for a TV movie can easily run up a $35,000 bill for three to four weeks of rentals.

21-07 Additional Lighting and Equipment

You may find that even though you rent a fully equipped studio there will still be some lights that your gaffer wants to rent. Use this line item for any miscellaneous lighting expenditures.

Additional equipment could include special riggings, dimmers, or light tents. Sometimes the camera operator will own lights that can be rented as part of his or her package at bargain basement rates.

21-08 Generator/Driver

Whenever the power needs of your lights (or other equipment, like power tools) exceed what's available, you rent a generator. The Gaffer or Best Boy will tell you what kind and size to get, and how long it will have to operate. Some are self-contained in vans, others are small or large monsters that are towed in and left, or included in a 40-foot trailer/production truck. You will need a Driver/Operator, which on small shoots may be your Best Boy. On big shoots it will be a separate person. You'll also need fuel to feed the monsters, based on how many hours of running you expect.

$$$

• The smallest generators are in the 350 amps range. They can be hitched to a tow, and either delivered by the company, or picked up by someone on the production team. Average price is $335/day, plus about $30 in fuel for 10 hours of shooting.

• Mid-range units are 750 amps at $575/day, plus fuel at $75-$100/day.

• Larger units are 1,200 amps at $675 day, plus fuel at $120/day.

• Major features might need multiple units and/or a 2,500 amp unit pulled by a semi at $850/day plus fuel at $250/day, and an operator at $250/day.

22-00 Camera

22-01 Director of Photography

Key position—reports to the Director—translates the Director's vision into "paintings of light and shadow." DP's in film must know cameras, lenses, lights, film stock, basic editing, must match lighting and camera direction scene to scene, and must sometimes save the boss from his or her own ineptness. The same is true for the DP in video, but minus the film stock. (Many DP's know both film and videotape—but ask.)

The DP's job encompasses both the physical and creative aspects of production. Vision and ability to work fast and smoothly with others is key to the success of a film or videotape production.

There are four main types of DP's:
- Dramatic (TV episodic, TV movies, features, commercials, music videos)
- Documentary/Industrial (operates the camera, works with small crew)
- Aerial (in charge of air-to-air and air-to-ground photography)
- Underwater (working alone or with full crew)

In all of the above, the DP orders the type of camera and film stock, is involved with the selection of the lighting/grip package, checks the actors (hair, make-up, costumes), sets, props, etc., for photographic consistency. The DP supervises the camera crews, the lighting, sets the camera positions (with the Director), orders any special mounts (for boats, cars, planes, helicopters), and orders dollies and cranes. After shooting, the DP supervises the timing (color correction) and telecine (film to tape transfer), and screens dailies for quality control.

$$$
DP's earn about $1,000 per day for TV movies and most features. For commercials and music videos the rate can vary from $750 to $3,000 per day, with $1,500 being average. For documentary work, a DP might also operate the camera for a day rate of $450 to $600 per day, not including camera package.

In non-union situations, many DP's negotiate a day rate and count on going 14 hours or more with no overtime. That's because they are considered a department head, and as such a sort of "management" person.

Desperate Measures

There is usually a prep day, sometimes a scout, and sometimes travel. Try to negotiate half-day rates for travel, which is pretty standard, but ask the DP to throw in some prep or scouting at no extra charge. It's worth a try.

22-02 Camera Operator

For film cameras, this person operates the camera, and is the one who looks through the camera during the shot, carrying out what the DP wants in composition, movement, and focus. He or she has many other duties, such as checking the film gate for dust, checking the film thread on new rolls, checking the F-stop, and supervising the transportation of the camera.

For video shoots when the DP is not also the Camera Operator, this person operate the video camera, setting the white balance, replacing batteries, replacing tapes, and so forth. In studio situations, with the big cameras on moving pedestals, the Camera Operator follows the orders of the Director in the Control Room to change position, frame shots, and focus.

$$$

Rates for film Camera Operators go from $400 to $500 per 12-hour day. Video shooters get from $300 to $450 per 12-hour day.

22-03 First Assistant Camera (Film)

The First Assistant Camera Operator is also called the Focus Puller, at least in England. In addition to following focus on shots that require it, the First AC also maintains camera reports of takes and footage used, makes sure the right film stock is in the camera, and generally hovers over the camera with the rest of the camera crew like worker bees attending the queen. The First AC may also be a camera repair wizard, and it's not a bad idea to have someone on set who can fix the thing when it goes down.

The First AC will also need to be hired for a half to full day on each side of principal photography to check the film package, make sure that all the parts are there and that they work, and transport the equipment.

There is no First AC in video.

$$$
Figure $275 to $350 per 12-hour day.

22-04 Second Assistant Camera (Film)
This person is yet another attending to the camera's every need. He or she loads film magazines, logs and labels film cans, and often works the slate or clapper.

$$$
Figure $200 to $325 per 12-hour day.

22-05 Still Photographer
Production stills (sets, make-up, wardrobe, continuity, props) are different from publicity shots. The production stills are usually shot by the respective department person. So this category is really about publicity stills.

There is a difference between shooting "documents" of the production and taking photographs that can be used on posters or within the film itself. The former case involves a photographer who roams the set and clicks away during rehearsals of scenes. For the latter case, the photographer usually sets up in a professional studio.

Then there's the question of who owns the rights. Some photographers want to control the rights on their own negatives so they can make money selling to magazines and newspapers. (With all the movie stars around there's good pickin's.) The producer, however, wants control of the photographs to promote the film, and will need to own the material.

There are various ways people work this out. Sometimes the producer owns the material, but the photographer receives any monies from magazine publication. On the other hand, many publicity shots from films are supplied free to the media, and in these cases the photographer would not receive any remuneration. Sometimes the photographer may retain foreign rights if that is agreeable to all parties.

If the photographer retains some publishing rights, he or she may accept a lower day rate. After all, the photographer is being granted special access to movie stars, and may make money by selling to the publishers.

Professional still photographers have rates as varied as those of cinematographers, and are often based on experience and reputation.

$$$
To get high-quality, original work you may expect to pay $150 to $350 per 12-hour day or more for a top-notch documenting photographer, and $500 to $2,000 for a studio shoot, just for the photographer. The studio itself may be $500 to $1,000 per day. Your photographer will prepare a budget for you to include fees, studio and equipment, make-up and hair, lights, backdrops, props, film, processing, prints, and so on.

22-07 Camera Package (Film and Video)

Film Cameras
Are you shooting in 35mm or 16mm? Your Producer, Director, DP, possibly your distributor, and especially your budget will make that decision. Once made, everything you do from here on—the camera package, film stock, lab and processing, and film editing—will be affected by that choice.

In either 35mm or 16mm, your camera package will consist of a specific camera, either with sound or not ("MOS"), plus magazines, matteboxes, optical accessories, batteries, lenses, filters, heads, tripods and the like. Your DP will make the list. Naturally the price goes up the more you add on—just like options on a new car.

Here are some rates for various cameras, just to give you some idea of prices. For larger shoots, you may want a second camera body, both as a reserve for distant location work, and for simultaneous shooting with your first camera. In the latter instance, hire a second camera operator and First AC to run it.

$$$

The rates given are by the day, but if you rent by the week, in most houses, you multiply the day rate by 3, giving you 7 days of shooting for the price of 3. Longer term rentals give you even more leverage, so negotiate!

35mm sound cameras

Panavision, Arriflex, and Moviecam are three standards. We use Arriflex as examples here:

Arri 535	$790/day
Arri 35 BL4S	$490/day
Arri 35 BL3	$315/day

35mm MOS cameras

Arri 35-3 PL	$265/day
Arri 35 IIIC PL	$215/day
Arri 35 IIC PL	$120/day

16mm

Arri 16 SR3	$325/day
Arri 16 SR2	$180/day

A TV movie or feature will budget $6,000 to $7,000 per week for an entire camera package, including lens kit and accessories—more for a second camera.

Lens Kit

Special jobs require special lenses. Most DP's will want a set of prime lenses (fixed focal lengths) and a high-quality zoom lens, plus quite possibly a super-wide angle lens. These are add-ons to the camera package. Zoom lenses fetch from $100 to $375 in 35mm, and from $75 to $150 in 16mm. Prime lenses can go from $60 to $300 in 35mm, and from $40 to $300 in 16mm.

Camera Supplies
The camera will also require expendables like camera tape, filters, canned air, packing foam, and marking pens. Figure $200 to $400 for the first day and $50 to $100 for subsequent days, which will be ample for most documentary shoots. Sometimes this equipment can be rented from the First AC or Camera Operator for greater savings, since you pay only for what is used.

Video Cameras
Video is a different animal. We are recording images electronically rather than on a film emulsion.

Studio Video Cameras
These cameras are monsters attached to large, heavy pedestals on wheels. The operator can dolly (if the floor is smooth enough), move up and down (within a few feet—beyond that and you need a crane or jib), and zoom. They are connected electronically to the Control Room, which in turn sends the signal to videotape machines in a separate room. When you contract with a studio for complete services, you get their cameras (see 12-00 Stage).

Remember the gag on the David Letterman Show where the shot on him starts shaking and rolling? They cut to a wide shot of the set and there's a studio camera operator trying to make a monster camera act crazy—that's a studio camera. We cut back to the camera's point of view as it "breaks loose" and runs outside to terrorize Manhattan—that's a field camera (you couldn't possibly run with a studio camera).

Field Cameras (Video)
Lightweight (the cameras news crews carry). Capable of recording video images either in the camera (on-board), or running a cable to a record deck. They are often called Betacams because they use Beta (either oxide, SP, or Digital) format video stock (see 27-00 Film and Lab and Videotape Stock).

$$$
Video equipment houses rent Betacams, which usually include a simple light kit, tripod, and basic microphone setup for around $450 to $800 per day, depending on the model of the camera.

125

Another tape format gaining in popularity is Hi-8mm video. Most of these cameras are for home movies, but there are some professional level ones with three computer chips that lay down a pretty decent image for the price. You can rent these for around $100 to $425 per day. And ask for the Steadicam Jr attachment—a neat little device that lets you do hand-held work smoother than the Shaky-Cam style most home movies boast, but watch out, they break easily.

If you do use 8mm or Hi-8mm, expect a grainier, rougher image quality than with Beta (which may suit your show just fine). The tape itself is fragile, so resist the temptation to pop the popcorn and play back your tapes on your TV, since you may get permanent dropouts. Instead, go straight to your post-production house and transfer the footage to a Beta or digital format, which now becomes your new masters. Once you're sure you've got a good transfer, you can go home for the popcorn and TV.

Many DP/Operators own their own Betacam (or Hi-8) equipment , and may rent it to you cheaper than an equipment house. The advantage of going through a house, however, is maintenance or camera replacement in the time it takes the guy to get back to you. If you do go through a house, the weekly rate is usually four times the daily rate. (For monthly, figure 12 rental days.) If you shoot for an entire week or longer, you can save some money. Or, for short shoots, you can rent the camera on a Friday afternoon and return it Monday morning for a one-day rate. Many rental houses will give a discount of 10% to 25% or more, especially if your camera operator or DP is a preferred or repeat customer. Always ask for the biggest discount; even if you don't get it, they'll still give you something off the original bid.

22-08 Video Truck

When your show needs multiple cameras and you can't shoot in a studio with a complete camera setup, you call a video truck company. They send complete video studios on wheels to sports events, concerts, even situation comedies set up in converted warehouses. If you are shooting a concert and need multitrack audio, ask if they have a sound truck, or if they can recommend one.

126

Once you have a bid from a company you like, ask them to send someone over to the location with you for a technical survey. They'll help you work out how much cable to lay out, best places to load in equipment, where to put the generator, possible camera positions, and so forth.

$$$
Video trucks come in different sizes, so prices will vary. And the equipment menu is a la carte, so if you're shooting a sit-com with four cameras at $550 each, it'll be a lot less than shooting Pavarotti, Domingo, and Carreras at Dodger Stadium with nine cameras. For average situations, expect to pay between $7,500 and $10,000 for a day's work.

22-09 Video Studio or Truck Crew
Whether you're in a video studio or video truck, you'll need the same crew (Director, DP, Grip and Electric crew are in their respective categories elsewhere). Here's the rundown with day rates for a 10-hour day:

Camera Operators	$350- $450
Utilities (people who pull cable and are generally useful)	$250- $300
Audio	$375- $450
Audio Assist (A-2)	$300- $375
Boom Operator (Audio)	$300- $375
Technical Director (crew chief and camera switcher)	$400- $450
Video Control (quality control of video picture)	$375- $450
Video Tape Operator (runs record machines/changes reels)	$250- $350

A few other crew people unique to video stage or video truck production:

Lighting Director (reports to DP or lacking same, creates the lighting)
$400- $500

Assistant Director (DGA) (in Control Room with Director, readies shots
     for Director) $350

Stage Manager (DGA) (readies and cues all talent) $320

Video Field Package

When you do not need a video truck, but you do need more than one camera, you rent a Field Package through an equipment house. This consists of your cameras (usually no more than three or four), record machines (either on-board the cameras or separate decks), possibly a field switcher so the Director can cut the show on the spot, and a video package of scopes and paintbox for quality control. For this setup, you may or may not need all of the above crew, depending on the size of your shoot. Call your video camera rental company for a bid.

22-11 Steadicam Operator and Equipment (Film and Video)

The Steadicam is an outlandish contraption of springs, counterweights and shock absorbers worn by a Steadicam Operator. The camera is attached to it, and now the whole rig can walk, walk fast, run, climb or descend stairs, and generally move around—all the while delivering a steady, jerk-free image.

$$$

There's a real knack to it, so Steadicam Operators get paid a bit more than an average Camera Operator—about $500 per 12-hour day or more for real athletes of the genre.

Most Operators own and maintain their own Steadicam rig, and charge around $500 to $750 per day for the equipment.

22-12 Teleprompter/Operator (Film and Video)

Nobody memorizes lines anymore, so teleprompters fill the bill. They are standard equipment at most TV studios, and can be fitted to any studio or Betacam field camera, as well as a 35mm or 16mm film camera. When attached to the camera, you have a through-the-lens effect, meaning the actor or reporter reads the lines looking right at you, making you wonder how this person can be so eloquent and remember all those words.

When you want the talent to look at another person and pretend to be eloquent, the Operator places a monitor with the words just over the other person's shoulder and out of camera range.

$$$
Rates for Operator and Teleprompter run about $370 to $400 per 12-hour day. Some companies offer half-day rates as well.

22-13 Video Assist/Operator (Film)
A video tap is a piece of equipment that attaches to the film camera's reflex system, allowing you to see a video image through the lens of the film camera on a separate monitor. This is good for the Director, the DP, other crew, and nervous advertising account execs (when they aren't schmoozing or napping) to see what's being shot. If you want, you can add a VHS or 3/4" video recorder to the package (and an operator), so you can play back what you've shot. Agonizing over the playback of each take is a great way to waste time, so don't get suckered in.

$$$
Tap systems vary on the camera type, whether you want color or b&w, and record capability. The camera portion is supplied by the camera rental house. Prices go from $275 to $425 for the tap systems, plus various accessories like monitors ($35 to $60), wireless transmitters, extra cable, and such.

There are also companies that specialize in video taps. They supply playback services, and other support equipment such as accurate slow motion video playback from a high speed film camera. Operators on most features get union scale at about $31/hour. Non-union rates are in the $400 per 12-hour day range.

On simple, low budget shoots, when someone installs the tap into the camera, a Production Assistant can handle a VHS record and playback deck.

22-14 Aerial Photography

Shooting from airplanes and helicopters requires some specialized personnel and equipment. Pilots not experienced in the precision flying needed for this job can waste your time. The pilot is also the person who will set up the aircraft, and walk you through the process, so for safety as well as quality reason, go with someone experienced in aerial photography.

You'll hear talk of the "Tyler mount" as an indispensable piece of equipment. It is a camera mount, usually rented from the camera rental house, that stabilizes the camera and reduces vibration. Tyler is one system. Westcam and Continental are two others.

$$$
Figure $600 to $800 per day for the mount alone, plus the camera package (see above).

Expenses for aerial shooting vary on the camera package, the type of aircraft (jet helicopter, Cessna etc.), the experience of the pilot, and how long you shoot. Some samples:

Pilot	$750 to $1500 per 12-hour day
Camera Operator	$1000 to $1500 per 12-hour day
Jet Ranger helicopter	$1500 for 3 hours
Cessna	$100 per hour

22-15 Underwater and Topside Water Photography

Here's another specialty area for professionals only. Some underwater filming experts (Marine Coordinators) own and maintain their own film and video cameras, packages, housings, and some lights, as well as boats and dive equipment. Others are more free-lance. They may own a Beta Cam, but would rent the other gear from a camera house.

Michael says,

I produced an underwater special called Dolphin Adventures. *We had two underwater cameramen and one topside cameraman. Working underwater has its own very complex set of "do's" and "don'ts". Because our underwater guys were highly experienced they recommended numerous shots that gave the editor tremendous coverage with which to work.*

For topside work, Coordinators know boat behavior and can make it work the way you want for your shots. They also coordinate the water scene for safety and look. They know the various insurance rates and Coast Guard regulations.

$$$
You can spend anywhere from $2,500 to $75,000 or more for a day on or underwater, but here are some sample prices:

Marine Coordinator $500 to 750 per 12-hour day
Underwater camera operators $700 to $900 per 12-hour day
Crew people add $180 to standard rates
Underwater camera package $1,000 to $1,200 per day

22-16 Motion Control/Animatics
If you have still photographs that need to be shot, you'll want to go to a post-production house and rent time on their motion control (sometimes called Animatics) camera system.

In the best of situations, this is a huge contraption whose servo-mechanism is entirely run by computer. It holds a video camera pointing down at a large table, upon which you put your stills, one at a time. The operator can program camera moves on the still—pans, zooms, and moves along the still's x and y axis. The result is a completely custom job of shooting your stills exactly how you want.

It's good to bring in your script and actually read the narration copy that will go over the still. That helps you plan the speed of the move and what parts of the still to focus on as you move.

$$$
These cameras and operators command hefty fees, but the look is usually worth it. Expect to pay from $300 to $450 an hour (includes the operator) plus stock. If you rehearse reading the copy over the stills back at the office, and make notes, you can shorten the session considerably.

Desperate Measures

If the above is too rich, you can also shoot stills by putting them on clean, black art cards with graphics spray cement, place them on an easel, and shoot them with your rental camera. The problem is, the tripod and head may not be smooth enough for really good work (remember, you're working in extreme close-up, and every camera shake will show). You can get smoother heads at slightly more expense—talk it over with your camera operator in advance.

23-00 Sound

If the sound you record in the field is the sound you'll use in the master, it had better be good. Feature films do a lot of "looping," or ADR work (Automatic Dialogue Replacement) in audio post to correct problems with recordings in the field. Sometimes those problems are unavoidable, but a good mixer will help prevent those that are avoidable.

23-01 Mixer

Good ones have an uncanny ability to hear what the rest of us ignore. Background sounds like air conditioning (especially when it cuts on and off, causing havoc in editing), dripping faucets, chattering squirrels or distant school children all land on the Mixer's sensitive eardrums. Even 35mm camera noise can cause a problem.

$$$

Rates for Mixers average $300 to $550 per 12-hour day.

23-02 Boom Operator

These people develop amazing triceps from holding aloft a microphone attached to a fish pole for hours at a time. They are also good (hopefully) at keeping the mike out of the frame, yet as close as possible to the talent, and properly pointed.

On sound stages, the Boom Ops handle the mechanical Microphone Booms.

$$$

Rates average $250 to $350 per 12-hour day.

23-04 Sound Package (Film and Video)

Film

In film, the Sound Package is a high-end 1/4 inch recorder such as a Nagra, or Digital Audio Tape (DAT), plus assorted microphones (maybe wireless radio mikes), a stereo mixer unit, fish poles, booms, batteries, and baffles. The tape recorder can be either an analog or a time-code-based system. Analog is used when you are editing on film and require the 1/4 inch production sound to be transferred to Mag Film. Time-code-based systems are used when you want to transfer your film footage to videotape, and edit on a Digital Work Station all the way through. The time-code machine generates time code onto the 1/4 inch audio tape, and displays it on a "smart slate," a clapstick with a time code window display. In the telecine transfer process, the sound and picture are synced and are time code accurate.

$$$

Film Sound Packages go for around $200 to $400 per day, depending on the accessories. Analog packages should be $50 to $100 cheaper than time code. Don't forget audio stock.

Video

In video, the Mixer records sound directly to the video tape, so you need everything in the Film Sound Package, except the Nagra. The mixer unit and other equipment can be rented through the camera house and included in the camera package, although some Mixers insist on bringing their own gear because they know they can rely on it.

$$$

The package without the recorder ranges between $50 and $150 per day, depending on specific equipment.

Sound Truck

You've just been asked to produce the Beatles Reunion Concert for TV. When it's time to consider the sound, you'll want to go to an audio services company that rents sound trucks. If the music is to be remixed later, you want multitrack recording capability—probably up to 48 tracks for the Beatles. The Mixer will mix the band, orchestra, chorus, and whatever else they throw at you. When the concert is over, you'll remix at a recording studio or post-production sound facility.

If the sound is going out live and you have no time for a remix (now or later), then you can save money because you won't need multitrack recording—only a good audio board to send the mixed stereo sound over to the video truck where it is added to the picture and beamed out to the waiting world.

$$$
Basic rate (with no travel) for a truck plus crew will be in the $5,000 per day range.

23-05 - 08   Walkie-Talkies/Beepers/Portable Phones
Now standard issue on shoots big and small, walkies are a pain to lug around, even with belt holsters and headsets, but they are convenient. Whenever you have people spread out (and it's too far to yell), or you have to hold traffic, or cue the stampeding baboons, equip your key people.

$$$
Walkies go for about $8 a day, weekly at $17 (for 8 channel units)
Beepers go for $5 a week.
Portable Phones rent for $25 a week and 65 cents per minute.

24-00 Transportation

Getting there is half the expense, at least for TV movies and features. Moving everything and everyone from location to location is a formidable job. What follows is for TV movies and features. For smaller, non-union shoots, your drivers will probably be your crew and PA's.

If you are using Teamsters on your shoot, consult the IATSE rate card job categories, work rules, and rates.

24-01 Transportation Coordinator

This person coordinates the whole enchilada, and hires the Captains and Drivers, and administrates the operation. The Captains report to him, and handle the parking, the moving of vehicles, and so forth.

$$$

Rates: $1,800 to $2,200 five-day week flat rate.

24-02 Drivers

Captains

$1,400 to $1,700 per five-day week.

Drivers

Rates vary on the type of vehicle driven. Some samples by the five-day week:

Auto/Station Wagons/Small Vans	$900 to $1,200
Forklifts/Tractors	$1,000 to $1,300
MaxiVans, Buses	$1,000 to $1,400
Camera Car Driver	$1,400 to $1,700

24-03 Transportation Equipment Rental

The Transportation Coordinator will make the truck rental deals according to your budget. If you're on your own, consult the local production guides.

Star Dressing Room

In the real old days, a nearby barn would do. Now, a mobile home or trailer is often part of the contract negotiations handled by the Casting Director. How big it is reflects the status of the star. Dressing rooms therefore range in size from huge to a shared room in the honeywagon.

$$$

Some of the larger mobile homes or trailers range from $400 to $900 per week, plus towing or driving costs.

$$$

Here are some typical rates of other vehicles:

Crew Cab	$60/day
Production Van	$300/day
Camera Truck	$90/day
20' Stake Bed	$100/day
Set Dressing 5 ton	$95/day
Set Dress Van	$65/day
Prop 5 ton	$165/day
Make-Up/Wardrobe	$300/day
Cast Trailer	$120/day
3-Room Cast Trailer	$180/day
Honeywagon	$300/day
Gas Truck	$80/day
Maxi Van	$70/day
Water Truck	$200/day
Camera Car	$300/day

Other transportation expenses:
    Gas & Oil
    Repairs & Maintenance
    Honeywagon pumping

25-00 Location Expenses (also see Chapter 2)

25-01 Location Manager

A good Location Manager, after finding the perfect places, makes the deals for the locations, gets permits, police, parking, fire, and approvals for same including those from the neighborhood. He or she also troubleshoots the location during production. The Location Manager may also need an assistant to handle the troubleshooting, while he works ahead of the shooting company to set up the next place.

$$$

Rates are $300 to $400 per 12-hour day, or $1,300 per week for low budget projects.

25-03 First Aid

A location nurse or other qualified medical person with kit will run around $300 per 12 hr. day.

25-04 Fire Officers

Local regulations may require Fire Officers on the set whenever you use any electric lights, but especially if you're using open flame or blowing anything up. Check with the local permit office for details and rates. A Fire Marshal or set Firefighter can run $500 per 12-hour day.

25-05 Security

A Watchman will cost about $100 per 12-hour day, but you and/or your sets and equipment may need 24-hour protection. On a TV movie or feature, this figure can run into the thousands.

25-06 Police

Depending on local regulations, you may need police. In some cities they charge you, in others they don't. Check locally with the film commission or permit department. Big city rates can hover around $400 per 12-hour day.

25-07 Permits

Every big city and many small ones have Permit Departments. Since there can be many twists and turns to getting the right permit for your shoot, call them and get the local scoop while you're budgeting—not the day before cameras roll.

25-09 Catering Services

Most caterers are sensitive to the variety of palates and diets on a movie set, and most do a good job of designing a menu. A good menu, therefore, has a meat dish for those who feel cheated without a leg of something, as well as a vegetarian dish, like pasta, and a salad bar for the light eaters, veggies, and dieters.

Most services stock tables and chairs, although there may be a setup charge. You may also need tents, and even heaters if you're shooting a winter scene.

$$$

Caterers charge by the head, with average prices for a two-entree meal being from $10 to $14 per person, with a minimum of 20 or 30 people. They also charge "Server's Fees" or "Setup Fees", so ask about those.

Don't forget to budget for second meals on those days you expect to go long.

Desperate Measures

On low-budget shows, if you don't have enough people to warrant hiring a caterer, pass around the menu from a good local restaurant and have a PA take orders. Or, if it's tighter than that, say for a student film, order in a pizza.

High budget or low, don't overlook the eating place. People use meals as a break from the job, and an opportunity for a little fellowship, so keep them warm or cooled, as required, and away from unpleasant distractions like traffic exhaust, barking dogs, or gawking humans. Sometimes, a little quiet music from a boombox helps set the mood.

25-13 Location Office Space Rental

If you are all staying at a hotel, it may be convenient to rent an office or an extra room and have office furniture brought in, or make it part of the overall hotel deal and get the office for free. Another ploy is to rent a motor home or trailer equipped with desks, office gear, and a generator to run lights, computers, copiers, et al. Main occupants are the Production Coordinator and the Production Accountant.

$$$

A fancy motor home or trailer decked out as an office rents for about $1,500 per week.

25-17 Location Site Rental Fees

Whether you're shooting the Brooklyn Bridge or your aunt's backyard, allow whatever appropriate for both fees and permits. If you are going through a location service, or using a Location Manager, they'll apprise you of the likely costs. On private property, the fee might be negotiated for less on prep and wrap days than on shoot days, saving a few dollars.

The price can be anything from a barter agreement (a cassette of the film in exchange for a few days in someone's apple orchard) to thousands of dollars. In Los Angeles, some home owners are well used to movie companies, and actually design their homes to attract the lucrative fees. Other places in town, people have been so burned by the local tie-ups and traffic congestion that movies create that you must go through the neighborhood association, obtain signatures of neighbors, and generally pacify the natives before shooting (also see Chapter 2).

26-00 Picture Vehicles/Animals

The vehicles we see in the show—from buckboards to magic buses—are the Picture Vehicles. Animals are animals.

26-01 Animal Trainers

Boss Wrangler
He works with the Stunt Coordinator and Director to map out stunts, and otherwise handles the animal's care, feeding, transportation, shelter, tack, and working conditions. He'll prepare a budget including all of the above.

$$$
Boss Wranglers earn from $300 to $500 per 12-hour day and up in special situations.

Assistants and Wranglers earn from $200 to $300 per 12-hour day.

26-02 Animals
The cost for the critters themselves varies, as you might expect, on their level of expertise. If you want a chimp to sharpen a pencil, and he doesn't know how, you'll be charged to have the trainer teach him.

$$$

Otherwise, here are some sample rates:

Chimpanzee	$600/day
Snakes	$50 - $250/day depending on size
Zebra	$500/day
Tarantula	$50/day
Scorpion	$75/day
Flies	$300 per thousand/day
Horse	$100/day (trained is $300 and up)
Herd of cows	$200 each/day

26-03 Picture Cars

You need a yellow taxi, armored truck, pink Ferrari, bus, cop car, limousine, or hearse? You need a picture vehicle rental company. Costs depend on the scarcity and value of the vehicle, whether it will have to be painted, trailered, and so forth. Different rates often apply for commercials, features and TV. Students should always ask for discounts.

$$$

Some sample day rates:

Contemporary police car	$250
Contemporary taxi	$250
Vintage London cab	$350
Armored car	$750
Cobra	$550

27-00 Film and Lab / Videotape Stock - Production

This category is for the production period only, and therefore includes:
- Raw stock (film and videotape).
- For film: lab processing and dailies.
- For film to tape editing: telecine, and video dailies stock.

All other Film and Lab and Stock items are found in Editorial and Post-Production.

The prices quoted here are <u>rate card</u>, and tend to be high. As you establish relationships with stock houses, film labs, video and audio post facilities, you'll do much better. Keep shopping around, and keep asking for better prices.

27-01 Raw Stock

The DP decides the stock, the amount of stock, and the brand—Kodak, Fuji, Agfa, or Ilford. Prices slip and slide frequently, and depend on quantity.

You'll be buying raw stock for both your First Unit and Additional or Second Unit cameras, and don't forget to add sales tax. When you order your film, ask them to set aside stock with the same batch and emulsion numbers.

As to 16mm vs. 35mm? It's almost always a budget decision. If you expect theatrical release, or you are shooting something that has to look the absolute best, shoot 35mm if you can afford it. Always ask for discounts.

$$$
These are some fairly typical prices for popular film stocks:
<u>35mm</u>
Kodak   #5298 $0.4732 per foot
Fuji   #8570 $0.4495 per foot

<u>16mm</u>
Kodak   #7298 $110.40 per roll
Fuji   #8670 $110.34 per roll

Desperate Measures
Film stock companies sometimes keep "short ends," "long ends," and "re-canned" film stock. Short ends are leftover reels with less than 400 feet per reel (they can be hard to use if they're too short).

Long ends have 700 feet or more. Re-canned stock means they may have put the film in the magazine and changed their minds. Long ends and re-cans are used by productions big and small, but there are some possible snags.

As mothers like to say, "Don't touch that, you don't know where it's been." Insist that the film be tested. The good stock houses do this anyway, processing a strip from each can at a lab to check for density levels, scratches, fogging, and edge damage. Testing is also the only way to verify what kind of film is in the can, since cans are often mis-labled or de-labled in the field.

Also, if you are a student, some film and tape companies provide automatic discounts. If you are a member of Independent Feature Project (IFP) West or East, ask them about discounts for stock.

27-02 Lab - Negative Processing

Same story as raw stock—prices vary with labor and stock increases, so get quotes. These prices are rate card , so you can do better. In choosing a lab, whether a big one or a small one, go for impeccable credentials. You really don't want to reshoot hard-earned scenes.

$$$
Typical processing costs:
35mm $0.2174 per foot
16mm $0.2080 per foot

27-03 Videotape Stock (Production)

Like film, videotape stock prices vary by the brand and the quantity. Three-quarter inch is still used as a production stock on low budget projects, but most often used as an Off-Line editing format because it is cheaper. Most video production uses BetaSP stock, although Digital Betacam tape will probably catch up. Beta oxide tape is a lot cheaper, and some reality broadcast shows do use it (where a grittier look is desired). The problem is, you're likely to get more video dropouts on oxide than on SP, so caveat emptor.

3/4 Inch
30 min. $13   60 min. $17

3/4 Inch SP
30 min. $17   60 min. $22

Beta (oxide)
20 min. $7.55   30 min. $9.45   60 min. $24.00

BetaSP
20 min. $22.50   30 min. $25.00   60 min. $33.50

Digital Betacam is a digital, composite metal tape format. It's more expensive than BetaSP, but if you want to stay in the digital component domain from shooting through post, this is it. It also comes in lengths of 6 minutes up to 124 minutes.

One inch
30 min. $41.95   60 min. $58.95   90 min. $87.95

Desperate Measures

Conventional wisdom says to buy decent stock no matter how broke you are—it's just not worth risking your picture for a few bucks saved. But what if you're really stone cold seriously dead broke and even Beta oxide is too expensive? Some film and tape stock companies, or post-production houses, have recycled tape stock that has one or two passes on it. The tape should be checked for picture and audio dropouts, degaussed (de-magnetized), and cleaned. Studio Film & Tape in Los Angeles and New York pioneered recycling tape, and markets it in all formats as ECOTAPE. If shooting with recycled stock sends shivers up your spine, you can certainly use it for Off-Line Editing.

27-04 Film Dailies

These are your workprints. Have the lab quote you up-to-date prices per foot. Don't forget to add stock costs.

35mm (one light) $0.3748 per foot
16mm (one light) $0.3156 per foot

27-05 Sound

While the film lab processes your negative and prints Dailies, you take the original production sound to an audio post house to transfer the 1/4 inch audio tape to Magnetic (Mag) Tape. The Editor or assistant then syncs the Mag Tape with the Film Dailies for screening.

$$$

Typical costs for transferring 1/4 inch to Mag Tape:
35mm and 16mm costs $0.05 to $0.09 per foot. Or you can pay a stock charge of between $70 and $90 per hour.

Stock:
35mm $7 per 7 inch reel (1200 ft.)
16mm $5 per 5 inch reel (600 ft.)

If you want to have a video cassette made of your Dailies, for screening purposes only, you take the Mag Tape over to the lab, where they sync it with the workprint and do a transfer to video.

$$$

For 35mm, a video screening cassette will cost about $.05 a foot. For 16mm it's about $0.125 per foot.

27-08 Telecine

As the name implies, Telecine is the process of transferring filmed images to videotape, usually because you plan to edit on videotape either all the way through to a videotape master, or you plan to edit on tape Off-Line, then return to the film negative, conform it to the edited show, and finish the process on film.

Telecine is done on extremely expensive machines by highly trained people called "Colorists," who "color correct" your images any way you want, from a realistic, balanced look to the color-saturated look in commercials, to the impressionism seen on music videos. A good Colorist can work wonders. Be careful, however, because scene to scene color correction is like an auto repair shop we know whose motto is, *"We're slow, but we're expensive."*

Since Telecine is so expensive, you want to use it wisely, and so there are a number of approaches. Simply put, you can go:

(1) "scene to scene," meaning you'll spend upward of five hours of color correction for every one hour of shot film, getting every scene just right.

(2) "one light," meaning you run the film through Telecine without any stopping for color correction. Why? Because all you want at this stage is videotape you can edit with (often called Video Dailies—and don't forget to budget for this stock). Later, you'll do the real color correction on your finished show.

(3) "best light," a cross between the two.

Which one you choose depends on how much material you have to transfer, how much time you have, how much money you have, and what your editing process is. We suggest you review all this with your editing facility and decide on a plan.

Here are some examples of how others handle the process.

• A commercial producer will often do a one light film to tape transfer to 3/4 inch, edit Off-Line (usually on a non-linear system), then cut the original negative into a "select reel" of all the best takes. The select reel is then transferred scene to scene, and the commercial is finished On-Line.

• A TV movie producer might do a best light transfer to 3/4, and whatever the master format is (D-2 for example). They then edit Off-Line, and go directly to On-Line using the best light D-2 as a play-back source. Now they have an edited master that is not color corrected. To get the color right, they now do a <u>tape to tape</u> color correction in Telecine. Since they are editing on D-2, a digital format, there is no discernable loss of picture quality by going down a generation.

By the way, your production sound will have been recorded on a time-code recorder that puts time code to the 1/4 inch audio tape. In Telecine, the sound is then synced to the picture for the transfer from film to tape.

For other discussions of Post-Production, see Chapter 2 under the sub-heading "Post-Production." Also see in this chapter Editorial (30-00) and Post-Production Film and Lab (31-00).

$$$
Prep and Clean Negative for Telecine:
35mm and 16mm $100/hour
Also quoted as $25 per 1,000 feet

Rates for Video Dailies (one light):
35mm to 3/4 inch or 1/2 inch $0.05 per foot
16mm to 3/4 inch or 1/2 inch $0.125 per foot
(Many places will have a minimum, say around $75. Stock is additional.)

Scene to Scene Telecine Color Correction:
35mm or 16mm to D-2 $475/hour
35mm or 16mm to BetaSP $375/hour

How much time do you allow for color correction? (You can really punch a hole in your budget if you shilly-shally with this.) A starting place is to allow five hours for every one hour of show.

28-00 Travel and Living—Crew

28-01 Air Fares

Economy fare is sufficient for most crew. The exceptions are Directors of Photography and Production Designers, who are sometimes open to negotiation. Also, some contracts may demand flight insurance.

When working non-union, the issue of first-class travel becomes negotiable. For long trips, first class might be justifiable, but generally, "we'd rather see it on the screen."

Sometimes flight packages may be negotiated with airlines, and a promotional deal may be worked out. It's remarkable what a short shot of a plane taking off in your film can get you. Explore promotional tie-ins for savings on air travel.

Don't forget that humans are only one half of your travel expense. Equipment has to fly too, so allow for extra baggage and/or shipping.

28-02 Hotel
By multiplying the number of crew times the hotel day rate times the number of days, you come up with the hotel line budget. Sometimes promotions or package deals can be arranged for long stays. "It's remarkable what a short shot of the hotel can..." Never mind, you already know that one!

If you're going to be on location for a long time, say a month or more, check out renting apartments. It's probably cheaper and more like home. Try your location manager or local film commission for tips on where to look.

Gratuities
Gratuities are sometimes added to the budget. Especially when working in large cities, there will be hands out everywhere—from the doormen to the taxi drivers.

28-08 Per Diem
Meals on the set have been accounted for in Catering (25-00 Location Expenses), but what about breakfast and dinner when you're all in Calcutta? The producer can either pay all meal expenses as they occur or more frequently distribute the per diem ($40 to $50 per day per person depending on local prices) and let each person take care of his or her own meals. This way, the more frugal members of the cast and crew will go home with some pocket money and the producer will know, before the shoot, what to allot for meals.

If the producer provides all meals through catered breakfasts, lunches, and dinners, no per diem is needed, although you may want to give $10 per day for incidentals. In any case, when the producer serves a lunch, you can either deduct it from the per diem, or make for a happy crew and not deduct it. Generally, serving meals on location keeps the production more focused and moving along.

In any case, don't shortchange the crew on meals. As Confucius is so fond of saying: "Crew with empty stomach is like camera with no film. No food, no picture."

29-00 Below-The-Line Fringe

These folks are mostly employees (although you may have a few "loan outs" among your Line Producer, Production Designer, etc.). Once again, these are the employer contributions:

- <u>Social Security and Medicare</u> (FICA-SS and FICA-HI) 7.65%.

- <u>Federal Unemployment Insurance</u> (FUI) 0.8% of first $7,000 in salary.

- <u>State Unemployment Insurance</u> (SUI) adjustable by state. In New York and California it's 5.4% on the first $7,000 in salary.

- <u>Workers' Compensation</u> rate is set annually by state and differs with each industry. Workers' Comp. is less for office people than for grips. Call your state agency or payroll service to ask how much to average for your project. For purposes of illustration, let's say 6%.

For Guild members, add:

DGA   20.2% (AD's, Stage Managers, UPM's only—12.5% P&H + 7.719% Vac./Holiday)

SAG 12.8% (Extras, Day Players, etc.)

AFTRA 12% (Extras, Day Players)

AFM 9% Pension (Theatrical/TV/Film/Videotape/Industrial) $15.54 per 12-hour day for musicians. Other AFM functions are different.

For IATSE members add:

Pension and Health $2.46 per hour (based on straight time rate for any OT hours worked)
Vacation and Holiday 7.719% on day rates based on straight time (weekly rates already include it)
For Teamsters add:
Pension and Health same as IATSE

30-00 Editorial (Film and Video)

30-01 Film Editor
The Editor's creative decisions, under the Director's supervision, contribute tremendously to the success of the film. The Editor (usually with an assistant) screens dailies, edits the work print into an assembly (usually while shooting continues), and later into a rough cut and a fine cut, marks the workprint for the Negative Cutter, edits the voice tracks, prepares picture loops for Automatic Dialogue Replacement (ADR, also called "looping"), checks the sync accuracy for all tracks (voice, music, and sound effects), preps and approves orders for opticals, and screens the answer print for quality control.

When no Sound Effects Editor is on the show, the Editor may also select sound effects, build the sound effects track to conform with the work print, check sync, and prepare cue sheets for sound effects dubbing.

If no Music Editor is on board, the Editor may also build the music track to conform with the work print, check sync, and prepare music cue sheets for dubbing.

149

On large projects there will be an entire editing team with a Music Editor, Sound Effects Editors, and perhaps others. A film like *Jurassic Park* requires a veritable army of editors. On small projects an editor with possibly an assistant editor can manage.

How long will editing take? For a TV movie, or feature, the Editor starts assembly when principal photography begins, and continues through production. There should be a finished assembly or Editor's cut within a day or two of completion of photography. If it's a DGA feature, the Director has a minimum of 10 weeks to complete the Director's cut. For low budget features (under $1.5 million), the Director has 6 weeks.

Scripted television shows of 30 minutes usually get edited in a couple of days. A one-hour show may go 4 to 5 days. A 90-minute show up to 15 days.

A one-hour documentary, on the other hand, can take two months, six months, or a year. Commercials and music videos are usually edited in a few days or weeks. Short films can take a week or two. It all hangs on the quantity of material shot, quality of the Script Supervisor's notes, the speed of the Editor, and the ability of the Director and Editor to communicate.

If the prerequisites for editing are carefully orchestrated so the Editor isn't waiting around for sound or picture elements, the process will be cheaper and more efficient.

$$$
A Film Editor (16mm or 35mm) earns $400 to $600 per 12-hour day.

30-02 Assistant Editor
Editors usually hire their own assistants, who sync and code the dailies, break down dailies after viewing, catalogue and file each scene and take by roll number and edge numbers, mark and order opticals, book screenings, editing rooms and equipment, order dupe negatives,

workprints and optical effects, and maintain a clean and orderly editing room and a cheerful attitude.

$$$
Rates go from $200 to $300 per 12-hour day.

30-03 Music Editor
He or she builds the music track to conform with the work print, checks sync, and prepares music cue sheets for dubbing, and again when dubbing is finished. (For a more complete description of what the Music Editor does, see 34-00 Post Production Sound.)

$$$
Rates are $200 to $500 per 12 hr. day.

30-04 Sound Editor
The Sound Editor works with the Director and Producer to spot for sound effects, pulls the effects from an effects library, supervises the Foley effects sessions, and syncs the effects to picture (which in video is called the "Pre-Lay"). (For a more complete description of what the Sound Editor does, see 34-00 Post-Production Sound.)

$$$
Sound Editors earn $300 to $400 per 12-hour day.

30-05 Cutting (Editing) Room Rental (film)
The Editor will order everything you need, including rooms, Flatbeds or Moviolas (smaller version of flatbed), benches, supplies, and so forth.

$$$
The cost of editing room equipment depends on how much you use, and whether you set up in your own office or use a facility's rooms. Here are some sample basic equipment packages for both 35mm and 16mm.

Room with Bench Setup $212/week or $850/month

Bench Setups include:
> Synchronizer w/one Magnetic Head
> Amp
> Splicer
> Two Split Reels
> Two Spring Clamps
> Tape Dispenser
> Tightwind Attachment w/Core
> Adapter
> Editing Bench w/Rack and Rewinds
> Trim Bin
> Floor Rack
> Swivel Base
> Chair
> Lamp

Room w/16mm 6 plate Moviola Flatbed
> $312/week or $1,250/month

Room w/35mm 6 plate KEM Flatbed $537/week or $2,150/month

Room w/35mm 6 plate Moviola Flatbed
> $398/week or $1,595/month

Bench rentals are sometimes seasonal, and if they are plentiful you may find lower prices. (This is increasingly true as more and more producers are editing on videotape.) Or, your editor may have his own editing room and flatbed, all of which you can get for a package price, including his or her fee.

Telecine (see 27-00 Film and Lab, also discussion of different film and tape editing paths in "Post-Production," Chapter 2.)

Videotape Editing

Whether you shoot on film or tape, videotape editing is becoming more and more popular. The non-linear Off-Line systems give you so many creative choices, it's hard to resist. In fact, many producers succumb to the siren's call and fritter away precious time and money playing around too much. That's where a good Editor comes in.

30-08 Off-Line Editor

Good Editors are enormously helpful in visualizing how a scene can play best, and even how an entire show can be structured best (given the material that's been shot). If you are a hands-on producer, you'll be spending many days and nights with your Editor cooped up in a dark little room. It helps to like each other.

Many Off-Line edit sessions work off a "paper cut."

<u>A Note about Paper Cuts</u>

Paper cuts have that name because they represent the proposed sequence of shots, with appropriate time code, all laid out on paper for the Editor to follow. They are often used with shows that are unscripted, such as documentaries.

Paper cuts begin with VHS or 3/4" copies of all the footage that was shot, with time code burned in a window. The other essential element is the logs. Someone, perhaps an able PA, has screened every window burned tape, and written out what happens in each shot, including any dialogue spoken. Time code marks each in-cue and out-cue for each shot. It is a laborious but essential process.

An example of a log:

12:04:06 - 12:04:17	Wide shot - crowded beach. Sally and Jack's yellow umbrella visible in center frame. Beach sounds.
12:04:21 - 12:05:32	MS - a seagull flies in - lands at water's edge - takes flight as small boy runs in from frame right. Beach and surf sounds.
12:16:34 - 12:16:59	Long shot - Sally (standing) pours Jack (sitting) water from thermos into cup.

Beach sounds + Director giving camera instructions.

12:17:03-12:17:12   Hand-held - topless woman lies on stomach as small girl piles sand on mom's back. Girl turns to cam, stares. Beach sounds.

12:24:09 - 12:24:45   Full body shot - Sally and Jack lie on towel under umbrella. Hand-held cam follows Jack - he stands, walks down beach 10 feet, then returns.

JACK: "You always do this. You always say you love me and then ask me to do something for you."
SALLY: "I do?"
JACK: "You can go get your own popsicle."
Sally stands, walks past Jack and down beach.
JACK: (shouts) "Get me one too."

Then it's time to assemble the paper cut, and even though you are seeing the footage, it takes a practiced eye to put it together in a way that will edit together effectively.

A paper cut can be tight or loose. A tight one means the Producer, Director, or whoever does the paper cut has a clear idea of exactly what shot will go where, and with what audio, in order to best tell the story. A loose one can be merely a sequence of interview bites that lays out the audio narrative in broad strokes. The Editor then assembles that sequence and looks for picture coverage.

Here's an example of a paper cut:

	SALLY - SOT
SALLY - SOT (sound-on-tape)	Usually Jack and I get along
Interview	great. Only lately, um, he's
Reel 3	been strange...um..kind of
03:12:56 - 03:13:09	weird... evasive.

SALLY - Audio only
Interview
Reel 3
03:13:07 - 03:13:16

SALLY - Audio Only
I think he may be seeing
someone. I really do.
Um...he usually is a sloppy
person (LAUGHS). Well, he
is. Only lately he's been
cleaning up his act.

JACK
Washing the car.
Natural sound under.
Reel 6
06:13:11 - 06:13:29

Depending on how complicated the show, and how much footage is shot, a paper cut can be a piece of cake or a real brain teaser. In either case it takes time, anywhere from a few days to weeks and weeks. From a budget standpoint, therefore, it is essential to allow for this, and agree on who is to do it, and for how much.

Also, don't try to create a multicolumn document with a standard word processing program unless you know how to format the document. It will drive you insane. There are several programs on the market that piggyback on your word processing program and give you great looking multicolumn scripts and/or paper cuts. One of them is called Side by Side (Simon Skill Systems, Rancho Santa Fe, CA.). It currently works with Mac and Windows.

So...back to the Off-Line Editor.

In Off-Line Editing you make all your creative decisions. (If you start making changes in On-Line, the much higher hourly rate will make you pay dearly.) A good Editor will show you different ways to cut a scene, but the decision to keep trying or move on is up to you. When the creative choices have all been made, you want the Editor to submit a clean, perfect Edit Decision List (EDL) so that On-Line Editing runs like clockwork.

Many producers have relationships with several favorite Editors whose work they know and trust. If you don't know any, get recommendations from other producers and directors and go meet them and see their reels.

$$$

Off-Line Editors earn from $400 to $500 per 12-hour day average. There are stars, however, particularly in the feature and commercial areas, where you'll pay a premium.

30-09 Off-Line Edit System

For Off-Line, you can go with a traditional linear system, such as a 3/4 inch Case system, or, for about the same amount of money, you can jump into the low end of the non-linear, digital domain.

There are two ways to go. You can Off-Line edit at a post-production house, or you can hire a free-lance editor, rent an edit system, and set it up anywhere you want. The former is usually more expensive, because you are also buying the house's overhead (the fancy bathrooms, free meals, free snacks, and instant maintenance). On the other hand, if you do both your Off-Line and your On-Line at the same house, they may cut you an all-in deal that's worth it.

$$$

The following prices are the cheap method—renting the system and setting up in your, or your editor's extra bedroom. The brand names mentioned (AVID, DVision, Lightworks) are some of the current standards, but more will probably show up on the scene.

Off-Line Systems - Linear
- 3/4 Case systems cuts only. $850/week
- Multisource dissolve systems. $1,600/week

Off-Line Systems - Non-Linear
- AVID Media Composer outputs a 30 fps Edit Decision List (EDL), so is good for editing that will end with a video master.
$1,250/week

- AVID Media Composer can digitize at 24 fps, and outputs an EDL that conforms to a Negative Cut List, so is good for editing that will end with a film master. $2,000/week

- DVision is a DOS based system that is simple and not difficult to learn. Often used for documentaries and low budget features. $850/week

- Lightworks is comparable to the AVID Film Composer in capabilities. $2,000/week

Prices vary depending on the amount of storage. The AVID has Removable Hard Drives (R-Mags). The Lightworks has Towers, the smallest is a 10 gigabyte tower, the "10 hour tower." Each tower is $350/week, and can store about 10 hours of material at medium resolution. Compression schemes are always improving, so you'll be able to pack more material into storage.

Why edit in a non-linear format? Instant gratification sums it up.

In <u>linear</u> editing, once you edit the show into a rough cut, there are only two ways to change the sequence of shots, or add or delete shots. First, you can recut the whole show downstream of the changed edit. Second, you can make the change, then dub your original version from the edit point downstream. Either way it's a chore, and you lose image quality every time you go down a generation.

In <u>non-linear</u> editing you are in the digital realm, and can make changes anywhere you want and see the scene instantly.

Non-linear does have its drawbacks: software bugs, computer down time, and a picture quality (when using the lowest resolution) that looks like your film spent the night on the floor of a taxicab. But the resolution quality is improving (or we're getting used to it) and all in all, non-linear is the way of the future.

Desktop-Based Non-Linear Off-Line Editing
The computer hardware and software for desktop off-line editing is improving fast, but as of this publication date, the storage of moving images and sound is still not up to snuff for any project longer than

a few minutes. Stay tuned, however, because the day is coming when for $20,000 or so, anyone can set up a spiffy off-line non-linear editing system.

30-10 On-Line Editing (Mastering to Video)

For the picture path, this is the final stop. You have made all your creative decisions in the Off-Line Editing, the Editor has made an Edit Decision List (EDL), cleaned it of digital debris, and put it on a floppy disc that is compatible with your On-Line system. Now you go into a luxurious edit bay with deep leather sofas and try to stay awake as an On-Line Editor assembles your show from the EDL, using your video camera originals, or your film-to-tape transferred video masters.

You will have already discussed with your Off-Line Editor and On-Line Editor the *mode of assembly* you will use. There are basically two choices:

- A Mode assembly—the Editor makes all edits in sequential order, from the top of the show to the end. This mode usually takes the longest, because a Tape Operator is constantly putting up and taking down reels. But it is also the only method in which you can watch the show build. If you need to color correct shots, or create any On-Line graphic effects, A Mode is for you.

- B Mode assembly—the EDL is organized by reel number. When a reel is put up, the computer automatically selects all the shots from that reel that will go into the final show. Then the next reel goes up, and the next - until *voila*, the show is done. This is the fastest method, and the most tedious, because you have no idea if everything came together perfectly until the end. B Mode is good for shows with no color corrections and no On-Line Graphics.

There is also C Mode, D Mode, and E Mode assembly, which are variations of the B Mode.

30-11 On-Line Effects—Digital Video Effects (DVE)

Also called the "bells and whistles," these are the myriad effects we've come to expect for television shows—the page turns, curls, flips, spins, wipes, image enlargement, boxes, supers,and so on. Most of the time, Video Effects achieved in the On-Line session are to provide a transition from one shot or scene to another. But Effects can also be used to dress up images, putting colored boxes around them, moving the boxes around, superimposing other images, and so on. A good On-Line Editor can advise you on your project, and tell you how much time it will take to achieve a given effect.

If you have a lot of effects, and/or if they are too complex (or time consuming) for the On-Line session, you are better off having them done by a Graphic Artist on one of the several computer work stations available. Ideally, all of your graphic effects are done before On-Line, laid off to a playback tape, and brought into the On-Line session all wrapped up and pretty—ready to be dropped into the show just like any other shot. (See 35-00 Titles and Graphics.)

Rates for On-Line and Effects are listed by the hour, and include the edit suite, a record machine in the format of choice, one playback machine, the On-Line Editor, and usually a Tape Operator. If you add more playback machines, any of the Digital Video Effects (DVE) available, character generator time, or extra dubs, you pay more. It's like having lunch in an expensive restaurant. You have prepared yourself for the high price of the entree, but when you get the bill and see how the soup, wine, dessert, and expresso doubled the price, it always makes you gulp.

That's why it's important to negotiate a good deal going in, since On-Line Editing is highly competitive. Work out what services you think you'll need. Include your best estimate of how many hours you'll need (ask your Off-Line Editor), what effects you'll use, how much character generator time you'll need (show your credits list and other on-screen verbiage to the On-Line sales person), and allow plenty for Dubs and Transfers, which includes master coded stock, and any duplicate masters (ask the sales person for an estimate).

Now you have a plan that can be compared apples to apples with several different post houses. Call a few and get bids. Then try playing one house against another to get the rates down even lower. They'll ask if you'll work nights and weekends. Say "yes." But always insist on a fully qualified On-Line Editor—no apprentices.

$$$

Here are some average On-Line and Effects Rates (but you can beat them).

D-1 Mastering
One D-1 Playback to one D-1 Record

$450 - 600/hour

Digital Betacam or Betacam to D-1 Record
One Digital Betacam playback to one D-1 Record

$500/hour
One BetaSP playback to one D-1 Record $425/hour

Digital Betacam or BetaSP to Digital Betacam
One Digital Betacam to one Digital Betacam Record

$400/hour
One BetaSP to one Digital Betacam Record $345/hour

D-2 Mastering
One D-2 playback to one D-2 Record $400/hour

Interformat Editing to D-2 Record
One BetaSP playback to one D-2 Record $300 - 345/hour

Additional On-Line Services and DVE
Sony System G (creative image distortion) $400/hour
Kaleidoscope - per channel (page turns, curls etc.) $375/hour
ADO 100 (reposition of image, zoom past normal size) $250/hour
Chyron Infinit! (character generator - with operator) $135/hour

30-12 and 30-14   Videotape Stock - Editing

The next item of business you will have already discussed is what format you are editing to. This was decided months ago when you called your distributor and asked how they wanted the edited masters delivered. They may have said one inch videotape, D-1, D-2, D-3, or whatever else has been invented since this book was published. (There's a new format every Tuesday.)

One inch video is the pre-digital workhorse. It's still reliable, and plenty of shows are still mastered and broadcast on one inch. It's also the cheapest of the lot.

$$$
60 minute black and coded stock is about $230.

D-1 is a component digital tape format. *Component* means the video signal is split into three components—red, green, and blue. Its component status makes it the format of choice for high-end effects and graphics work, where precise colors are prized.

$$$
76-minute black and coded stock is $400 or so.

D-2 is a composite digital tape format. *Composite* means the red, green and blue elements of the video signal are combined, or composited, into one signal. Because of its lower cost (lower than D-1, that is), it is the format of choice for editing and broadcast.

$$$
64 minutes of black and coded D2 stock is around $300.

A popular feature of any digital format is that even several generations away from the original, there is no discernible signal loss. Compare that to one inch or BetaSP, where you really see the difference after three or four generations.

There are three formats you probably won't use because of their relative obscurity, but you should know about them anyway, just in case.

D-3 is another composite digital tape format—Panasonic's answer to D-2. NBC is the only broadcaster at present requiring delivery on D-3.

D-5 is a component format, also by Panasonic, similar to D-1.

DCT (Digital Component Transport) is a compressed digital component format from Ampex. Like D-1, its machines can read both PAL and NTSC.

(PAL and NTSC are two of the more common technical methods used around the world for recording and playing back video. Different countries use different methods, and none is compatible with any other. PAL, used in the United Kingdom and much of Europe, displays 25 frames of video per second, and has 625 lines of video information per frame.

DCT is a high-end editing format usually used by commercial clients who require precise colors and the ability to layer multiple images without generation loss.

Digital Betacam is an up and coming favorite as both a production and an editing format. It is component, and digital, and has four channels of digital audio (compared to Betacam's two channels).

$$$
60 minute black and coded stock is about $235.

31-00 Post-Production - Film and Lab

In category 27-00 Film and Lab, your film was developed at the lab and dailies were made. The dailies are broken down by the Editor or assistant and become the Work Print, which is reworked until a fine cut is achieved. This is the film equivalent of Off-Line Editing in video where all the creative decisions are made.

Some Lab expenses to budget for:

31-01 Duplicate Work Prints
These are made from the Work Print, and while they used to be in black and white, they are now in color. When you're in Seattle, and a studio executive in N.Y. wants to see the dailies, you make a Dupe Work Print.

A close cousin of the Dupe Work Print is the "Dirty Dupe," a black and white print made from the cut Work Print for the Sound Effects Editor, Music Editor, and for ADR (Automatic Dialogue Replacement, or "Looping").

35mm	$0.20 - $0.30 per foot
16mm	$0.20 - $0.30 per foot

162

31-02 Negative Cutter

Now the Work Print has been approved, the Editor has clearly marked where all optical effects are to occur, and it's time to turn it into a finished film. So off it goes to the Negative Cutter.

Working with the original camera negative is a delicate job, so don't scrimp on an amateur—you don't want a scratched or damaged negative. The Negative Cutter breaks down and catalogues the original negative and the optical or mag track, records and catalogues edge numbers of the final work print, orders necessary dupes, matches and cuts the negative to conform to the work print, and cleans and repairs the negative, as necessary. Once Optical effects have been approved, the Neg Cutter edits them into the final negative.

$$$

Rates (non-union):

$550 to $850 per 1,000' reel (standard features are 10 - 12 reels) . Allow about one day and a quarter per reel. Also budget for supplies, leader, etc. ($75 per reel).

Opticals

Opticals are the same basic effects you get in your Video On-Line and Effects (dissolves, freezes, flips, skip frames, reverse action, wipes, zooms, etc., as well as titles), except achieved through a completely different technology.

In the sequence of things, Opticals are usually ordered before the Negative Cutting. The Assistant Editor prepares a *count sheet*, giving precise instructions to the Opticals House. "This fade begins at this frame, lasts for three feet and ends at that frame." Then the original uncut negative is sent to the Opticals House. They make a pin-registered Interpositive for each optical effect, and use it to put the effect onto a negative. That negative is returned to the Negative Cutter to be cut into the film.

(See 32-00 Optical Effects for budget breakdown)

31-03 Develop Optical Negative
There is one intermediate step and expense. The Optical House does the shooting but the Lab must develop the Optical Negative. Here are some prices.

$$$

35mm	$0.34 - $0.37 per foot
16mm	$0.34 - $0.37 per foot

31-04 Answer Prints
Now that the negative has been cut, and the opticals are all included, it's time to get the the colors and densities in the film looking just right. That process is achieved through the Answer Print, and is the job of the Timer. If you see colors or densities that are off, you have another Answer Print made until you get it right. Finally, you have the perfect formula for your Release Prints, but to get to the Release Print, you must make an Interpositive and an Internegative.

$$$

(If you "wet gate" the Answer Print to smooth out scratches add $0.10 per foot.)

35mm (from A/B rolls) $0.75 - $1.5887 per foot
16mm (from A/B rolls) $0.75 - $1.4514 per foot

31-05 Intermediate Positive (IP)/Intermediate Negative (IN)
The IP (also called "Interpositive") is made from the original cut negative. The reason to make an IP is so you can make an IN. (Remember, we're going from negative to positive, and the only way to make a positive print you can watch is from a negative.) Now that you have an IN, you'll want to check it for any dirt, scratches, or other problems that may have cropped up. So you make a Check Print, until you're sure you have a perfect IN. It has to be perfect because that IN is what you'll use to make your Release prints.

(Think twice before making IP's and IN's or even titles until a distribution deal is worked out. You may be asked to make editorial changes and a new, expensive internegative.)

$$$

Most labs give you a break if you make the Answer Print, IP, IN, and Check Prints at their place.

Intermediate Positive	
35mm	$1.6038 per foot
16mm (from A/B rolls)	$1.1273 per foot
Intermediate Negative	
35mm	$1.3975 per foot
16mm	$0.9517 per foot

31-07 Release Prints

This is it. The actual prints that will journey far—illuminating darkened theaters with the brilliance of your movie magic. The Release Prints are made from two sources, a picture source (the IN; intermediate negative), and the sound source (the Optical Sound Track). Together, they are used to make a composite Release Print.

Normally, the Release Print expenses are paid by the distributor, and the more prints, the greater the lab discount. Therefore, wait until you've completed a distribution deal before ordering prints (for yourself) in quantity. You can then piggyback on the distributor's rate.

$$$

When figuring footage for the Release Prints, add 30 to 40 feet for the head and tail leader the lab will require for Release Prints, Optical Negatives, or Internegatives. A production company logo will increase the total footage as well.

35mm (from Internegative)	$0.3128 per foot
16mm (from Interneg)	$0.2666 per foot

Lab Rush Charges

Labs are always asked to produce miracles and meet impossible deadlines. They'll do it but it costs. Rush charges can amount to

100%-300% above standard rates. If you know that processing or printing must be done at night, on weekends or holidays, add this line item. Avoid rush charges with proper planning. This goes for rush shipping as well.

32-00 Optical Effects (Film)

If you are delivering your master on videotape, and/or if you do not need to project your film in theaters, you can skip this line item. If you are delivering on film, you need an Optical House for any effects like dissolves, fades, and wipes, and any text on screen, including titles and credits.

The Optical House receives the marked work print from the editor, and/or the count sheet from the editor with specific instructions for every effect. They make a pin-registered Interpositive (IP) for each Optical effect, and use it to print the effect onto a negative in an Optical printer. That negative is returned to the Negative Cutter to be cut into the film.

Text, like titles and credits, are type set, shot on hi-con film, and composited over the IP, creating a "texted" IN.

For an average feature, the Opticals process may take two to three weeks or longer if there are changes.

$$$

There are three expenses in Opticals: the shooting of the IP's, the developing of the IP's, and the effects themselves. (The developing costs are covered above in category 31-00, under Develop Optical Negative.)

Shooting the IP's can run $1.60 to $2.40 per foot. If a negative has been scratched, or if you have old footage that has been mishandled, the Optical House puts the negative through a wet gate process to smooth out the defects. As a setup to the IP process, it usually runs about $75.

There are tons of effects you can order, but here is a sample menu (prices are per each effect, and are the same for 16mm and 35mm):

Dissolve	$300 - $700
	(variable is length of effect)
Fade	$200 - $500
Freeze Frame	$200 - $500
Repositioning	$300 - $500

(What is repositioning? Here's an example: the love scene is steamy, but in the corner of the shot we can make out the reflection of a grinning Grip in the shiny knob of the brass bed. We need to reposition the shot, enlarge it a bit, to lose the offending leer.)

Step Printing	$300 - $500
	(Speeding up or slow motion)
Compositing text over picture	$500 per card
Text over black	$150/hr. overhead camera
Artwork	$50 - $75 per card

Many Optical Houses give student discounts of 30% to 50% or better. If you're a student, ask about this.

Digital Visual Effects

These days, many optical and title houses provide more services than titles and standard effects. They're now into main title design, traveling mattes, blue screen composites, and high-end 3D animation effects.

The compositing of images and text for film is done on one of several possible computer systems. The Domino is one. Cineon is another. They'll also remove any film damage and make wires used in mechanical effects disappear.

For 3D special effects, you'll probably be into Macintosh or SGI systems. Let's say you have an actor playing an android, and he has to unbutton his shirt, open up his rib cage, and pull a damaged chip from where the liver usually lives. That's 3D special effects.

If you are planning anything like this, it's imperative that you meet with the Director and the Artist doing the effect before you shoot—first to see if you can afford it, and second to prepare for the shoot. Artists are fond of saying that a one-hour conversation before shooting the scene can save tens of thousands of dollars in post. It's true.

The pre-production meeting can also help you avoid a common misconception about computers. They take time. On some effects, it may take the computer two weeks just to render what the artist has finished.

$$$

These are the (simplified) steps you travel through to produce computer generated effects, with some sample rates:

Inputting - film or video transfer to exabyte - a storage medium. $5 per frame for film. $225/per hour for tape.

Modeling - computer wire frame models to create 3D images.
$150/hr.

Compositing - layering live action or other images with the computer images. $150/hour

Animation - making the images move over time. $150/hour

Rendering - every frame is re-drawn by the computer. $50/hour at about 10 minutes per frame for fairly complex work.

Output mediums - exabyte back to tape or film. $2.50 - $5.00 per frame for film and $225 per hour to tape.

33-00 Music (Film and Video)

This category covers the getting or creating of music. The technical methods of recording and editing it are in 34-00 Post-Production Sound.

There are three common ways to get music for your project:

(1) Have it composed.
(2) License pre-recorded music from a music library.
(3) Buy CD's with pre-recorded music from a buy-out music library.

Composer
A composer (preferably one accustomed to scoring to movies) screens your final work print (in video, it would be your On-Line edited master), and composes music directly to picture. If you get a good composer, this is the best way to go. You get the personal touch.

Costs depend on the composer's reputation, the number of musicians used, recording studio time, and total number of minutes of music needed. But you don't always need a symphony orchestra, not since the synthesizer.

The synthesizer has probably put a lot of musicians out of work, which is sad, but nonetheless it is now a permanent "player" on the scene. Many composers create the score and play all the music parts on a synthesizer. That's usually the cheapest method. If the resulting sound is too synthesized for you, composers can lay down a synthesized foundation, then bring in some musicians to sweeten the sound. A few real violins or French horns over the electronic ones can make a world of difference.

If you don't know any composers and don't really know what you can get for your budget, call some agents who handle composers, and tell them how much you want to spend. They'll refer you to some of their clients appropriate for your show.

If you know or have been referred to some composers, ask them to bid on the music package, which may include composing, arranging and producing all necessary music, studio time, musicians, and equipment. It's called an "all-in" or a "package" deal. The composer ultimately presents you with a finished tape ready for audio post.

$$$

Some sample package budgets:

- A composer for a TV movie might receive $40,000 to $60,000 as a package deal.
  - A half-hour TV show might pay as little as $3,000 to $5,000.
  - A three-minute promotional might pay $1,500 to $2,500.

When you do a package deal with a composer, you avoid having to deal directly with the musician's union, the American Federation of Musicians (AFM). Not that they are bad people, but if you are unfamiliar with the complexities of union wages and extras, you have a steep learning curve ahead. That's why many producers like packages.

Other producers go one of three other routes:

(1) If the composer is a signatory company to the AFM, he can hire union people and take care of the union payrolls himself.

(2) If the composer is not signatory, he or she can use a payroll service that is signatory, and administrate the union payrolls through the service. This works for film projects only, not for videotape (it's a union agreement thing).

(3) The composer can hire union people, but bring them in outside of union payroll, that is, pay cash. In this last scenario, the musicians will probably want more than scale, since they are forgoing their union benefits. Also, the composer is advised to bring in the musicians one at a time, since they don't want to be seen by other musicians working a non-union gig.

<u>Music Line Items</u>

If for whatever reason you decide to hire the composer for creative talents only and put the rest of the music package together yourself, there are hard costs to contend with.

Composer's Fee (creative only)

Composers are outside the jurisdiction of the AFM. A negotiable amount that can be as little as $2,000 for an episode of a half-hour weekly prime time series, to $100,000 for a feature if you're dealing with an established master.

Musicians

If you are working with non-union musicians, fees are negotiable, although you can get some clues by reading the American Federation of Musicians basic agreements (or see The Industry Labor Guide in the Resources section). The union work rules are complex. There are different fees for features, trailers, shorts, commercials, industrial/documentary, television, home video, and so on. Length of the program is important. Musicians who "double" (play more than one instrument) get more money. (Since it is possible to produce very different sounds by changing instruments, this is a very cost effective way of broadening the sound landscape of the musical score.)

Figuring a union music budget requires an experienced hand. Study the AFM basic agreement or the section of The Labor Guide to gain a basic understanding. Even then you may need help the first time. Other costs must be taken into consideration, such as leader fees, rehearsals, meal penalties, overtime, and instrument rental and cartage.

Other contractual considerations will be the publishing and auxiliary rights to the music produced (sound track and songs), which may affect the composer's and musicians' fees. A music rights lawyer should be consulted on these issues. The union commitment does not stop after the musicians walk out the door. There is a back end for musicians if the music is released as a sound track, or in foreign or other supplementary markets, and for commercials there are residual fees. Contact the music payroll service about these issues.

$$$

Some sample rates from the AFM agreement:

TV Movies and Theatrical Films (budgets of $6 million or less)
Sideman (regular player) 3 hrs. or less $208 (35 men or more)
$240 (23 men or less)
Double (plays a second instrument) $360

<u>Television</u> (one hour variety special)
Sideman
(with 4 hours rehearsal same day) $316

<u>Documentary/Industrial</u>
Sideman (2-hour session) $147
Overtime after 2 hours $18/hour

Again, these are just sample rates. They don't include cartage, rental, pension, health, and other fringes. If you are putting together your own package, consult the agreement and work with someone who knows how the agreement applies to your show. Discuss it with a music payroll service (See Resources section).

Music Prep

Once the harmonic, rhythmic, and melodic structure has been established by the Composer, either the Composer or an Orchestrator/Arranger assigns the various voices (including instruments) in the form of an orchestra score. Then a Copyist produces a finished score for each musician.

$$$

Music Prep people get paid by the page, but at the beginning of a project you won't know how many pages there will be or how many musicians, so here's a rule of thumb. For an orchestra of 40 people for a 3-hour session, budget an extra 50% of the musicians' gross wages for the Music Prep folks. Adjust it later when you know what you've got.

Studio Costs

Studio costs include the room rate, the setup, piano tuning, outboard gear, tape stock, and a 2nd Engineer. (The 1st Engineer is either a staff person or a freelancer whom you will pay separately.)

$$$

Costs are $145 to $250 per hour. Try to get a flat deal (called a "lock-out") with the studio—a set number of hours for less than the combined hourly rate. Recording for commercials that only use a few hours may cost twice the usual rate, since the studio has pretty much blown the day on you.

Cartage and Rentals

This one always amazes first time producers. In certain cities, Los Angeles and Nashville, for example, the producer must either pay cartage for some instruments, or pay the musician a set fee for bringing it in himself. For some reason, there is no cartage fee in New York City.

Cello players, for example, get $6, but percussionists with a van full of congas, bull-roarers, and slit gongs can get up to $400, as do synth players. Amps for guitars are extra, and grand pianos are way extra. (If you do need a grand piano, see if you can get the rental fee waived in exchange for a screen credit, and just pay the cartage.)

Even working non-union, musicians who play more than one instrument will expect an additional rental and playing fee, but that is small compared to what it would cost to hire additional musicians.

Synth Programming

If your composer is laying down a synth foundation, the machine needs to be programmed. This is also a handy place to hide additional creative fees to the composer (assuming he or she is actually playing the synth).

Singers

Singers are covered by the SAG and AFTRA union agreements, and are paid according to a complicated formula based on what the show is, whether they are on camera or off, whether they over-dub, if they "step out" from a group and sing solo up to 16 bars, and so on. Consult the SAG or AFTRA agreements or <u>The Labor Guide</u> (see Resources) for rates.

$$$
Some sample rates:
Television (off-camera)
4-hour session solo or duo $544/day
Overdubbing   100% of the day rate.

Payroll Service

Because music is so complicated to budget and track paperwork and residuals, there are payroll services that specialize. Their fees may be the same as for a production payroll service (2%-3% of gross payroll) or higher if they become a signatory to the AFM for you (up to 4%). Still, it's probably well worth it. A good service will really work with you to help get the best deals on the union contracts and keep you straight with the paperwork.

Miscellaneous

Music hard costs suffer the same slings and arrows as production hard costs, so allow for office expenses, phones, postage, messenger, and other expenses (see 38-00 General and Administrative Expenses for a master checklist).

Desperate Measures

Another route is to hire student composers and musicians from music schools who can often provide reasonable work for bottom-dollar. The student composer may well do the job for no fee (he or she gets a sample reel and a credit out of the deal) if you cover the hard costs of studios, instrument rental, cartage, tape stock, etc. Yet another way is to ask the composer for any unreleased recordings you can license directly, provided the composer owns 100% of the publishing rights (sync and master rights).

Licensing Pre-Recorded Music

Music libraries license music for a fee, based on how much music you use and in what markets it will appear. This is still called "needledrop" music, because each time the needle (remember those?) was moved on the record, it was another charge. Per "needledrop" means one continuous use of a single piece of music. You can also purchase a "production blanket," which gives you unlimited use of music within a single production.

Some libraries charge "search fees" if you use their people to search for music. In most cases, you are the searcher. You tell them what styles of music you seek, and they put you in a room with a stack of CD's and a pair of earphones.

Do not pay music license fees until after you've completed your film and know for sure what cuts you'll use. Many filmmakers mistakenly purchase music rights and then do not use the music. Finally, if you are a student filmmaker, or producing for a non-profit, ask for discounts.

$$$

Sample Needledrop fees:
Broadcast (Free TV and Basic/Pay Cable)

	$300/needledrop
Basic/Pay Cable TV only	$150
Commercial (national network + cable)	$400
Commercial (local Free TV + cable)	$125
Corporate (up to 150 copies)	$70

Sample Production Blanket fees:
Broadcast (Free TV, Basic/Pay Cable, 45 to 60 min.)

	$1,600/program
Cable TV only (45 to 60 min.)	$1,065
Home Video (up to 10,000 copies, 45 to 60 min.)	$2,925
Corporate (unlimited copies, 15 to 20 min.)	$800

Buy-Out Music Library
Some producers amass a collection of CD's from Buy-Out Libraries, and then use any music for anything anytime they want. Like the Licensing Libraries, what you get is commissioned music, mostly from synthesizers, that is organized according to the *feeling* of the music you want. Hence categories like, "Corporate Image," "Forward Progress," and "Pensive." Single cuts have titles like, "Shopping Spree," "Cash Flow," "Japan Nights," and "Action Central News."

$$$
Sample rates:

Package #1 (19 CD's of assorted styles)	$800
Package #2 (11 CD assortment)	$400
Package #3 (any 2 CD's)	$49
Package #4 (6 CD's of sound effects)	$269

Purchasing contemporary pop music by recording stars is extremely expensive and presents enormous legal problems. You must deal with the composer, the publisher and the record company, and pay additional "reusage" fees to the musicians who performed on the original recording. Costs can run in the thousands. For a discussion of music rights, see Chapter 2.

34-00 Post-Production Sound (Film and Video)

Your dialogue is on your originals, and has been part of the picture editing process all along. Now it's time to fill out the sound dimension with music and sound effects. First we'll follow the film path, then the video path.

The Film Process

On a large production, there will be a Supervising Sound Editor to ride herd on all the post sound elements. On a small project, that may be you, with help from technical people as you go. At this point, there are lots of sounds to prepare: music, sound effects, "Looped" dialogue (ADR), Foley (sound effects), and possibly narration. The preparation of all these elements should happen as simultaneously as possible, just to keep a lid on the overall length of the project. Let's take each element one at a time, starting with music.

34-01 Spotting (Music and effects)

The Music Editor, the Composer, the Director, and the Producer watch the finished picture edit of the film in what is called a "spotting session." They all talk about where music should be, and what kinds of feelings it should evoke. (The Director and Producer also spot for sound effects with the Sound Effects Editor.) The Music Editor takes careful notes, which go to the Composer, who writes the music, and plays it for the Director and Producer in "listening sessions." Once the creative aspects of the score are approved, it is ready to be recorded on a Music Scoring Stage. The Music Editor now edits "streamers"—yellow warning stripes—onto the picture to alert the composer to upcoming tempo changes, start points ("downbeats") and such.

Desperate Measures

If you can't afford to score with real musicians, then the composer writes the score, records it from synthesizer to some tape format, probably DAT. You then skip the Music Scoring Stage step, and go directly to Music Pre-Lay (see below).

$$$

Spotting is usually done off a 3/4 inch videotape with a window for time code, so all you're paying for is people's time.

34-02 Music Scoring Stage

This is a recording studio with projection capability, so the Composer/ Conductor can record the music in sync to picture. The music is recorded on multitrack tape, and/or 35mm film.

$$$

Scoring stages cost $160 to $700 per hour, depending on how elaborate you want your recording to be. An average feature score might take from five to ten days or longer to record.

34-03 Music Mix Down

After the musicians go home, the Composer, and the Music Editor work with the engineer to mix the multitracks down, usually into two stereo tracks. Some Music Editors like to record the mix on Digital Audio Tape with time code, and make a 4 track analog tape as a back-up. Since some mixing studios still do not have DAT playback capability (and it costs a lot to bring in a DAT machine), the analog copy might come in handy.

Here's another tip for the music mix. Let's say there's a big cymbal crash on "Rex" and "Veronica's" first screen kiss, and you fear it may be over the top. You can keep any of those dubious elements on a third track, saved for the final mix, where you can use it or lose it. The flip side of that ploy is that if you have too many dubious cues, you'll drive the Recording Mixer crazy—he or she already has enough to do with all the ADR, Foley, and sound effects to mix in as well.

$$$
The Mix Down can happen on the same board used in the scoring session, or, less preferably, on another board. The rate is $160 to $400 per hour, depending on how "high-end" you are .

Desperate Measures
If your "orchestra" is a combo of friends, and you can't afford a scoring stage, try packing into a friend's garage recording studio rigged for video projection. Remember, if you have not recorded a synth foundation, the recording machine needs to be electronically locked to the picture; otherwise music cues may be out of sync Consult an audio engineer at an audio sound house.

If you did record a synth foundation, and have transferred the music to a multitrack tape with time code, you are already synced to picture, and your combo can jam along to the synth—no picture or picture lock may be needed. On the other hand your musicians lose the opportunity to put in stings which are musical accents which illuminate visual action.

Music Pre-Lay
The music has been mixed, and the Music Editor now needs to correctly place it to picture in a process called *pre-lay*. The music cues are transferred to a multitrack tape which will become the playback source in the Final Dub, or Final Mix.

$$$
Pre-Lay rooms go for $150 to $275 per hour. A TV movie or low-budget feature might take up to 20 hours or so.

178

34-04 Automatic Dialogue Replacement (ADR) Stage

Now that the music is underway, it's time to consider ADR. Prior to booking your ADR Stage, you had a "spotting" session at your audio post house, in which you confirmed the worst: portions of dialogue are unusable (the neighbor refused to silence his yapping yellow Chihuahua, or your lead actor just couldn't deliver that morning). You identify exactly what dialogue needs to be replaced. Your ADR Editor prepares actor's lines and cue sheets for the ADR Mixer. You now bring your actors to the ADR stage, project the film or tape, and have them try their darndest to lip sync to picture as they listen to their original lines through earphones.

Desperate Measures:

For bare bones ADR, you need a quiet place, a film loop of each scene to be looped, or a video playback, some earphones, decent microphones, a decent recording machine such as 1/4 inch, multi-track, or video (Beta deck or better), and the ability to lock your recording machine to your picture. If you only have some small ADR to do, you could squeeze it in during the final mix. Be sure the Mixer knows all about it beforehand, and don't be too surprised if he looks at you in horror.

$$$

ADR rates vary from $200 to $350 per hour for one Mixer.

34-04 Foley Stage/Foley Artists

A Foley Stage is a specially designed soundproof room in which Foley Artists watch a projection of the film, and make sound effects that sync up with the picture. The Artists are masters at finding ingenious ways to make sounds, and include footsteps, horses walking, body punches, and a zillion other effects in their repertoire.

$$$

Foley Stages go for about $275 to $350 per hour. Foley Artists earn $350 to $425 per day. But the "Walla Crew" (true term), the people who make crowd scene sounds (like "walla walla!"), earn less, between $200 to $300 per day.

179

Desperate Measures
Features, TV movies, and prime time episodics Foley every foot-step in the show. But you can save money by selecting only the sections that really need it. You may also use library sound effects, but be careful—the editor may spend so much time on it in you would have spent the same money in Foley.

34-05 Narration Recording
Some producers like to record a rough, or "scratch" narration track during Off-Line editing, using themselves as unpaid talent. This gives you freedom to make copy changes as you go, and tailor the copy to scenes as they change.

When the cut is approved, a professional Narrator is called into the recording studio to record the final track. Some like to record to a running picture, others find this a distraction, and prefer to just record it to the producer's cues for length of each speech. We've found the latter approach to be the most successful.

To save money some producers record the Narrator with a Nagra recorder outside the studio, but the quality may suffer from ambient sounds.

Depending on the complexity of the copy and the ability of the Narrator, figure one to three hours for a 30-minute documentary script. Take the time necessary to do the job right.

For long documentaries, calculate additional time to return to the studio to record "pick-up" lines, should re-editing become necessary. Use the same studio so the sound quality and microphones will match. Be sure your rate for a narrator includes these pick-up sessions whenever possible.

$$$
Narrators are in either SAG or AFTRA. AFTRA announcer's scale for a one-hour documentary is $616.

To record the Narrator "wild" (i.e., without a simultaneous picture) to Digital Audio Tape (DAT) in an announce booth, with

Recordist and engineer, costs $150 - $250/hour, plus stock. To picture is $285/hour plus stock.

Desperate Measures

To save money some producers record the Narrator with a Nagra or comparable recorder in their shower stall, with blankets over the windows at four in the morning, but the quality may suffer from the ambient sounds of other family members snoring. A friend may also have a home recording studio that will work.

34-06 Laydown

After all the different sound elements have been prepared, they are ready to be synced to the picture in the Pre-Lay (see Music Pre-Lay above, and Sound Editor below). The audio post house takes the approved Answer Print, which has the production sound either on an optical track attached to the print, or on mag tape, and does a *laydown*, wherein the production sound is stripped from the picture, and laid down to one track on a multitrack tape. Time code goes to another track for reference. All the other sound elements, music, ADR, Foley, and so forth are Pre-Layed — synced to picture—on different tracks of this multitrack tape.

$$$

Laydown rates are in the neighborhood of $150 to $275 per hour.

34-07 Conforming on Mag Film

Now that you have recorded the ADR, Foley, and sound effects, Sound Editors edit them at the right place in the picture in a process called Conforming. This can be done either with mag film and a work print, or on a Digital Work Station (see below).

If you are having this done on mag film and syncing to film work prints, you can't hear any of it played together until the mix. But if you are using one of the Digital Work Stations now common in most audio post houses, you can hear it played in relation to almost everything else.

$$$

-When a Sound Editor works on mag tape with a work print for picture, the room and equipment costs around $500 per day.

- Mag film stock is $80 per reel. A $4 million feature might average 60 reels ($4,800).

- 24 Track stock is $250 per one-hour reel. A $4 million feature can use up to 30 reels ($7,500).

34-08 Pre-Lay on Digital Work Stations

Let's say the Sound Editor wants to edit in all the sound effects. He has all the effects ready for playback (from your Foley sessions, your effects library, etc.). He now sets up a multitrack recording system, say 24 tracks. Then he goes through the show editing in all the footsteps onto one track. Next pass he'll do all the crowd cheers on another track, and so on. Then he'll edit in the ADR material on another track. He edits in everything except the music. When he's done, he has everything on the multitrack correctly placed to picture, and he has a finished cut on a 3/4 inch video cassette with a time-code window. That 24 track will become the effects and ADR playback source in the final mix. But first, there's a Pre-Dub session.

$$$

Digital Work Stations cost anywhere from $175 to $300 per hour.

34-09 Pre-Dub (Pre-Mix)

In this session, the picture is projected and the 24 track is played. Now the Mixer works with levels of the various effects, or dialogue, getting them one step closer to the final mix.

$$$

Pre-Dub sessions cost $150 to $450 per hour.

34-10 Final Dub (Mix)

In the final mix session, all your sound elements, including production dialogue and sound, ADR dialogue, narration, Foley, music, and sound effects are combined, usually into a stereo four track configuration (left, center, right, and surround) on a new multitrack tape or mag film.

$$$
Mixing can cost anywhere from $300 to $700 per hour, depending on what equipment you use, where you mix, how many margaritas you have, and how many Mixers are in the session (big or complicated projects can use up to three).

34-11 Printmaster
Now the mixed audio on multitrack is combined, through either a Dolby or ultra-stereo matrix encoder to create the Printmaster. This will then be used to transfer to 35mm negative for sound.

$$$
Print masters cost from $250 to $500 per hour.

Dolby
This may be a bit obscure for most producers, but since great sound is fast becoming the standard for home entertainment centers, and already exists for movie theaters, we want to include it. Dolby Laboratories has several technologies producers should know about.

Dolby Noise Reduction (DNR) is a technology to reduce tape hiss—good to have on your master. An audio post facility already equipped with DNR will probably include it in your package. If they don't have the equipment, it has to be rented, and you'll pay for that. By the way, DNR is standard on all BetaSP, which means your production audio hiss is already reduced.

If you are releasing your project on VHS cassettes, and you want DNR, you, or the legal owner of the property (maybe the distributor), must become a licensee of the DNR technology. Most of the major distributors and studios already are, but in any case, the fee is only $150.

Dolby Surround is a technology applied to any consumer media such as VHS, CD, video games, CD-ROM, etc., that encodes the audio. When the audio is played back on your similarly equipped home entertainment system, you get 4 channel sound, just like in a movie theater. The technology will probably be standard for most home systems within a few years.

If you want Dolby Surround on your project, work at an audio post facility that has it. Otherwise, contact Dolby Laboratories for further information (see Resources).

Dolby Stereo is a similar technology for the theatrical release of 35mm films. There is a basic license fee of $7,500 per feature, which includes the prep of the master. Most major studios include it, and the list of independents is growing.

Mag Stock/Transfers

On low budget projects stay away from Mag stock—24 track is cheaper. Most sound edit rooms are now set up so you don't need Mag transfers. It's all done on the Digital Work Station.

34-12 Optical Sound Transfers

After the final mix, you end up with a completely mixed sound track on Mag film. The optical house shoots an optical neg of the track, which becomes the sound track for the Internegative, and ready to make release prints.

$$$

Optical Sound Transfers cost $0.35 to $0.38 per foot. An average feature will therefore be $3,500 to $4,000.

Video

Audio post for video follows a similar path as film, but with different technology.

34-14 Laydown

First you take your edited master (which has production audio on it), and go through a process called *laydown*, in which the audio is stripped off the videotape and put on to a multitrack audio tape. The sound is kept in sync with the picture by the master's time code, which goes to a dedicated audio track.

34-15 Pre-Lay

The other audio elements, the music, sound effects, ADR, Foley, and narration all may exist on different pieces of tape, some on Digital Audio Tape (DAT), on multitrack, or 1/4 inch. In the pre-lay session, they are rerecorded onto multitrack audio tape, and synced to their correct places in the picture.

34-16 Mix

In the Mix Session, you and the Mixer decide on the appropriate levels for each of the elements.

34-17 Lay-Back

When everyone agrees that the Mix is a success (given the time/budget parameters), the mixed audio is *laid back* to the video master. Now you have a Sweetened Edited Master, the final stop. Except you'd better make a protection copy from which you can strike any dubs. Put the Master master away in a vault.

$$$

How much does all this cost? A $10 million feature may spend from $300,000 to $7,500,000 on audio post. A TV movie or low-budget feature ($3 million to $4 million) might spend $60,000 to $150,000 on audio post. A half-hour children's home video with music, dialogue, and effects could spend $3,000 to $5,000. If you have only a few elements, say music, a half-dozen sound effects, and production dialogue, you might do the same half-hour for $1,000 to $2,000.

Since audio post is often budgeted as a package "all-in" deal, first figure out exactly what you'll need and about how much you can afford, then call two or three audio post houses and get bids.

Desperate Measures

As with video post, you can try to play one facility against another to get the bids down, but don't make up stories. All these people know each other and word quickly spreads if you're faking low quotes. If the price is still too steep, sit down with the house of your choice and work out what services you can cut to fit your budget.

35-00 Titles and Graphics

35-01 Graphic Designer and Workstation

The computer has taken hold of the graphic design industry and swallowed it whole. Every graphic element you see on TV, from local news titles to Olympics openings, has been designed on a computer. When it's time to think about your opening titles and internal graphics, work out what you have in mind, and then meet with two or three graphic designers. Your post-production facility can recommend a few, or may even have one in-house. Get some bids, look at some reels, and go with the one who seems to grasp what you have in mind, and can do it for the money.

Text Effects

It used to be that to get text in your show, you had to produce an "art card," actual letters pressed onto a piece of cardboard, then shoot it on a video camera. They've been replaced by *video graphic workstations*, which can work with both text and images, and by *character generators*, which can also produce text and images, but at a lower level of complexity. The simplest thing a character generator does is your closing credit roll. But if you need text sized in different fonts, colored, designed with simple shapes, put into 3D, and the like, a character generator can do the trick. Ask your post-production facility for a demonstration.

Desperate Measures

Can't afford time on a graphics workstation or character generator? Art cards still work, and you can get quite creative, even wild, using simple press-on letters, paint, ink, and drawing tools. Talk over your ideas with your Editor. The art cards can be shot during your regular production period, while you're still renting your camera package, or you can shoot them during post-production on an overhead camera. The text images can be moved around on screen, and made bigger or smaller, in On-Line. We once saw an opening titles piece for a network sitcom done by a single artist painting one or two brush strokes at a time, and "clicking off" a few video frames. It was a great effect.

Special Graphic Effects

Designers can also create special effects on your images. If your script calls for a magic Santa to wave his hand, producing a shower of magic dust that reveals a fully decorated Christmas tree, go to a graphics designer. But go before you shoot, because you'll need to work out exactly how to integrate your live action with your special effect.

There are cheap ways and expensive ways to achieve effects, so you'll need to have at least a ball park figure for your graphics budget. Either way you go, ask the designer to show you an example of the effects in the discussion stage, so you can all agree on the look.

$$$

How much money? The more images move, the more you pay. If you are having a lot of frame by frame work done on a Composium or a Harry or a Hal (all different computer graphics workstations), it can take many hours at $300 to $650 per hour, depending on the machine. A ten-second network opening title sequence for an episodic series or a special can run from $5,000 to $15,000 and up for more complex animation. A national evening news show open might cost $50,000 to $100,000 because the network's ego image is at stake. A 45-minute home video with opening titles and a dozen internal graphic elements might have a $3,000 to $8,000 graphics budget. You can get a simple but dramatic effect by flying a single graphic element on screen (through the DVE in the On-Line switcher), and placing it over a live action shot, like the flashing blue light on a cop car. The design of the single element might cost you from $800 to $2,000.

35-03 Motion Control
A really fun (and potentially cheap) way to make title graphics is to build or use actual 3D pieces, and shoot them under a motion control camera. You can use a snorkel lens, which gets you right down among the pieces. The overall effect gives a lot of texture and 3D reality (because it is!) compared to the high cost of high-end 3D computer graphics.

One creative Graphics Designer we know was hired to design and produce an opening title sequence for a network comedy show. He built a little 3ft. x 3ft. scale model of Hometown, USA, with little streets, buildings, and store fronts. He took it to a post house with a motion control camera (@ $350/hour) and shot moves on the set with a snorkel for a couple of hours. Then he edited the footage, designed the text logo for the show, composited it over the footage, and there it was—a delightful, unique open for a total cost to the producer of $5,000. (Also see Motion Control/Animatics in 22-00 Camera)

35-04 3D Graphics and Computer Generated Animation
This is still the domain of high-end ads for TV, but costs are dropping all the time. In fact, software originally developed for architects (to "walk" clients through imaginary buildings), and insurance companies (to show how car accidents happen) has led to its use in television. It is a lower end 3D look, but acceptable.

$$$
3D designers with their own studios can output the lower end images at around $200 per second. Higher end platforms can put you in the $500 per second and up stratosphere.

35-05 Cel Animation
This is such a specialized area, it's really outside our scope for this book. Suffice to say that if you want animation in your show, either

188

standing alone or composited over live action, there are many excellent animation houses and independent artists who can work for you.

$$$

Costs are all over the map. Animators will ask: How smooth must your images move? How many backgrounds? Do the backgrounds move? Do you want shadows and reflections? Just to give you a frame of reference, the cartoon shows on Saturday morning TV have all-in budgets (producers, writers, directors, music, and all animation) of around $225,000 per half hour (actually about 22 minutes). That's around $170 per second. Prime time cartoon shows have budgets in the $400,000 to $650,000 per half hour range. That's around $300 to $500 per second — again, all-in.

As memory gets cheaper and the various platforms get more powerful, the technology will continue to decentralize, so that you'll be able to contract graphic design services for your opening titles and internal graphics from a neighbor down the street—maybe even do it yourself.

Desperate Measures

If your graphics budget really is below standard for the kind of show you're producing, go to a Graphic Designer and say, "I have $2,000 (or whatever), do you want to get creative and take on the job?" If the Designer is busy, he or she will have to turn you down, but perhaps will say something like "I'm swamped now, but in two weeks I'll have time. Can you wait?"

36-00 Stock Footage

Need a shot of the Colorado State Capitol's golden dome in fresh snow? How about a close-up of a red robin eating a worm? Or World War I footage of life in the trenches? A stock footage house somewhere has your shot. If they don't, you might find one that will go out and shoot it for you, and only charge you the regular stock footage rate. (See the discussion of feature film clip clearance and stock footage in Chapter 2.)

Archive Film Clips and Stock Footage.

Studios have a stock footage department where you can get generic looking shots pulled from their own movies. Or go to a stock footage library. Some have both stock and archival footage, while some specialize in one or the other. If it's contemporary sports footage you want, you'll have to go through the professional sports leagues like the NFL, the NBA and the NHL. Ask for the clip licensing departments.

$$$

Standard fees for movie studio footage average $50 per foot (on 35 mm) with a ten-foot minimum cut ($500). Stock footage libraries and archive houses usually charge by the second ($25 to $50 per second is average). They may charge you a research fee of $50 to $150 average for putting together a screening reel. Professional sports footage goes by the league. The NHL, for example, licenses hockey footage for broadcast (North American rights) at about $22 per second with a ten-second minimum. For home video rights, the same footage costs $63 per second.

- **Feature Film Clips.** (See Chapter 2.)

37-00 Insurance

You'll need a standard Producer's Entertainment package, and your distributor will probably insist on an Errors and Omissions policy as well. If you have a star whose sudden disappearance or indisposition on shoot day sinks your project, you'll want Cast insurance as well. (See discussion of insurance in Chapter 2.)

$$$

Some producers allow 3% of the total budget for insurance. The safer route is to call an entertainment insurance broker and get a precise quote for your project.

38-00 General and Administrative Expenses

Inexperienced producers always seem to get stung on this one because they forget or underestimate what it costs to just show up at the office and do business. (See the discussion of Setting Up in Chaper 1, and many parallel references in Chapter 2.)

38-01 Business License
Technically, your company needs a business license to operate in your city, although many people whose offices are in the garage don't bother. The fee is based on a percentage of your company's annual gross income, and it varies by city. Call the City Clerk for an application. (See Chapter 1)

38-02 Legal Fees
Have a heart-to-heart with your entertainment attorney about each project and what he or she estimates in fees. Some producers allow anywhere from 3% all the way up to 12% of the budget. With that kind of spread, it's better to talk it out. (See Chapter 1 "Attorney," and Chapter 2 "Legal")

38-03 Accounting Fees
Hopefully, you have hired a Production Accountant or Bookkeeper as part of your Production Staff (budget category 10-00) to keep track of the books during and immediately after production. If you are using a Payroll Service (see Chapter 2, "Payroll Services"), you are already factoring in accounting costs for personnel into your Payroll Tax percentage. Even so, you may have accounting costs beyond those mentioned, and this is the place to put them. Many producers allow about 1% of the budget here. (See Chapter 1 - "Accountant," and Chapter 2 - "Tracking Costs.")

38-04 Completion Bond

Hopefully, you won't need this, but if you do, see Chapter 2 "Completion Bond."

38-05 Telephone and FAX

Estimate a monthly telephone and FAX fee, and multiply by the number of months you'll be chained to the project. Include the basic monthly charge, connection fees, and local and long distance calls. Pre- and Post-Production telephone bills could be higher because of long distance calls for research and to distributors and others. Two or more lines in an office may be needed, especially during production and to accommodate other staff members.

38-06 Copying

Copies of treatments, scripts, legal contracts, releases, invoices, correspondence, and news clippings are entered here. The volume of copying will determine whether it would be worthwhile to rent a copy machine on a monthly basis as opposed to making numerous runs to the copy shop. It's usually worth the rental.

38-07 Postage and Freight

Include postage for research, promotion, mailing VHS screening copies, and distribution activities. Freight and shipping costs will be incurred if there are shoots on distant locations. Film and tape masters, equipment, scripts, cassettes, release prints, promotional materials, and a host of other unknown expenses will be included here.

38-08 Office Space Rental

Allow for Pre-Production, Production, and Post-Production, but keep track of your needs for space. In Pre-Production, for example, if your writer and researchers are working out of their homes and billing you for telephone and other expenses, you may not even need an office for a month or more, or at most, only one room. In Production, if it's local, you may need to add a room or two or three for meetings, and additional staff, like Production Coordinator, Production Manager, and Production Assistants. In Post-Production, your needs will shrink again, probably back to one office, or two if you are setting up your Off-Line Editing there as well.

38-09 Office Furniture

Some office buildings offer a furniture package, or you can rent from a rental company or visit Goodwill. Handy items are desks, filing cabinets, shelves for books and cassettes, and 8-foot tables for meetings and plenty of spread-it-out room for artwork, and so forth.

38-10 Office Equipment and Supplies

Include computer/printer rentals, computer programs, calculators, projectors, VHS video playback/recorder and TV, and stereo/CD system. People often bring in their own computers for a show and rent them to the company for less than the cost of a standard rental.

On the supply side, what will it cost to take a grocery cart through the local office supply shop? Probably three times more than you think. It's expensive to set up a production office for the first time. Costs will depend on how many people are on your office staff.

38-11 Computer Rental

If you have to rent computers from a rental house, do the math and see if it's cheaper to buy. Sometimes your producer or coordinator or production assistants bring in their own computers. On a low budget show, they may do it as a favor. On bigger budgets, pay them a weekly rental fee that is less than the fee you would pay to a rental house.

38-12 Software

There is some dandy production software out there. Screenplay Systems, Inc. in Burbank, CA, has "Movie Magic" Budgeting and Scheduling. Then there are numerous script formatting, script collaborating, and storyboarding programs, plus others to make your life simpler.

There is a floppy disc of the budgets in this book available as an Excel document (Macs only). Ordering this template and then adapting it for your own budgets will save you a lot of time in setting up a budget format and formulas. You may order it from MWP.

For the latest hot software programs, call MWP at (818) 379-8799 or The Writers Computer Store in West Los Angeles at (310) 479-7774.

38-13 Transcription

Whenever you have long interviews you need to cut into pieces and edit into a show, get them transcribed - it will save your sanity many times over. The usual process is to make audio cassette dubs while you are having VHS or 3/4" window dubs made from your source reels. The transcriber has a special audio playback machine operated by foot, so hands are free for typing.

Be sure to specify whether you want the interviewer's questions transcribed or not, and whether you want a *verbatim* copy. Verbatim gives you all the "uh's and ahh's" and coughs and laughs. It's good to go with a verbatim copy because you need to know exactly what the subject is saying, and how it is said.

When you get the pages back, sit down with the window dub and mark up the transcription copy with time code in's and out's, as well as marks that tell you whether a given phrase ends at a clean edit point or not. This saves you time in off-line when you are riffling through pages of the transcript looking for just the right quote. You'll know where it is on the source reel (through your good time code notes), and you'll know if it is a clean edit in and out.

$$$

Transcribers usually allow a 3 to 1 ratio, that is, 3 hours of typing for every one hour of audio. Rates are in the $20 to $27 per hour range.

38-14 Messenger/Overnight

For a production office in a large city like New York or Los Angeles, it's probably more cost effective to use a messenger service than to use a production assistant's time and mileage fees on his or her car.

38-15 Parking

Is there a fee for parking on the office lot? If so, it may be worth it, especially if there is metered parking on nearby streets, or if it's dangerous for your people to get to their cars after hours.

38-16 Storage

Any project will generate countless boxes of scripts, receipts, tax statements, income statements, bank statements, financial journals, records, originals, work prints, dupes, magnetic stock, mixed music masters, narration tracks, sound effects etc. Film or tape will need to be stored in a dust-free, safe, temperature-controlled environment. Years later, you may choose to destroy stuff you no longer need, but for the two or three years after production, keep and file everything— you'll be surprised at what you may need to retrieve.

38-17 Still Photographer

(See 22-00 Camera)

38-18 Publicity

This expense may be covered by the distributor, but if you want to send flyers or VHS cassettes to your own list, or throw a screening party and hand out souvenirs, this is the line item.

38-19 Wrap Party

Your hard-working staff and crew deserves to bend the elbow at the show's expense, right? If you can afford it, it is nice to either bring in some pizza and beer on the last day of production, or at a later date.

38-20 Hospitality

When your distributors come to visit you'll want to take them to something nicer than Casa de Vicky's Mexican Diner.

38-21 Overhead (Production Fee)

In preparing a bid for a commercial or a client-sponsored industrial, many producers add overhead (also called the Production Fee) to represent the company's profit on the project. The fee is usually 20%-35% of the budget. If regular production expenses can be held down, then profits will be increased. If there are cost overruns, profits will be reduced—-or, in the worst of situations, it will cost the production company out-of-pocket money, that is, your salary.

Contingency

There are hundreds, if not thousands of variables involved in any project. The ability to foresee all these expenses is beyond that of most soothsayers, but that is exactly what a producer must do. It's easy to forget something. By carefully studying the script, breaking it down, and preparing the budget, and by maintaining strong control during production, a producer will come close to the estimated budget.

But when the terrain is unknown, or the script has not been fully developed, an experienced producer will add a "contingency" to the budget. How much depends on what 's available: 5% is helpful, 10% is a good average, 20% is high but maybe necessary if you're wading into a swamp.

Weather, changes in the script, music, recasting, reshooting, change of location ad infinitum conspire to push budgets upward. There will always be unforeseen expenses and a contingency comes to the rescue.

Clients and grant foundations, on the other hand, may not want to see a contingency line in the budget. They may think it is unprofessional, that it's simply the producer's way of saying, "I don't know, so I'll slop in some more money here."

Rather than showing a contingency, it can be built in (padded) into the line items. Sometimes it's necessary for a producer to make two budgets—an actual cost and a padded client budget. This way a producer can be assured that there is money for omissions, errors, and the great unknown.

The budgets in this book are "actual" budgets. They are not padded except where specified to prove a point.

The Bottom Line

Holy moley! This is the estimated total cost of the project. It's the first place a client's eye will go. The bottom line. If the total exceeds an acceptable bid, a grant application, or the amount of money a producer can raise, the production must be replanned and the budget reduced.

What things can be eliminated? Now begins the delicate dance of deletion. But be careful here. In your zeal to get the job, you may cut too much. There is a point beyond which the show cannot be produced, at least without revising the concept (and the script). The budget cannot be too high (or the bid won't be accepted) or too low (to allow actually doing the work).

SUMMARY

The figures quoted in this chapter, and in the next, "Sample Budgets," are based on average "book" rates in Los Angeles and New York, the two biggest production centers in the U.S. Some cities will offer lower rates, others will be higher. **It is absolutely essential that you research costs with the people and facilities where production will actually take place, and negotiate your own good deals.**

These figures are only meant to guide and assist you in the preparation of your own budgets. Hopefully, by studying the budgets that follow, you'll be able to construct your own to include all your necessary line items. If this book does nothing more than identify one oversight in your own planning, it will have been the price of the book.

The sample budgets which follow in this book (Chapter 4) do not have all the master list categories because most projects will not have the people, equipment, and special effects found in most major features—thank goodness!

SAMPLE
BUDGETS

SAMPLE BUDGETS

Few things are harder to put up with than the annoyance of a good example.
Mark Twain in *Pudd'nhead Wilson's Calendar*

First there are the budget *categories*-the big picture. Then there are the *line items* —the nitty gritty details without which we have no budget at all. This chapter grasps the budget and shakes it so all the line items fall out into the daylight. Now we can study them in situations that resemble real production.

Let's be clear that this chapter is for illustrative purposes only. We want to show examples of producers planning and budgeting for real world situations, albeit hypothetical ones. Please do not fall into the trap of taking a sample budget and applying it to your project lock, stock and barrel. Every project is different, and cries out for its own creative thinking and budgeting.

The sample budgets that follow may help you avoid stumbling where others have stumbled before you.

$5 MILLION FEATURE FILM BUDGET

SUMMARY BUDGET	
Fringe assumptions:	Production: "Skylark"
Payroll Tax 18.00%	Shoot Days: 24
WGA 12.50%	Location: New Orleans
DGA 12.50%	Unions: WGA, DGA, SAG
SAG 12.80%	Shoot Date:
Overtime 10%	Exec. Producer:
	Producer/Prod. Mgr.:
	Director:

01-00 Story-Rights	0
02-00 Script	149,032
03-00 Producers Unit	197,560
04-00 Direction	203,365
05-00 Cast	760,049
06-00 Travel & Living – Producers	35,866
07-00 Travel & Living- Cast	31,762
TOTAL ABOVE-THE-LINE	**1,377,634**
10-00 Production Staff	321,202
11-00 Extra Talent	107,400
13-00 Production Design	43,917
14-00 Set Construction	191,807
15-00 Set Operations	115,851
16-00 Special Effects	75,664
17-00 Set Dressing	156,533
18-00 Property	69,115
19-00 Wardrobe	104,915
20-00 Make-Up and Hairdressing	53,959
21-00 Electrical	112,248
22-00 Camera	127,968
23-00 Sound	44,420
24-00 Transportation	311,645
25-00 Location Expenses	280,319
26-00 Picture Vehicle/Animals	42,516
27-00 Film & Lab	146,018
28-00 Travel and Living-Crew	166,121
TOTAL PRODUCTION	**2,471,618**

	Amt.	Units	x	Rate	Sub-Total	Total
30-00 Editorial					124,852	
31-00 Post-Prod. Videotape/Film & Lab					81,508	
32-00 Optical Effects					37,050	
33-00 Music					85,000	
34-00 Post Production Sound					118,370	
TOTAL POST-PRODUCTION						446,780
37-00 Insurance					85,470	
38-00 General & Administrative					101,275	
TOTAL OTHER						186,745
Total Above-The-Line						1,377,634
Total Below-The-Line						3,105,143
Total Above and Below-the-Line						4,482,777
Contingency @ 10 %						448,278
GRAND TOTAL						$4,931,055

ABOVE-THE-LINE

	Amt.	Units	x	Rate	Sub-Total	Total
01-00 Story-Rights						
01-01 Options					0	0
01-02 Rights Purchases					0	0
Total for 01-00						0
02-00 Script						
02-01 Writer's Salaries						
Treatment	1	Allow	1	28,741	28,741	
First Draft	1	Allow	1	28,741	28,741	
Final Draft	1	Allow	1	14,365	14,365	
Polish	1	Allow	1	9,580	9,580	
Production Bonus	1	Allow	1	20,000	20,000	101,427
02-02 Research	1	Allow	1	5,000	5,000	5,000
02-03 Title Registration	1	Allow	1	385	385	385
02-05 Script Copying	1	Allow	1	1,500	1,500	1,500
02-06 Script Delivery Service	1	Allow	1	500	500	500
02-08 Script Timing	1	Allow	1	750	750	750

02-10	Development	1	Allow	1	7,500	7,500	7,500	
	Payroll					107,177	19,292	
	WGA					101,427	12,678	
					Total for 02-00			149,032
03-00	**Producers Unit**							
03-01	Executive Producer	1	Allow	1	175,000	175,000	175,000	
03-02	Producer					0	0	
03-03	Associate Producer					0	0	
03-04	Assistant to Exec. Prod.	15	Weeks	1	800	12,000	12,000	
03-06	Consultants	1	Allow	1	5,000	5,000	5,000	
03-07	Producer's Misc. Expenses	1	Allow	1	2,500	2,500	2,500	
	Payroll					17,000	3,060	
					Total for 03-00			197,560
04-00	**Direction**							
04-01	Director	1	Allow	1	175,000	175,000	175,000	
04-02	Assistant	10	Weeks	1	550	5,500	5,500	
	Payroll					5,500	990	
	DGA					175,000	21,875	
					Total for 04-00			203,365
05-00	**Cast**							
05-01	Lead Actors							
	Role of Frances	1	Allow	1	250,000	250,000		
	Role of Skylark	1	Allow	1	200,000	200,000	450,000	
05-02	Supporting Cast (6 day weeks)							
	Role of Harry	2	Weeks	1	3,750	7,500		
	Role of Edna	2	Weeks	1	4,000	8,000		
	Role of Sheriff Riz	1.4	Weeks	1	3,000	4,200		
	Role of Hoot	1	Week	1	2,500	2,500		
	Role of Charlene	1	Week	1	2,500	2,500		
	Role of Lady Jane	1	Week	1	2,500	2,500	27,200	
05-03	Day Players (Includes agency fees at 10%)							
	Role of Balthazar	3	Days	1	700	2,100		
	Role of Rudnick	2	Days	1	650	1,300		
	Role of Shorty	3	Days	1	600	1,800		
	Role of Soda Jerk	1	Day	1	555	555		
	Role of Waitress #	1	Day	1	555	555		

	Role of Waitress #	1	Day	1	555	555	
	Role of Wilty	1	Day	1	555	555	
	Role of Ruth	1	Day	1	555	555	
	Role of Man in Car	1	Day	1	555	555	
	Role of Dispatcher	1	Day	1	555	555	
	Role of Cleaning Lac	1	Day	1	555	555	
	Role of Plumber	1	Day	1	555	555	10,195
05-04 Casting Director/Staff - L		1	Allow	1	25,000	25,000	25,000
Casting - New Orleans		1	Allow	1	10,000	10,000	10,000
05-05 Casting Expenses		1	Allow	1	1,000	1,000	1,000
05-06 Choreographer		2	Weeks	1	2,200	4,400	4,400
05-07 Assistants (Choreographe		1	Week	1	850	850	850
05-10 Stunt Coordinator		3	Weeks	1	3,500	10,500	10,500
05-11 Stunt Players (6 day week		1.4	Weeks	4	2,051	11,485	11,485
		20	Mandays	1	504	10,080	10,080
05-12 Stunt Costs/Adjustments		1	Allow	1	5,000	5,000	5,000
05-13 Stunt Equipment		1	Allow	1	2,500	2,500	2,500
05-14 Looping (Actor's fees)		1	Allow	1	10,000	10,000	10,000
05-15 Cast Overtime		1	Allow	1	15,000	15,000	15,000
	Payroll					543,145	97,766
	SAG					539,630	69,073
				Total for 05-00				760,049
06-00 Travel & Living – Producers/Director							
06-01 Airfares - LA - New Orlea		2	1st	1	2,008	4,016	4,016
06-02 Hotels (Incl. 4 weeks prep		60	Nights	2	125	15,000	15,000
06-03 Taxi/Limo		1	Allow	1	500	500	500
06-04 Auto		2	Months	2	800	3,200	3,200
06-05 Rail						0	0
06-06 Excess Baggage						0	0
06-07 Phone		1	Allow	1	850	850	850
06-08 Gratuities		1	Allow	1	300	300	300
06-09 Per Diem		60	Days	2	100	12,000	12,000
				Total for 06-00				35,866
07-00 Travel & Living· Cast							
07-01 Airfares							
	Role of Frances	1	1st	1	2,008	2,008	2,008
	Role of Skylark	1	1st	1	2,008	2,008	2,008
	Role of Harry	1	1st	1	2,008	2,008	2,008

	Role of Edna	1	1st	1	2,008	2,008	2,008	
07-02	Hotels							
	Role of Frances	26	Nights	1	125	3,250	3,250	
	Role of Skylark	26	Nights	1	125	3,250	3,250	
	Role of Harry	16	Nights	1	125	2,000	2,000	
	Role of Edna	16	Nights	1	125	2,000	2,000	
07-03	Taxi/Limo	1	Allow	1	750	750	750	
07-04	Auto	32	Days	2	45	2,880	2,880	
07-05	Rail					0	0	
07-06	Excess Baggage					0	0	
07-07	Phone					0	0	
07-08	Per Diem	32	Days	4	75	9,600	9,600	
					Total for 07-00			**31,762**

BELOW-THE-LINE

10-00 Production Staff

10-01	UPM/Line Producer							
	Prep/Travel	7	Weeks	1	5,000	35,000		
	Shoot	4	Weeks	1	5,000	20,000		
	Wrap	3	Weeks	1	5,000	15,000		
	Severance	1	Allow	1	5,000	5,000	75,000	
10-02	Assistant Directors							
First A.D.								
	Prep/Travel	3.4	Weeks	1	3,595	12,223		
	Shoot (Incl. 6th da	4	Weeks	1	3,595	14,380		
	Prod. Fee (shoot da	24	Days	1	146	3,504		
	Severance	1	Allow	1	3,595	3,595		
	Overtime Allow	12	Days	1	300	3,600	37,302	
Second A.D.								
	Prep/Travel	1.8	Weeks	1	2,406	4,331		
	Shoot (Incl. 6th da	4	Weeks	1	2,406	9,624		
	Prod. Fee	24	Days	1	119	2,856		
	Severance	1	Allow	1	2,406	2,406		
	Overtime Allow	24	Days	1	201	4,812	24,029	
10-04	Production Coordinator							
	Prep/Travel	6	Weeks	1	1,200	7,200		
	Shoot	4	Weeks	1	1,200	4,800		
	Wrap	2	Weeks	1	1,200	2,400	14,400	

Asst. Coord.							
	Prep	6	Weeks	1	750	4,500	
	Shoot	4	Weeks	1	750	3,000	
	Wrap	1	Week	1	750	750	8,250
10-05 Script Supervisor							
	Prep	5	Days	12	21	1,286	
	Shoot	20	Days	14	21	6,000	
	Saturdays Worked	4	Days	18	21	1,543	
	Wrap	3	Days	12	21	771	
	2nd Camera Days	8	Days	1	40	320	
	Overtime	1	Allow		9,921	992	10,913
10-06 Production Auditor/Accountant							
	Prep/Travel	7	Weeks	1	2,100	14,700	
	Shoot	4	Weeks	1	2,100	8,400	
	Wrap	4	Weeks	1	2,100	8,400	
	Post Production	7	Weeks	1	800	5,600	37,100
Assistant Auditor							
	Prep/Travel	6	Weeks	1	1,300	7,800	
	Shoot	4	Weeks	1	1,300	5,200	
	Wrap	4	Weeks	1	1,300	5,200	18,200
10-07 Technical Advisors		1	Flat	1	15,000	15,000	15,000
10-08 Production Assistants							
Office PA							
	Prep	30	Days	12	7	2,574	
	Shoot	20	Days	14	7	2,002	
	Wrap	10	Days	12	7	858	
	Saturdays Worked	9	Days	12	7	772	
	Overtime	1	Allow	1	5,434	543	6,750
Set PA #1							
	Prep	3	Days	12	7	257	
	Shoot	20	Days	14	7	2,002	
	Saturdays Worked	4	Days	18	7	515	
	Overtime	1	Allow	1	2,774	277	3,052
Set PA #2							
	Shoot	20	Days	14	7	2,002	
	Saturdays Worked	4	Days	18	7	515	
	Overtime	1	Allow	1	2,517	252	2,768
10-09 Teachers/Welfare Worker		4	Weeks	1	1,250	5,000	5,000
10-10 Secretaries						0	0

	Payroll					257,763	46,397	
	DGA					136,331	17,041	
					Total for 10-00			**321,202**
11-00 - Extra Talent								
11-01 Stand-ins @ 12 hr. days		24 Days	4	158	15,120	15,120	
11-02 Extras (non-SAG)		300 Extras	14	8	34,146	34,146	
11-03 Extras Casting Fee @ 10%		1 Allow	1	49,266	4,927	49,266	
	Payroll					49,266	8,868	
	SAG does not rep extras in New Orleans							
					Total for 11-00			**107,400**
13-00 Production Design								
13-01 Production Designer								
	Prep/Travel	6 Weeks	1	2,750	16,500		
	Shoot	4 Weeks	1	2,750	11,000	27,500	
13-03 Assistants								
Assistant #1 Prep/Travel		30 Days	12	9	3,344		
	Shoot	20 Days	14	9	2,601		
	Overtime	1 Allow	1	5,946	595	6,540	
13-07 Purchases/Rentals		1 Allow	1	1,000	1,000	1,000	
13-08 Research/Materials		1 Allow	1	500	500	500	
13-09 Car Expense		10 Weeks	1	150	1,500	1,500	
13-10 Polaroid Film		1 Allow	1	750	750	750	
	Payroll					34,040	6,127	
					Total for 13-00			**43,917**
14-00 Set Construction								
14-01 Construction Coordinator								
	Prep	20 Days	12	25	6,000		
	Shoot	20 Days	14	25	7,000		
	Saturdays Worked	4 Days	18	25	1,800		
	Overtime	1 Allow	1	14,800	1,480	16,280	
14-02 Labor - Foreman								
	Prep	20 Days	12	21	5,143		
	Shoot	20 Days	14	21	6,000		
	Saturdays Worked	4 Days	18	21	1,543		

	Overtime	1	Allow	1	12,687	1,269	13,955
	Labor - Crew	1	Allow	1	50,000	50,000	50,000
14-03 Scenic Painters							
	Lead Scenic Painter						
	Prep	10	Days	12	21	2,572	
	Shoot	20	Days	14	21	6,000	
	Saturdays Worked	4	Days	18	21	1,543	
	Overtime	1	Allow	1	10,115	1,011	11,126
	Labor - Painters	1	Allow	1	25,000	25,000	25,000
14-05 Greens		1	Allow	1	5,000	5,000	5,000
14-06 Purchases (Bldg materials		1	Allow	1	25,000	25,000	25,000
14-07 Rentals (Tools/Paint kit)		1	Allow	1	7,500	7,500	7,500
14-08 Equipment		1	Allow	1	12,000	12,000	12,000
14-09 Set Strike		1	Allow	1	5,000	5,000	5,000
	Payroll					116,362	20,945
					Total for 14-00		191,807
15-00 Set Operations							
15-01 First Grip							
	Prep/Travel	7	Days	14	25	2,450	
	Shoot	20	Days	14	25	7,000	
	Saturdays worked	4	Days	18	25	1,800	
	Wrap	1	Day	14	25	350	
	Overtime	1	Allow	1	11,600	1,160	12,760
15-02 Second Grip (Best Boy)							
	Prep	5	Days	14	21	1,500	
	Shoot	20	Days	14	21	6,000	
	Saturdays worked	4	Days	18	21	1,543	
	Wrap	1	Day	14	21	300	
	Overtime	1	Allow	1	9,343	934	10,278
15-03 Other Grips							
	Grip #1						
	Prep	4	Days	14	18	1,000	
	Shoot	20	Days	14	18	4,998	
	Saturdays worked	4	Days	18	18	1,285	
	Wrap	1	Day	14	18	250	
	Overtime	1	Allow	14	7,533	753	8,286
	Grip #2						
	Prep	4	Days	14	18	1,000	

	Shoot	20	Days	14	18	4,998	
	Saturdays worked	4	Days	18	18	1,285	
	Wrap	1	Day	14	18	250	
	Overtime	1	Allow	14	7,533	753	8,286
Grip #3							
	Prep	4	Days	14	18	1,000	
	Shoot	20	Days	14	18	4,998	
	Saturdays worked	4	Days	18	18	1,285	
	Wrap	1	Day	14	18	250	
	Overtime	1	Allow	14	7,533	753	8,286
Additional Grips		40	Mandays	14	16	8,999	
	Overtime	1	Allow	3	8,999	900	9,899
15-04 Dolly Grip							
	Prep	1	Day	14	21	300	
	Shoot	20	Days	14	21	6,000	
	Saturdays worked	4	Days	18	21	1,543	
	Overtime	1	Allow	1	7,843	784	8,628
15-05 Craft Service							
	Prep	4	Days	14	13	720	
	Shoot	20	Days	14	13	3,598	
	Saturdays worked	4	Days	18	13	925	
	Wrap	2	Days	14	13	360	
	Overtime	1	Allow	1	5,603	560	6,163
Purchases		24	Days	1	275	6,600	6,600
Rentals		1	Allow	1	500	500	500
15-06 Grip Rentals							
	Package	4	Weeks	1	1,250	5,000	
	Dollies	4	Weeks	1	1,250	5,000	
	Cranes (Incl. Driv	2	Days	1	1,000	2,000	
	Addl. Equip.	1	Allow	1	2,000	2,000	14,000
15-07 Grip Expendables		1	Allow	1	7,500	7,500	7,500
15-08 Box Rentals							
	Key Grip	4	Weeks	1	250	1,000	1,000
	Craft Service	4	Weeks	1	150	600	600
	Payroll				72,585	13,065	13,065
				Total for 15-00			115,851
16-00 Special Effects							
16-01 Special Effects Person							

	Prep/Travel	12	Days	12	25	3,600	
	Shoot	20	Days	14	25	7,000	
	Saturdays Worked	4	Days	18	25	1,800	
	Overtime	1	Allow	1	12,400	1,240	13,640
16-02 SFX Assist.		20	Days	14	21	6,000	
	Saturdays Worked	4	Days	18	21	1,543	
	Overtime	1	Allow	1	7,543	754	8,298
16-03 Additional Labor							
	Shoot	100	Mandays	14	18	24,990	
	Saturdays Worked	20	Mandays	18	18	6,426	
	Overtime	1	Allow	1	31,416	3,142	34,558
16-06 Manufacturing Labor		1	Allow	1	1,500	1,500	1,500
16-07 Fabrication		1	Allow	1	1,000	1,000	1,000
16-08 Expendables		1	Allow	1	5,500	5,500	5,500
16-09 Rentals		1	Allow	1	1,000	1,000	1,000
	Payroll				56,495	10,169	10,169
					Total for 16-00		75,664
17-00 Set Dressing							
17-01 Set Decorator							
	Prep/Travel	17	Days	14	25	5,950	
	Shoot	20	Days	14	25	7,000	
	Saturdays Worked	4	Days	18	25	1,800	
	Wrap	5	Days	14	25	1,750	
	Overtime				16,500	1,650	18,150
17-02 Lead Man							
	Prep/Travel	17	Days	14	21	5,100	
	Shoot	20	Days	14	21	6,000	
	Saturdays Worked	4	Days	18	21	1,543	
	Wrap	5	Days	14	21	1,500	
	Overtime				14,144	1,414	15,558
17-03 Swing Gang							
Swing Gang #1							
	Prep	10	Days	14	18	2,499	
	Shoot	20	Days	14	18	4,998	
	Saturdays Worked	4	Days	18	18	1,285	
	Wrap	5	Days	14	18	1,250	
	Overtime				10,032	1,003	11,035
Swing Gang #2							

Prep	10	Days	14	18	2,499		
Shoot	20	Days	14	18	4,998		
Saturdays Worked	4	Days	18	18	1,285		
Wrap	5	Days	14	18	1,250		
Overtime				10,032	1,003	11,035	
Swing Gang #3							
Prep	10	Days	14	18	2,499		
Shoot	20	Days	14	18	4,998		
Saturdays Worked	4	Days	18	18	1,285		
Wrap	5	Days	14	18	1,250		
Overtime				10,032	1,003	11,035	
17-04 Additional Labor	1	Allow	1	1,400	1,400	1,400	
On-Set Dresser (Shoot)	20	Days	14	16	4,500		
Saturdays Worked	4	Days	18	16	1,157		
Overtime				5,657	566	6,222	
17-05 Expendables	1	Allow	1	1,500	1,500	1,500	
17-06 Purchases	1	Allow	1	25,000	25,000	25,000	
17-07 Rentals	1	Allow	1	35,000	35,000	35,000	
17-08 Loss & Damage	1	Allow	1	1,500	1,500	1,500	
17-09 Box Rentals					0	0	
Set Decorator	8	Weeks	1	200	1,600	1,600	
Lead Person	8	Weeks	1	150	1,200	1,200	
17-10 Car Expense							
Set Decorator	8	Weeks	1	150	1,200	1,200	
Lead Person	8	Weeks	1	150	1,200	1,200	
17-11 Film	1	Allow	1	500	500	500	
Payroll				74,435	13,398	13,398	
Total for 17-00							156,533
18-00 Property							
18-01 Property Master							
Prep/Travel	22	Days	14	25	7,700		
Shoot	20	Days	14	25	7,000		
Saturdays Worked	4	Days	18	25	1,800		
Wrap	5	Days	14	25	1,750		
Overtime				18,250	1,825	20,075	
18-02 Assistant							
Prep	20	Days	14	21	6,000		
Shoot	20	Days	14	21	6,000		

	Saturdays Worked	4	Days	18	21	1,543	
	Wrap	5	Days	14	21	1,500	
	Overtime				15,044	1,504	16,548
18-03 Purchases		1	Allow	1	10,000	10,000	10,000
18-04 Rentals		1	Allow	1	10,000	10,000	10,000
18-05 Loss & Damage		1	Allow	1	2,000	2,000	2,000
18-06 Box Rentals							
	Prop Master	4	Weeks	1	250	1,000	1,000
18-07 Car Expense							
	Prop Master	9	Weeks	1	150	1,350	1,350
	Assistant	7	Weeks	1	150	1,050	1,050
18-08 Film		1	Allow	1	500	500	500
	Payroll				36,623	6,592	6,592
				Total for 18-00			69,115
19-00 Wardrobe							
19-01 Costume Designer (6 day flat)							
	Prep/Travel	4	Weeks	1	2,250	9,000	
	Shoot	4	Weeks	1	2,250	9,000	
	Wrap	1	Week	1	2,250	2,250	20,250
19-02 Costumer							
	Prep/Travel	17	Days	14	18	4,251	
	Shoot	20	Days	14	18	5,001	
	Saturdays Worked	4	Days	18	18	1,286	
	Wrap	5	Days	14	18	1,250	
	Overtime	1	Allow	1	11,788	1,179	12,966
19-03 Additional Costumer							
	Prep	15	Days	14	18	3,751	
	Shoot	20	Days	14	18	5,001	
	Saturdays Worked	4	Days	18	18	1,286	
	Wrap	5	Days	14	18	1,250	
	Overtime	1	Allow	1	11,288	1,129	12,416
	Additional Costumers (Sho	15	Mandays	14	18	3,751	
	Overtime	1	Allow	1	3,751	375	4,126
19-04 Expendables		1	Allow	1	500	500	500
19-05 Purchases		1	Allow	1	10,000	10,000	10,000
19-06 Rentals		1	Allow	1	25,000	25,000	25,000
19-07 Alteration & Repairs		1	Allow	1	3,000	3,000	3,000

19-08 Cleaning & Dyeing		1	Allow	1	3,000	3,000	3,000	
19-09 Loss & Damage		1	Allow	1	1,500	1,500	1,500	
19-10 Box Rentals								
	Costume Designer	9	Weeks	1	150	1,350	1,350	
19-11 Car Expense						0	0	
	Costume Designer	9	Weeks	1	150	1,350	1,350	
19-12 Film		1	Allow	1	500	500	500	
	Payroll				49,758	8,956	8,956	
				Total for 19-00				104,915
20-00 Make-Up and Hairdressing								
20-01 Key Make-Up Artist								
	Prep/Travel	4	Days	14	25	1,400		
	Shoot	20	Days	14	25	7,000		
	Saturdays Worked	4	Days	18	25	1,800		
	Wrap	1	Days	14	25	350		
	Overtime	1	Allow	1	10,550	1,055	11,605	
20-02 Additional Make-Up Artist		15	Days	14	21	4,500		
	Saturdays Worked	4	Days	18	21	1,543		
	Overtime	1	Allow	1	6,043	604	8,053	
20-03 Hair Stylist								
	Prep/Travel	7	Days	14	25	2,450		
	Shoot	20	Days	14	25	7,000		
	Saturdays Worked	4	Days	18	25	1,800		
	Wrap	1	Days	14	25	350		
	Overtime	1	Allow	1	11,600	1,160	12,760	
Additional Hair Stylist		15	Days	14	21	4,500		
	Saturdays Worked	4	Days	18	21	1,543		
	Overtime	1	Allow	1	6,043	604	8,158	
20-05 Purchases		1	Allow	1	2,000	2,000	2,000	
20-06 Rentals		4	Weeks	1	250	1,000	1,000	
20-07 Box Rentals								
	Key Make-Up	24	Days	1	30	720	720	
	Addl. Make-Up	19	Days	1	30	570	570	
	Hair Stylist	24	Days	1	30	720	720	
	Addl. Hair	19	Days	1	30	570	570	
20-08 Film		1	Allow	1	500	500	500	
	Payroll				40,575	7,304	7,304	

					Total for 20-00			53,959
21-00 Electrical								
21-01 Gaffer								
	Prep/Travel	7	Days	14	25	2,450		
	Shoot	20	Days	14	25	7,000		
	Saturdays Worked	4	Days	18	25	1,800		
	Wrap/Travel	1	Days	14	25	350		
	Overtime	1	Allow	1	11,600	1,160	12,760	
21-02 Best Boy								
	Prep	5	Days	14	21	1,500		
	Shoot	20	Days	14	21	6,000		
	Saturdays Worked	4	Days	18	21	1,543		
	Wrap	1	Days	14	21	300		
	Overtime	1	Allow	1	9,343	934	10,278	
21-03 Electrics								
Electric #1								
	Prep	4	Days	14	18	1,000		
	Shoot	20	Days	14	18	4,998		
	Saturdays Worked	4	Days	18	18	1,285		
	Wrap	1	Days	14	18	250		
	Overtime	1	Allow	1	7,533	753	8,286	
Electric #2								
	Prep	4	Days	14	18	1,000		
	Shoot	20	Days	14	18	4,998		
	Saturdays Worked	4	Days	18	18	1,285		
	Wrap	1	Days	14	18	250		
	Overtime	1	Allow	1	7,533	753	8,286	
Electric #3								
	Prep	4	Days	14	18	1,000		
	Shoot	20	Days	14	18	4,998		
	Saturdays Worked	4	Days	18	18	1,285		
	Wrap	1	Days	14	18	250		
	Overtime	1	Allow	1	7,533	753	8,286	
21-04 Additional Labor		30	Mandays	14	18	7,497		
	Overtime	1	Allow	1	7,497	750	8,247	
21-05 Purchases		1	Allow	1	7,000	7,000	7,000	
21-06 Rentals		4	Weeks	1	5,500	22,000	22,000	
	Addl. Equip.	1	Allow	1	5,000	5,000	5,000	
	Condors	1	Allow	1	7,000	7,000	7,000	

	Additional Generate	1	Allow	1	2,000	2,000	2,000	
21-09 Loss & Damage		1	Allow	1	2,000	2,000	2,000	
21-10 Box Rentals								
	Gaffer	4	Weeks	1	250	1,000	1,000	
	Payroll				56,142	10,106	10,106	
				Total for 21-00				112,248
22-00 Camera								
22-01 Director of Photography/OP								
	Prep/Travel	7	Days	1	1,200	8,400		
	Shoot	4	Weeks	1	7,200	28,800	37,200	
22-02 Camera Operator (B Cam)								
	Prep/Travel	2	Days	12	29	686		
	Shoot	8	Days	14	29	3,200		
	Saturdays Worked	2	Days	18	29	1,029		
	Overtime	1	Allow	1	4,228	423	5,337	
22-03 1st Asst. Camera								
	Prep/Travel	4	Days	14	25	1,400		
	Shoot	20	Days	14	25	7,000		
	Saturdays Worked	4	Days	18	25	1,800		
	Wrap	2	Days	14	25	700		
	Overtime	1	Allow	1	10,900	1,090	11,990	
	B Cam 1st Assist.	10	Days	14	25	3,500		
	Saturdays Worked	2	Days	18	25	900		
	Overtime	1	Allow	1	4,400	440	4,840	
22-04 2nd Asst. Camera								
	Prep	2	Days	14	21	600		
	Shoot	20	Days	14	21	6,000		
	Saturdays Worked	4	Days	18	21	1,543		
	Wrap	2	Days	14	21	600		
	Overtime	1	Allow	1	8,743	874	9,618	
	B Cam 2nd Assist.	10	Days	14	21	3,000		
	Saturdays Worked	2	Days	18	21	771		
	Overtime	1	Allow	1	3,772	377	4,149	
22-05 Still Photographer		1	Week	1	1,500	1,500	1,500	
22-06 Expendables		1	Allow	1	1,200	1,200	1,200	
22-07 Camera Package Rental		4	Weeks	1	7,000	28,000	28,000	

22-10 Additional Equipment		1	Allow	1	5,000	5,000	5,000
22-11 Steadicam Operator & Equi		2	Days	1	1,500	3,000	3,000
22-17 Maintenance/Loss & Damag		1	Allow	1	1,500	1,500	1,500
22-18 Box Rentals							
	1st Assist. Cam	4	Weeks	1	300	1,200	1,200
	Payroll				74,634	13,434	13,434
					Total for 22-00		127,968
23-00 Sound							
23-01 Mixer							
	Prep	2	Days	14	25	700	
	Shoot	20	Days	14	25	7,000	
	Saturdays Worked	4	Days	18	25	1,800	
	Wrap/Travel	2	Days	14	25	700	
	Overtime	1	Allow	1	10,200	1,020	11,220
23-02 Boom Operator							
	Shoot	20	Days	14	21	6,000	
	Saturdays Worked	4	Days	18	21	1,543	
	Overtime	1	Allow	1	7,543	754	9,318
23-03 Expendables (Batteries, e		1	Allow	1	1,500	1,500	1,500
23-04 Sound Package		4	Weeks	1	1,900	7,600	7,600
23-05 Walkie Talkies		4	Weeks	25	20	2,000	2,000
23-06 Radio Mics & Head Sets		4	Weeks	5	15	300	300
23-07 Beepers		3	Months	15	30	1,350	1,350
23-08 Cellular Phones/Service		1	Allow	1	5,000	5,000	5,000
23-09 1/4 inch Mag Stock		24	Days	3	13	936	936
23-10 Misc. / Loss & Damage		1	Allow	1	1,500	1,500	1,500
	Payroll				20,538	3,697	3,697
					Total for 23-00		44,420
24-00 Transportation							
24-01 Transportation Coordinator (6 day flat)							
		6	Weeks	1	2,500	15,000	15,000
24-02 Drivers							
Captain							
	Prep	10	Days	10	19	1,900	
	Shoot	20	Days	18	19	6,840	
	Saturdays Worked	4	Days	21	19	1,596	

	Wrap	5	Days	18	19	1,710	12,046
Star Trailer Drivers							
Driver #1							
	Prep	1	Day	10	19	190	
	Shoot	20	Days	18	19	6,840	
	Saturdays Worked	4	Days	21	19	1,596	
	Wrap	1	Day	18	19	342	8,968
Driver #2							
	Prep	1	Day	10	19	190	
	Shoot	20	Days	18	19	6,840	
	Saturdays Worked	4	Days	21	19	1,596	
	Wrap	1	Day	18	19	342	8,968
Production Van Driver							
	Prep	3	Days	10	19	570	
	Shoot	20	Days	18	19	6,840	
	Saturdays Worked	4	Days	21	19	1,596	
	Wrap	2	Days	18	19	684	9,690
Camera Truck Driver							
	Prep	3	Days	10	19	570	
	Shoot	20	Days	18	19	6,840	
	Saturdays Worked	4	Days	21	19	1,596	
	Wrap	2	Days	18	19	684	9,690
Stakebed Driver (Construction)							
	Shoot	5	Days	18	19	1,710	1,710
Set Dressing Driver							
	Prep	10	Days	10	19	1,900	
	Shoot	20	Days	18	19	6,840	
	Saturdays Worked	4	Days	21	19	1,596	
	Wrap	5	Days	18	19	1,710	12,046
Second Set Dressing 5 Ton		10	Days	18	19	3,420	3,420
Props Driver							
	Prep	6	Days	10	19	1,140	
	Shoot	20	Days	18	19	6,840	
	Saturdays Worked	4	Days	21	19	1,596	
	Wrap	5	Days	18	19	1,710	11,286
Make-Up/Wardrobe Driver							
	Prep	6	Days	10	19	1,140	
	Shoot	20	Days	18	19	6,840	
	Saturdays Worked	4	Days	21	19	1,596	
	Wrap	5	Days	18	19	1,710	11,286

Prod. Office Trailer Driver							
	Prep	1	Days	10	19	190	
	Shoot	20	Days	18	19	6,840	
	Saturdays Worked	4	Days	21	19	1,596	
	Wrap	1	Days	18	19	342	8,968
Honey Wagon Driver							
	Shoot	20	Days	18	19	6,840	
	Saturdays Worked	4	Days	21	19	1,596	
	Wrap	2	Days	18	19	684	9,120
Maxi Van #1 Driver							
	Prep	6	Days	10	18	1,080	
	Shoot	20	Days	18	18	6,480	
	Saturdays Worked	4	Days	21	18	1,512	9,072
Maxi Van #2 Driver							
	Prep	6	Days	10	18	1,080	
	Shoot	20	Days	18	18	6,480	
	Saturdays Worked	4	Days	21	18	1,512	9,072
Car Carrier		10	Days	18	19	3,420	3,420
Insert Car (car to car cam platf		2	Days	18	19	684	684
Water Truck Driver		4	Days	18	19	1,368	1,368
Caterer	Shoot	20	Days	18	19	6,840	
	Saturdays Worked	4	Days	21	19	1,596	8,436
Caterer Asst.	Shoot	20	Days	18	18	6,480	
	Saturdays Worked	4	Days	21	18	1,512	9,588
Additional Drivers		1	Allow	1	3,500	3,500	3,500
24-03 Equipment Rental							
Star Dressing Trailers		4	Weeks	2	475	3,800	3,800
Crew Cab		38	Days	1	60	2,280	2,280
Production Van (40' w/ 2 gennies		27	Days	1	300	8,100	8,100
Camera Truck		25	Days	1	100	2,500	2,500
Stake Bed		7	Days	1	90	630	630
Set Dressing 5 Ton		34	Days	1	95	3,230	3,230
Addl. Set Dressing 5 Ton		14	Days	1	95	1,330	1,330
Set Dress Van		34	Days	1	65	2,210	2,210
Props 5 Ton		39	Days	1	95	3,705	3,705
Wardrobe/Make-Up		35	Days	1	300	10,500	10,500
Crew Stake Bed		28	Days	1	90	2,520	2,520
Prod. Office Trailer		25	Days	1	120	3,000	3,000
Honey Wagon (Portable Toilets)		25	Days	1	300	7,500	7,500
Water Truck		24	Days	1	200	4,800	4,800

Gas Truck		24	Days	1	80	1,920	1,920
Maxi Vans		30	Days	2	70	4,200	4,200
Car Tow Trailer		10	Days	1	70	700	700
Car Trailer		10	Days	1	70	700	700
Camera Car		3	Days	1	300	900	900
24-04 Gas & Oil		1	Allow	1	12,000	12,000	12,000
24-05 Repairs & Maintenance		1	Allow	1	3,500	3,500	3,500
24-06 Honey Wagon Pumping		1	Allow	1	500	500	500
24-07 Miscellaneous		1	Allow	1	5,000	5,000	5,000
	Teamster Fringes:						
	P&H - 6,400 hrs. @ $2.46				15,744	15,744	15,744
	V&H @ 7.719%				12,917	12,917	12,917
	Payroll				167,338	30,121	30,121
				Total for 24-00			311,645
25-00 Location Expenses							
25-01 Location Manager							
	(6 day flat)	11	Weeks	1	2,150	23,650	23,650
25-02 Assistants (6 day flats)							
	Assistant Location Mgr.	7	Weeks	1	1,800	12,600	12,600
	Local Contact Person	4	Weeks	1	1,000	4,000	4,000
25-03 First Aid		4	Weeks	1	1,400	5,600	5,600
25-04 Fire Officers							
	Shoot	24	Days	1	400	9,600	9,600
25-05 Security		1	Allow	1	18,000	18,000	18,000
25-06 Police		24	Days	1	400	9,600	9,600
	Additional Police	1	Allow	1	4,000	4,000	4,000
25-07 Permits		1	Allow	1	2,500	2,500	2,500
25-08 Parking		1	Allow	1	7,500	7,500	7,500
25-09 Catering Service							
Crew Meals		24	Days	80	13	24,000	24,000
Extras		300	Meals	1	13	3,900	3,900
Ice/Propane		4	Weeks	1	300	1,200	1,200
2nd Meals		13	Days	1	500	6,500	6,500
Sales Tax		1	Allow	1	3,050	3,050	3,050
Tent		1	Allow	1	1,500	1,500	1,500
25-10 Location Office Drinks/Sna		12	Weeks	1	200	2,400	2,400
25-11 Location Office Supplies		1	Allow	1	2,500	2,500	2,500

25-12 Location Office Equipment	1	Allow	1	3,000	3,000	3,000	
25-13 Location Office Space Renta	2.5	Months	1	4,000	10,000	10,000	
24-14 Location Office Telephone/F	1	Allow	1	15,000	15,000	15,000	
25-15 Shipping & Overnight	1	Allow	1	1,500	1,500	1,500	
25-16 Gratuities	1	Allow	1	2,000	2,000	2,000	
25-17 Location Site Rental							
Shoot	24	Days	1	3,500	84,000	84,000	
25-18 Location Survey	1	Allow	1	2,000	2,000	2,000	
Photos/Film	1	Allow	1	750	750	750	
25-19 Auto Rentals							
Location Manager	12	Weeks	1	250	3,000	3,000	
Assistants	2	Weeks	1	150	300	300	
25-20 Miscellaneous Expenses							
Mileage/DGA/SAG/	1	Allow	1	1,000	1,000	1,000	
Payroll				87,050	15,669	15,669	
				Total for 25-00			280,319
26-00 Picture Vehicles/Animals							
26-01 Animal Trainers							
Boss Wrangler	3	Weeks	1	1,700	5,100	5,100	
Assistant Wrangler	3	Weeks	1	1,200	3,600	3,600	
Wranglers	1	Week	5	1,000	5,000	5,000	
Riders/Handlers, etc	1	Day	20	125	2,500	2,500	
26-02 Animals							
Horses	1	Allow	1	8,000	8,000	8,000	
Veterinary Expenses	1	Allow	1	500	500	500	
Feed/Shelter	1	Allow	1	1,200	1,200	1,200	
Transportation	1	Allow	1	5,000	5,000	5,000	
26-03 Picture Cars							
Sheriff Rizzoli's Ca	1.4	Weeks	1	500	700	700	
Frances' Car	3	Weeks	1	500	1,500	1,500	
Skylark's Car	3	Weeks	1	500	1,500	1,500	
Background Cars	1	Allow	1	5,000	5,000	5,000	
Payroll				16,200	2,916	2,916	
				Total for 26-00			42,516
27-00 Film & Lab - Production							
27-01 Raw Stock (Film-Product	6000	Ft.	24	0	66,240		

Second Camera	2000	Ft.	10	0	9,200		
Sales Tax	1	Allow	1	75,440	6,224	81,664	
27-02 Lab-Negative Prep & Proc	164,000	Ft.	1	0	31,629	31,629	
27-04 Dailies /Workprints	90,000	Ft.	1	0	29,700	29,700	
Stock Included							
27-05 Sound Transfers	75	Reels	1	7	525	525	
27-06 Projection	1	Allow	1	2,500	2,500	2,500	
				Total for 27-00			146,018
28-00 Travel and Living-Crew							
28-01 Airfares-LA-New Orleans	24	Fares	1	489	11,736	11,736	
DP/Cam Op/1stAC/Gaffer/Key Grip							
Key Make-Up/Key Hair/Costume Des.							
Costumer/Props/Set Dec./Swing Lead/							
Spec. Efx/Prod. Des./Asst. Prod. Des.							
Tech Adv./Auditor/Asst. Auditor/Editor/Asst. Ed.							
Prod. Coord/1st A.D./2nd.A.D./UPM							
28-02 Hotels	1031	Nites	1	100	103,100	103,100	
28-03 Taxi	1	Allow	1	1,500	1,500	1,500	
28-04 Auto - UPM	64	Days	1	35	2,240	2,240	
28-05 Rail					0	0	
28-06 Excess Baggage	1	Allow	1	2,500	2,500	2,500	
28-08 Per Diem	1001	Days	1	45	45,045	45,045	
				Total for 28-00			166,121
30-00 Editorial							
30-01 Editor - Shoot/Post	16	Weeks	1	2,400	38,400		
Post Production Superviso	8	Weeks	1	2,400	19,200	57,600	
30-02 Assistant Editor - Shoot/P	16	Weeks	1	1,300	20,800	20,800	
30-03 Music Editor	6	Weeks	1	1,500	9,000	9,000	
30-04 Sound Editor	6	Weeks	1	1,500	9,000	9,000	
30-05 Cutting Room Rental	16	Weeks	1	200	3,200	3,200	
30-06 Purchases	1	Allow	1	1,500	1,500	1,500	
30-07 Cutting Room Equip. Rental	16	Weeks	1	400	6,400	6,400	
Payroll				96,400	17,352	17,352	
				Total for 30-00			124,852
31-00 Post-Prod. Film & Lab/Videotape							

31-01	Dirty Dupes (1)	12,000	Ft.	3	0	7,560	7,560	
	Film to Tape (3/4")	12	Reels	2	45	1,080	1,080	
31-02	Negative Cutter	12	Reels	1	750	9,000	9,000	
	Supplies	12	Reels	1	75	900	900	
31-03	Develop Optical Negative	1500	Ft.	1	0	510	510	
31-04	Answer Prints (3)	12,000	Ft.	3	1	30,600	30,600	
31-05	Internegative/Interpositive	12,000	Ft.	2	1	20,400	20,400	
31-06	Check Prints (2)	12,000	Ft.	2	0	7,920	7,920	
31-07	Release Prints	12,200	Ft.	1	0	3,538	3,538	
					Total for 31-00			81,508
32-00	**Optical Effects**							
32-01	Fades, Dissolves, Titles etc	50	Efx	1	600	30,000	30,000	
32-02	Shoot Inter-Positives	3000	Ft.	1	2	5,550	5,550	
32-04	IP Set up charge/color tim	1	Allow	1	1,500	1,500	1,500	
					Total for 32-00			37,050
33-00	**Music**							
33-01	Composer	1	Allow	1	85,000	85,000	85,000	
(All-In Package includes: Arrangers, Copyists,								
...Musicians, Instruments)								
					Total for 33-00			85,000
34-00	**Post Production Sound**							
34-01	Spotting for Music/Sound E	30	Hours	1	150	4,500	4,500	
34-02	Music Scoring Stage	4	Days	1	2,400	9,600	9,600	
34-03	Music Mix Down	2	Days	1	2,400	4,800	4,800	
34-04	ADR & Foley	7	Days	1	2,600	18,200	18,200	
34-06	Laydown	4	Hours	1	200	800	800	
34-08	Editing (Digital Work Station)							
	Sound Editing	90	Hours	1	225	20,250	20,250	
	Dialogue Editing	60	Hours	1	225	13,500	13,500	
	24 Track Stock	50	Reels	1	250	12,500	12,500	
34-09	Pre-Dub	45	Hours	1	250	11,250	11,250	
34-10	Final Dub (Mix)	45	Hours	1	250	11,250	11,250	
34-11	Printmaster + M&E	8	Hours	1	300	2,400	2,400	
34-12	Optical Sound Transfer	12000	Ft	1	0	4,320	4,320	

34-13	Stock/Dubs/Transfers (F		1	Allow	1	5,000	5,000	5,000	
						Total for 34-00			118,370
37-00 Insurance								
(Allow 3% of Below-The Line)			1	Allow	1	2,848,999	85,470	85,470
37-01 Producers Entertainment Pckg.								
Negative							0	0
Faulty Stock							0	0
Equipment							0	0
Props/Sets							0	0
Extra Expense							0	0
3rd Party Property Damage							0	0
Office Contents							0	0
37-02 General Liability							0	0
37-03 Hired Auto							0	0
37-04 Cast Insurance							0	0
37-05 Workers Compensation							0	0
37-06 Errors & Omissions							0	0
						Total for 37-00			85,470
38-00 General & Administrative Expenses								
38-02 Legal			1	Allow	1	45,000	45,000	45,000
38-03 Accounting fees			1	Allow	1	5,000	5,000	5,000
38-05 Telephone/FAX			1	Allow	1	10,000	10,000	10,000
38-06 Copying			1	Allow	1	1,500	1,500	1,500
38-07 Postage & Freight			1	Allow	1	1,000	1,000	1,000
38-08 Office Space Rental			1	Allow	1	12,000	12,000	12,000
38-09 Office Furniture			1	Allow	1	2,000	2,000	2,000
38-10 Office Equipment & Supplie			1	Allow	1	5,000	5,000	5,000
38-11 Computer Rental								
	Line Producer		14	Weeks	1	125	1,750	
	First A.D.		7	Weeks	1	125	875	
	Prod. Coordinator		12	Weeks	1	125	1,500	
	Prod. Accountant		22	Weeks	1	125	2,750	
	Office		8	Months	1	350	2,800	
	Printers		8	Months	1	350	2,800	12,475
38-12 Software			1	Allow	1	1,500	1,500	1,500
38-14 Messenger/Overnight			1	Allow	1	1,000	1,000	1,000
38-15 Parking			1	Allow	1	800	800	800
38-16 Storage			1	Allow	1	1,500	1,500	1,500

38-19 Wrap Party		1	Allow	1	2,500	2,500	2,500	
					Total for 38-00			101,275
Contingency @ 10%							448,278	448,278
	GRAND TOTAL							$4,931,055
Total Above-The-Line								1,377,634
Total Below-The-Line								3,105,143
Total Above and Below-the-Line								4,482,777
					Check budget totals		4,931,055	4,931,055

$5 MILLION FEATURE

01-00 Story Rights
This movie is not based on a book, or on anyone's life story. It's an original screenplay based on an idea by the Executive Producer, who jotted it down on the back of an envelope as he stood in a line at the unemployment office.

02-00 Script
The Executive Producer interested an investor in the idea, who put up the money to hire a respected but unproduced screen writer.

02-01 Writer's Salaries
The Writer was paid WGA scale for the treatment through the polish, and negotiated a production bonus for himself (not required by the WGA) that pays him an additional $20,000 should the picture go into production.

02-02 Research
The Writer also convinced the Executive Producer to allow this line item for the purchase of books, and several trips to New Orleans to research background for the story, which takes place in the 1960s.

02-03 Title Registration
A legal fee paid to a clearance house to make sure there was no conflict with using the title.

02-08 Script Timing
Usually the script is timed after it has been approved for production, but in this case the script was long, and knowing that this might be a strike against him in getting a production deal, the Executive Producer wanted to know how long the movie would play as part of his pitch to the studio.

02-10 Development
The Executive Producer ran up a travel bill on his credit cards trying to get investors. This is his way of getting the money back.

03-00 Producers Unit

03-01 Executive Producer
His fee for the production period of the picture. He also has a "back end" deal to share profits with the investor, providing if there are any after the studio earns its production and promotion money back and takes its profit. But that's another book.

03-02 Producer
The Executive Producer has managed to do all the deal-making himself—that is, with no other "Producer" partners. He hires a Line Producer (10-01) to actually produce the movie, and the Editor to both edit and supervise post-production.

03-03 Associate Producer
Sometimes the Associate Producer is the Post-Production Supervisor, but in this case, the Executive Producer has hired the Editor to handle the post. So there is no AP on this one.

03-04 Assistant to the Executive Producer
This person helps the Executive Producer get through the days of pre-production, production, and half of post-production. The Executive wanted to keep him on until the end but had to cut somewhere, and post is quiet compared to production.

03-06 Consultants
This is a slop category. In this case, the Executive Producer had extensive production meetings with an established Producer who could not work on the project, but accepted an "honorarium" for his production advice.

03-07 Producer's Miscellaneous
Another slop category for unexpected expenses.

04-00 Direction

04-01 Director

The Executive Producer and the studio have selected a reasonably seasoned Director of low to medium budget films. He is paid over the DGA scale, and there is no payroll tax applied because his company is receiving the checks.

The Director is on location with the Executive Producer, Producer, and Location Manager a full 5 weeks before cameras roll. After the 24 days of shooting (and 4 days off), the Director will return to L.A., and, after a short break in which the Editor assembles the first rough cut, will spend the next two months creating the "Director's cut." After that he plans a vacation in Majorca with his three children from a failed marriage, and his current companion. It's the nineties.

05-00 Cast

05-01 Lead Actors.

These rates are way over-scale, but these are the stars. Current SAG pension and health rate is 12.8%, but if an actor earns over $200,000 in any single film, anything over that figure is not subject to the P&H. You can add it into the budget anyway, to create a secret pocket of cash for a rainy day, but check the actor's check requests to make sure you're not overpaying. Also, check with SAG for any changes to those rates or rules.

05-02 Supporting Cast

The roles of Harry and Edna are played by actors flying in from Los Angeles, so their pay for a 6-day week is calculated on a special formula. Check with SAG to figure out what your formula is, because there are several "if's," "and's," and "but's."

Similarly, because the other supporting players are local people, their pay is calculated differently from Harry and Edna's.

In this case, the actors playing Harry, Edna, and Sheriff Rizzoli are paid over-scale. Their fee includes a 10% agency fee. The other supporting cast players are local people, working a 6-day week, at SAG scale, plus an agency fee.

Note: This may be the first time you've encountered weeks with decimal points (Sheriff Rizzoli). This notation is often used for people who are hired by flat weekly rates. When a person is hired for one or more 5-day weeks plus a partial week, the partial week is divided into tenths. So one week and one day is shown as 1.2 weeks. A week plus 2 days is 1.4 weeks. A week plus 3 days is 1.6 weeks. And a week plus 4 days is 1.8 weeks. This makes budgeting simpler because you just multiply by the weekly rate instead of having to stop and figure out what the day rate is.

05-03 Day Players
The actors playing Balthazar, Rudnick, and Shorty are local character actors paid over-scale, plus agency fee. The rest of the Day Players are paid SAG scale plus agency fee.

05-04 Casting Director
This is a package price based on the number of cast, and the time allowed for the casting process. The price includes fees for the Casting Director and staff, room rental for auditions, video camera and stock to tape auditions, and other administrative costs of doing all of the actor's SAG paperwork. The lion's share goes to an L.A. based Casting Director to handle the principal parts. The rest goes to a New Orleans based person for the smaller parts.

05-05 Casting Expenses
An extra allowance is provided for copying of scripts, overnight delivery, and so on.

05-06 Choreographer
A Choreographer and one assistant are on board to stage a barn dance scene, and a steamy dance sequence between the two stars in a roadside honky tonk.

05-10 Stunt Coordinator

Since the stunts in this picture are pretty run of the mill as stunts go, (mostly fighting and falling), the Stunt Coordinator is only on for 3 weeks total. This includes all his prep time, which occurs during pre-production because the stunt scenes are near the start of the shoot. This rate is for 6-day weeks.

05-11 Stunt Players

Since only some of the stunt work is regular, only four stunt players are on weekly contracts (6-day weeks). The others are budgeted in a more general way as "man days," because they are called in on an "as needed" basis.

05-12 Stunt Costs/Adjustments

"Adjustments" are the extra monies stunt people get for doing what they do. This line is only $5,000 because the stunts are pretty basic. More dangerous stunts get higher adjustments.

05-13 Stunt Equipment

This figure is what the Stunt Coordinator has budgeted for some special rigging, padding, and so on, needed to pull off the fight scenes.

05-14 Looping

Since we have no idea how much looping (ADR) work there will be by the picture's end, this is a reasonable allowance.

05-15 Cast Overtime

Another reasonable allowance.

06-00 Travel and Living—Producers

06-01 Air fares

Two first-class fares and free champagne for the Executive Producer and the Director. Everyone else gets salted nuts.

06-02 Hotels
The Executive Producer and the Director are at the location for about one month of prep and one month of shoot.

06-09 Per Diem
Daily expenses for the Executive Producer and the Director

07-00 Travel and Living—Cast

07-01 Air fare
First class fares are standard for SAG players.

07-02 Hotels
The two stars are on location for practically all of the shoot period; "Harry" and "Edna" for a little over half of the period.

07-08 Per Diem
Daily expense allowances are part of the SAG agreement for players on location. The locals don't score here.

10-00 Production Staff

10-01 UPM/Line Producer
The Unit Production Manager/Line Producer (who will naturally prefer the latter title) is a nuts-and-bolts, up-through-the-ranks person with years of experience and know-how. This rate is about $500 per week over the DGA scale for UPM's on location—a "bump" for being the "Line Producer." It also includes his DGA production fee.

During the prep phase on location, the Line Producer checks in frequently with the head of each department, asking them to reassess their budgets in view of the Director's creative choices for specific setups and action. If any department budgets get too high, it's up to the Line Producer to either rob some other department, or confer with the Director to reduce costs.

His life span on the project is only through production and 3 weeks of cleaning up. Then he looks for work again.

10-02 First AD / 2nd AD
The 1st AD is on location with the Director from the start of prep through the shoot. The 2nd AD joins up about 2 weeks before the shoot. Payments for both are DGA scale for locations on a 6-day (Saturday included) shoot schedule. Also included on a separate line are the DGA "production fees" which are payable for every day cameras roll. First and Second AD's can be paid a "production fee" for prep days as well, at the Line Producer's discretion. This Line Producer opted not to, and made that clear at the outset.

10-04 Production Coordinator / Assistant Coordinator
On for almost the same prep, shoot and wrap time as the Line Producer, the Coordinators are essential in getting the myriad production elements ready. Payments are in the industry standard ranges for this level of budget, for a 6-day shoot schedule.

10-05 Script Supervisor
The Script Supervisor needs 5 days to get the script ready for shooting, and thereafter will be on hand for every frame of film shot.

Also, there are 8 days when the Script Supervisor will keep camera notes for two cameras, and he or she gets a "bump" or extra money for those days.

Note: If you are reading this budget from top to bottom, this is the first time you'll come across an hourly wage. The formula for paying people by the hour goes like this: The number in the *times* box (marked with an x at the top of the budget page) refers to the number of *pay hours* a person works. For this picture, the budget is calculated on a 12 work-hour day. So why enter the number 14 in most of the shoot lines? Because it represents *pay hours*, not hours worked. If a person works 12 hours, 8 of those hours are paid at straight time, and 4 hours are paid at time and a half (1.5). Four hours multiplied by 1.5 = 6 *pay hours*. So the total *pay hours* is the sum of 8 plus 6, or 14 pay hours.

The next number, for example with the Script Supervisor ($21.43), represents the person's hourly rate.

"Prep" and "Wrap" line items are self-explanatory, and vary according to the demands of each job. "Shoot" and "Saturdays Worked" need an explanation.

This is a 4-week, or 24-day shoot. Monday through Friday are straight time for 8 hours, and time and a half for 4 hours, which is 12 work hours per day, or 14 pay hours. Saturdays are also worked at a 12-hour day, but Saturdays are paid at time and a half. Twelve hours multiplied by 1.5 = 18 pay hours. That's why the number 18 sits in the "Saturdays Worked" box.

10-06 Production Accountant / Assistant
The Auditors or Accountants come on during prep to set up the books and handle payroll for all prep personnel. They are most active during the shoot period as they pay bills, payroll, and prepare daily and weekly Cost Reports that tell the Line Producer and the studio how much the picture is behind schedule and over budget.

10-07 Technical Advisor
An expert in law enforcement techniques is on hand during the shoot to keep Sheriff Rizzoli (and the Director) honest in the depiction of police methods of the 1960s.

10-08 Production Assistants
The Office PA is another indispensable person in the production chain of command. He or she, and the Set PA's, help on the set, reporting to the AD's. They must be bright, energetic, cheerful, efficient, and cheap.

10-09 Teacher/Welfare Worker
As the schedule turns out, there will be kids on the set during almost all of the shoot period. There are fewer than 10 at any given time, however, so only one Teacher/Welfare Worker is required. Also, since this is a summer time shoot, and the kids are on vacation, no school time is required, only daily periods of R&R.

11-00 Extra Talent

11-01 Stand-Ins
There is no SAG Extras agreement for the location, New Orleans, but this was figured on SAG minimums anyway, since these people will be on set for 12 hours a day during the entire shooting period.

11-02 Extras
There is one big barn dance scene that will employ 100 extras for one day. They will be required to stomp their feet and clap as two of the stars do a star turn. These are SAG rates, even though SAG does not represent extras in New Orleans. In some places, it's possible to get away with paying less, but not in New Orleans. The Line Producer does save a little by not paying SAG pension and health.

11-03 Extras Casting Fee
All the headaches of calling and organizing 300 people, and doing their paperwork, are handed off to an Extras casting agency for a 10% charge of Extras' salaries.

13-00 Production Design

13-01 Production Designer
The Production Designer must be on hand during prep to scout, help select, and design for all the locations. He or she is on a weekly (6 day) flat. The 1960s period look has to be resurrected for everything.

13-10 Polaroid Film
This is the first of many departments that requires Polaroids. They help in pre-production when the department head cannot lay eyes on the real thing. And they help in continuity during shooting, when something or someone has to be reconstructed more than once.

14-00 Set Construction

14-01 Construction Coordinator

For this picture, about one month is required to build the sets needed to start shooting. Sets needed later in production will be built after shooting begins. The Construction Coordinator works with the Production Designer on the plans, then gets the construction crew and painters in gear to get the sets ready on time.

Note: As a department head, the Coordinator gets the same rate, $25 per hour, as other similar department heads, such as Set Dressing, Set Operations, Property, and Electric. Their assistants and workers also get paid on a par with those in other departments. Consistency in the rate of pay keeps grumbling and jealousy about money in check.

14-02 Labor

The Foreman is a man with experience, knowledge of local deals, and good contacts for local crew. Based on conversations with the Production Designer and Construction Coordinator, an allowance of $50,000 is set aside for construction crew.

14-03 Scenic Painters

The Lead Scenic Painter is the Foreman to the painting crew. Like the Construction Foreman, this man knows local deals and crew contacts.

14-05 Greens

This is a fairly average allowance for plants, shrubbery, and the like, but there isn't all that much call in the script for action in and around the bushes. The Greens will also be used to mask an atrocious pink porch that the homeowner will not allow to be repainted—something about his wife spending three months to get the pink the exact right shade.

14-09 Set Strike

It's always unbelievable how much time, money, and effort go into making sets look perfect, sometimes for just one shot, only to have

them taken apart and destroyed a day later. This line item covers the
cost of taking sets apart and hauling them off to storage warehouses
or city dumps.

15-00 Set Operations

15-01 Key Grip
The Key Grip needs some prep time on location to pick a crew, and
scout the locations to get a sense of the equipment and pre-rigging
needs. This person is being flown in from L.A. because it's an
important position and the Line Producer wanted someone he had
worked with before.

15-02 Best Boy Grip
Once in New Orleans, the Key Grip and the Line Producer bring on
a Second Grip to assist with prep and shoot.

15-03 Other Grips
The three other Grips who will work the whole shoot are local as
well, and probably known to the Second Grip as reliable people. An
allowance of 40 man-days has been provided for extra Grips needed
for pre-rig, striking, and additional heavy days.

15-04 Dolly Grips
Prep time is allowed for these specialized Grips to check out the
dolly.

15-05 Craft Service
Because the crew needs coffee and donuts (and eggs, toast, bacon,
cereal) at the crack of dawn, and coffee to stay awake at night, these
necessary people are often first on and last off the set. An ample
overtime allowance is provided. At $275 per day for purchases,
there's a healthy sampling of good food on the table, including hot
"walking meals" for breakfast when needed.

15-06 Grip Rentals
During the prep period, the Director of Photography, Director, and
Line Producer determine what cranes and dollies, along with

standard grip equipment, will be needed to get the shots that will keep the story visually interesting. Then the equipment is ordered well in advance. Sometimes the shooting schedule changes, and specific equipment, like a big crane for example, may not be available. That's why good Line Producers, especially on location, have backup plans that include knowing where to get what they need.

16-00 Special Effects

16-01 Special Effects Person
This is another key person who flies in from L.A., in this case to have about 10 days prep time on location to survey the camera setups and troubleshoot any technical and safety problems that might come up to ruin his gags or get someone hurt.

He'll also have to time to pre-rig an effect involving Rain Birds (rain storm sprinklers), and huge fans that simulate a wind storm that blows two kids and a horse across an outdoor square dance platform. Fun.

16-02 SFX Assistant
This is a local guy who will also provide a mobile effects shop to fabricate or repair needed items on the spot (provided for in **16-09**).

16-03 Additional Labor
One hundred man-days are allowed for extra help in setting up the wind storm shot, a few car scrapes, and sundry other effects.

16-06/16-07/16-08 Manufacturing Labor/Fabrication/Expendables
These categories cover all the special rigging and materials needed to achieve the effects. The Special Effects Person has been key in estimating the cost of all this.

17-00 Set Dressing

17-01 Set Decorator
Working closely with the Production Designer, the Set Decorator arrives for three weeks of prep to scour New Orleans for the right period furniture, drapery, and other house and office accouterments that will make the scenes look right out of the 1960s.

17-02 Lead Man
The Lead Man is someone who has worked often with the Set Decorator. He works ahead of (i. e., "leads") the shoot unit, and is in charge of prepping locations, handling returns, and generally running the Swing Gang.

He and the Set Decorator scour New Orleans, often in separate cars (**17-10**), as well as hire the Swing Gang (**17-03**) who will physically move everything into place on the sets, hang the curtains and the lights, lay the carpet, and then take it all away when the shot is done.

17-06 / 17-07   Purchases and Rentals
Together, there's $60,000 to buy all the carpet set dressing used on the film. Anything that can be resold will be resold.

18-00 Property

18-01 Property Master
This is another fly-in from L.A., about 4 weeks prior to shooting. There are lots of props to buy and rent for this picture, including four antique blunderbuss muskets that must fire. The Prop Master also has a powder license to legally handle the firearms.

18-02 Property Assistant
This is a local person who knows where things can be found, and will help with buying and renting props.

19-00 Wardrobe

19-01 Costume Designer

The Designer works on a 6-day flat week, and flies in from L.A. for 4 weeks of prep. She works with the Director and Production Designer to make sure the styles and colors of the costumes blend in with the overall look of the film. Most of the 1960s fashions will be rented, but quite a few will be bought, made from scratch, or adjusted from contemporary clothing (**19-05 and 19-06**). The Costumer (**19-02**) and Additional Costumer (**19-03**), a local person, help do the adjustments. Lead and Supporting cast members are fitted well in advance, and all costumes are approved by the Director.

19-03 Additional Costumers

Fifteen man-days are allowed for more costumers to clothe certain extras for special business in the barn dance scene, and in several street scenes.

20-00 Make-Up and Hairdressing

20-01 Key Make-Up Artist

The Key Make-Up Artist has already had a discussion with the Director about the look of the actors. Since this is a realistic picture with no special make-up effects, it wasn't a very long conversation.

The Key Make-Up has 2 days to travel (one each way), like everyone else, and 2 days to check out any special setups, and gather any needed supplies.

The Line Producer, being the think-ahead kind of person that he is, heard through the grapevine that the actress playing "Edna" typically takes two and a half to three hours for regular make-up. He therefore worked with the 1st AD, who sets call times, to allow for that little glitch in the schedule.

20-02 Additional Make-Up Artist

Six days of the 24-day schedule are scenes that can be handled by the Key Make-Up alone, but the other 19 need help.

20-03 Hair Stylist

The Hair Stylist has three more days prep than the Key Make-Up—remember, this is the 60s when hair was king. The character of "Skylark" has a rich mane of long Hippie hair, but the actor just got off a picture in which he played a combat Marine. The answer is a wig, of course, which requires a bit more prep time each shoot day (**Rentals 20-06**). Other characters also sport long hair, but they've managed to grow their own.

20-04 Additional Hair Stylist

Same as the Additional Make-Up.

21-00 Electrical

21-01 Gaffer

The Gaffer is another key person who has been hired by the Director of Photography. They have a long relationship of working together, and the Gaffer usually second-guesses the DP. In addition, he tells good jokes, and since the DP is also operating the camera on this one, the stress level might be a little higher.

The Gaffer flies in for a week of prep on location, which involves a tech scout for each scene, hiring crew, conferring with the DP and the Key Grip for special equipment or crew needs, securing the right lighting equipment, and hiring the Best Boy and three local Electrics who will be the core team of his department.

21-02 Best Boy

The Best Boy is a New Orleans man with a good professional reputation and a recipe for a killer gumbo. He comes on for the same prep period as the Gaffer, and assists in running the crew and keeping track of all the lighting inventory.

21-03 Electrics

These three come on for 4 days of prep, during which they prepare and check all the lighting equipment, organize the truck, and do some pre-rigging for the first day's shoot.

21-04 Additional Labor

Thirty man-days has been allowed for the several setups that will require extra lights. The first is the now famous barn dance/wind storm scene, which requires substantial pre-wiring since it's a night shoot with water all over the place.

21-05 Purchases

This money covers the various "expendables" in the lighting budget, such as gels, black wrap, tape, replacement bulbs, and so forth.

21-06 Rentals

This is the basic lighting equipment package, which the Gaffer and the Line Producer have assembled per the instructions of the DP and within the limits of the overall budget. It comes from a New Orleans supplier, in a 40-foot production trailer truck with twin generators.

There is also Additional Equipment, Condors (crane-like devices that get lights up in the air and hold a man in a basket to adjust them), and an Additional Generator. These are for the barn dance night shoot, and for several other less elaborate night shoots.

22-00 <u>Camera</u>

22-01 Director of Photography/Operator

The DP and the Director are old collaborators who work well together. On this shoot he will also operate the A camera. He arrives on location for 5 days of prep, and walks through each proposed setup with the Director and the Gaffer. He is on a 6-day per week flat.

22-02 Camera Operator (B Cam)

A second camera will be used for 10 days of the 24 days of shooting, but 2 of those 10 days will be with a Steadicam Operator (22-11). The B Camera Operator flies in from L.A. with no more than an afternoon of prep before his 8 days of shooting. As a specialist, his rate is higher than the $25 per hour paid to Keys and most department heads.

22-03 1st Assistant Camera

This is another specialist whom the DP relies on to pull focus, change lenses, and set f-stops. He also knows how to repair the camera for minor problems, which can be especially handy on location.

The 1st AC arrives on location for 2 days of prep, and checks out the two cameras, lenses, magazines, and other attachments very carefully to make sure no schlock equipment gets on the set. He'll also make sure the right film is on hand, and the film loading room is shipshape.

The B Camera 1st AC is local, shows up on his first shoot day, and works for 10 days, 2 of which are assisting the Steadicam Operator.

22-04 2nd Assistant Camera

The 2nd AC's load magazines, make sure can labels are accurate, handle the clapboard or slate, and generally help the others on the camera crew. Both of these assistants are local.

The 2nd AC for the A camera has 2 days of prep, working right alongside the 1st AC. Similarly, the 2nd AC for the B camera sticks with the 1st AC for the B camera, working 10 days, 2 of which are with the Steadicam Operator.

22-05 Still Photographer

The Line Producer wanted to have a still photographer on hand for the whole period, but decided he couldn't afford it. So the one week in which the movie's stars and supporting cast are all working is the week the still photographer shows up for production and promotion stills. She's a good shooter from New Orleans.

22-07 Camera Package Rental

The DP orders one Arriflex 535 with lenses as the A camera package, and an Arriflex 535B (camera body only) as the B camera. It will also act as a reserve camera in case of major trouble. The lens package consists of Zeiss Standard Speed PL Primes, and includes 16mm, 24mm, 32mm, 50mm, 85mm, and 100mm, plus one 500mm telephoto. The entire package, with magazines, filters, accessories, and batteries, comes to $7,000 per week.

22-10 Additional Equipment
This account allows for extra rentals for things that come up in the course of shooting, like a special camera rig for a difficult shot.

22-11 Steadicam Operator and Equipment
This is a local man who rents himself and his harness out as a package for $1,500 per day. The Director wants a moving camera look for some of the square dance scenes, and several others. Two days' work.

23-00 Sound

23-01 Mixer
The Mixer and the Boom Operator are actually a local couple who rent themselves and their sound package. In the one day of prep, the Mixer checks equipment and loads it into the camera/sound truck.

23-02 Boom Operator
The Boom Op shows up on the first shoot day with her "fish pole" (the mike boom), and her strong arms.

23-04 Sound Package
Since this film is being edited in a traditional film style, that is, on film rather than video tape, a standard Nagra sound recorder is used, along with a small complement of microphones, including radio mikes. (If the film were to be edited on videotape, a Nagra with the ability to create time code would be used to sync up sound and picture during the telecine process.)

23-05 Walkie Talkies
Everybody wants a walkie, it seems, from the Line Producer to the Crafts Services person. While they can be a pain in the neck to lug around, they can also save a lot of walking and serious yelling. A relatively cheap convenience.

23-07 Beepers
Another seemingly indispensable apparatus to keep everyone on a short leash. A love/hate thing.

23-08 Cell Phones/Service

The cell phone and the beeper were made for each other. Expensive but worth it.

23-09 1/4 inch Mag Stock

For the Nagra, the Mixer figures on three reels for each of the 24 shoot days.

24-00 Transportation

24-01 Transportation Coordinator

A competent Coordinator is a glorious thing. This man is a local with years of experience. He knows how to help the production team analyze the schedule and break out all the transportation needs.

24-02 Drivers

The Captain is the first lieutenant to the Coordinator.

There are 18 drivers on this shoot. Some prep for merely a day, which means they check out the truck and drive it to the first location. Others, like the Props or Set Dressing Drivers, have up to 10 days of prep, during which time they run all over town picking up the various items ordered by the Production Designer, Set Decorator, Costume Designer, and so on.

Drivers get 18 pay hours per average day, because they work 14 hours to everyone else's 12. They're on the set an hour prior and off the set an hour later.

24-03 Equipment Rentals

The vehicles list itself is a monument to careful planning. Every day of the shoot has been mapped out according to vehicle needs. In as many cases as possible, trailers have been rented instead of trucks. This means a Crew Cab or Maxi Van can haul the trailer to its place, then unhook and do other things.

25-00 Location Expenses

25-01 Location Manager

The Location Manager agrees to an 11-week deal on a weekly flat fee that includes Saturdays during production and as needed during prep.

A full 7 weeks before production begins, she starts scouting. She takes tons of pictures and video (25-18 Location Survey) and sends them back to the Executive Producer, Line Producer, and Director in Los Angeles. They spend hours on the phone with her, going through all the details: several property owners are balking at the size of the crew; a special fire permit is required for one scene; the seasonal rains may interrupt some shooting; tide charts show that the schedule must be adjusted to shoot during low tide; a holiday occurs that will cause traffic jams on the day a company move is planned.

Two weeks later, now 5 weeks before production, the Director, Executive Producer, and Line Producer show up in New Orleans to finalize all the locations.

In addition to locations for shooting, the Location Manager also helps the Line Producer select and make deals for housing for cast and crew. In this case, a pleasant, nearby hotel lowered its rates sufficiently to accommodate everyone. It could not, however, provide any production office space, which was a blow to the Line Producer who likes to roll out of bed and crawl to his desk in the morning. (See Production Office Space Rental 25-13.)

25-02 Assistants

The Assistant Location Manager joins up for three weeks of prep, to help the Location Manager get all the location paperwork and permits in shape. She stays on for the whole shoot.

The Local Contact Person is one Melville Oliver Bollineaux, a retired local politician whom residents call "Righteous Mel." He knows every alley, bog and bayou in 50 miles, and half the people too. Best of all, he is a master in the art of southern sweet talk, and will probably save the company thousands of dollars in grief.

25-03 First Aid
A local nurse is on hand each shooting day for anything from cuts and bruises to worse. She has good connections to local doctors, hospitals, and ambulance services.

25-04 Fire Officers
A county ordinance says a fire officer must be on hand for all shooting.

25-05 Security
This is a fairly healthy allowance for security guards, but production vehicles and parked crew cars need protection during all shooting, gear needs to be guarded during meals, and several nights the trucks will be left in remote areas. It's good insurance.

25-06 Police
A county ordinance says a police officer must be on hand for all shooting. Additional police will be used for traffic and crowd control during some shooting on city streets.

25-07 Permits
The $2,500 goes to the city and county.

25-08 Parking
This estimate is probably high, but the Line Producer stuck it in as cash for a rainy day.

25-09 Catering Service
The Location Manager has recommended *Frank's Finger Lickin' Kitchen* to cater the shoot meals. Frank agrees to $13 a head, which includes a vegetarian and a meat entree for each meal, plus choice of two salads, side dishes, drinks, and dessert. That price also includes servers, and table and chair setup and strike. It also includes a "walking breakfast" of hot food that the crew eats without a formal sit down. The tent is separate, as is the lunch for the 300 extras, and

2nd meals for the estimated 13 days when the shoot will go over the estimated 12 hours a day.

25-13 Location Office Space Rental
Home base for the production office is found at an office building two blocks from the hotel. It's a bit pricey for the neighborhood, but convenient.

25-17 Location Site Rental
This $3,500 per day is an average cost that includes prep and strike days. There's a house in the French Quarter that's going to run $5,000 per day for 5 days. But at the other extreme, there's a field and forest property in a remote section of the county that will only cost $750 per day for 4 days.

25-18 Location Survey
All those pictures and video and various expenses the Location Manager incurred while surveying are paid back to her here.

25-20 Miscellaneous Expenses
Mileage for DGA (.31/mile), SAG, and crew (.30/mile) is reimbursements for local people who drive their own cars to the far-flung reaches of the county for the field and stream stuff.

26-00 Picture Vehicles/Animals

26-01 Animal Trainers
The Boss Wrangler and the Assistant Wrangler come on for a week of prep to walk through the scenes with horses, including the big dance scene in which 20 extra horses will be used. A nearby rancher agrees to feed and keep the horses for the 2 weeks they're needed, and even throws in horse trailers to get them to and from the set each day for a reasonable fee.

The 5 Wranglers come on for the second week, and the 20 Riders/Handlers come on for the day of the dance scene.

26-02 Animals
Regular horses go for about $150 per day, but the horses for the stars and supporting cast are naturally better looking and better trained than most, and go for $300 per day. One little break—the Boss Wrangler was able to negotiate a half day rate for horses with a day off from shooting.

26-03 Picture Cars
The three main picture cars are 1960s vintage, and cherry, so they have to be trailered to every location. The background cars are just that, and can be driven on the short hops. For the one long hop back into the city, a larger car trailer will be used.

27-00 Film and Lab—Production

27-01 Raw Stock
The A camera is budgeted for 6,000 feet of film a day. That's about 1 hour and 7 minutes of exposed film per day, or about 26 hours and 40 minutes total for the 24-day schedule. If the finished movie is 2 hours, as expected, that's about a 13:1 ratio.

The B camera is estimated to shoot 2,000 feet per day (about 22 minutes), for 10 days, for a total of about 3 hours and 42 minutes. That brings the grand total ratio to about 15:1.

The stock prices were negotiated at .46 per foot from a Los Angeles supplier.

27-02 Lab - Negative Prep and Process
Negative will be developed at .19 per foot from an L.A. lab.

27-04 Dailies/Work Prints
Of the 164,000 feet of exposed film, about 90,000 feet (16 hrs. and 40 min.) of circled takes are transferred to Dailies.

27-05 Sound Transfers

The circled takes from the 1/4 inch audio is transferred to mag tape for editing. It will take up about 75 reels (1,200' each) of mag tape, at $7 per reel.

27-06 Projection

Costs for location projection of Dailies is allowed at $2,500 to rent a screening tent and a double system projector.

28-00 Travel and Living—Crew

28-01 Air Fares

All air fares Los Angeles to New Orleans and return are coach (this is a non-union shoot). The personnel flying from L.A. includes all production department heads with the exception of Sound, Set Construction, and Transportation. That is: Camera, Electric, Set Operations, Make-Up and Hair, Wardrobe, Props, Set Dressing, Special Effects, Production Design, Production, and Editing. These departments are considered so essential to the Director's creative concept for the picture that they should be headed by people whose work the Director and/or Line Producer knows—hence all of them come from L.A. The other people flying in are in turn key to the effectiveness of the department heads.

There are 24 fares in all, each arriving according to the timetable for prep established by the Line Producer.

28-02 Hotels

The total number of weeks in the hotel, including prep and shoot time, is obviously different for different people. Each one is calculated, and the total is given as 143 weeks, or 1,001 room/nights. With visitors and studio people dropping in, the Line Producer allows another 30 room/nights, bringing the total to 1,031 room/nights.

DP	5 weeks
Cam Op B	2 weeks
1st AC	5 weeks
Gaffer	5 weeks
Key Grip	5 weeks
Key Make-Up	5 weeks
Key Hair	5 weeks
Costume Designer	6 weeks
Costumer	5 weeks
Property Master	7 weeks
Set Decorator	6 weeks
Swing Lead	6 weeks
Special Effects	5 weeks
Production Designer	7 weeks
Asst. Prod. Designer	6 weeks
Technical Advisor	7 weeks
Auditor	9 weeks
Asst. Auditor	9 weeks
Production Coordinator	9 weeks
1st AD	7 weeks
2nd AD	6 weeks
Line Producer/UPM	9 weeks
Editor	4 weeks
Asst. Editor	<u>4 weeks</u>

144 weeks

28-08 Per Diem
The same formula applies to Per Diem—1,001 man-days at $45 each.

30-00 <u>Editorial</u>

30-01 Editor
Both the Editor and the Assistant Editor (30-02) fly in at the start of production to set up an editing room where they can sync the dailies and begin assembly of the film itself, as the dailies are screened.

When the shoot is over, they turn in their New Orleans editing gear, fly home to L.A., and set up shop there to continue. With a little luck, the film is assembled soon after the shoot, and ready for the Director to make his cut.

The Editor has also been hired to supervise the entire post-production process for additional compensation beyond his editing fee. He edits for 12 weeks after returning to L.A., cutting the Director's idea of the movie, then making fixes with respect to the studio's and the Executive Producer's notes.

As the picture gets closer to being "locked," the Composer, Music Editor and Sound Effects Editor come on board, and the Editor, now functioning as a Post-Production Supervisor, orchestrates their various functions, and guides the film through opticals, negative cutting, the final sound mix, and several answer prints. That entire process, from locked picture to delivery of a release print, takes about 8 weeks.

30-03 Music Editor
When the picture is locked, or enough locked that it makes sense to bring in the Music Editor, she sits down with the Composer, the Director, and the Executive Producer to spot the film for music. She attends the scoring session, in which the music is recorded, and then actually edits the music track to the picture on a flatbed at the post-production sound facility. That process takes about 6 weeks.

30-04 Sound Editor
The exact same process occurs with the Sound Editor, only he brings in sound effects and matches them to picture.

30-05 Cutting Room Rental
This 16 weeks includes 4 weeks in New Orleans syncing dailies and assembling, and 12 weeks back in L.A. going for the final cut.

The room includes the usual bench setup of a synchronizer with one Mag head, an amp, a splicer, two split reels, two spring clamps, a tape dispenser, a tightwind attachment with core, an adapter, a bench with rack and rewinds, a trim bin, a floor rack, a swivel base, chair and lamp.

30-07 Cutting Room Equipment Rental
In New Orleans, the Editor gets a 4-plate flatbed. In L.A., an 8-plate KEM Flatbed to accommodate more picture and sound tracks.

31-00 Post Production Film and Lab

31-01 Duplicate Work Prints
By now the Editor has cut the film down to its approved running time of 2 hours and 13 minutes (12,000 feet), has ordered the Opticals (see 32-00 Optical Effects), and needs one "dirty dupe" (b/w) of the Work Print for the Music Editor. The Sound and Dialogue Editors each get a film to videotape transfer of the Work Print, onto 3/4 inch tape with the film edge numbers in a window. This is for their sound effects and ADR/dialogue work respectively. The lab charges .21/ft. for the dirty dupe, and $45/reel plus stock for the 3/4 inch dubs.

31-02 Negative Cutter
Once the opticals are done, they are sent to the Negative Cutter, as well as the negatives of course. He cuts the original camera negative according to the Editor's marks on the final Work Print, and cuts in the opticals as well. About two weeks later, he's done, and the cut negative is ready for the first Answer Print.

31-03 Develop Optical Negative
This step is part of the opticals process. Each of the 50 optical effects (see 32-00 Opticals) is printed onto a negative in the optical printer, then sent to the lab to develop into an optical negative. Then they make a Work Print from the optical neg, both for evaluation of the effects, and for cutting them into the locked Work Print.

31-04 Answer Prints
It takes three Answer Prints to get it right, but finally the color and film density is as perfect as money and time will allow.

31-05 Internegative/Interpositive

Thanks to the Answer Print, the Editor now has the perfect formula to create a Release Print, but to get there, he has to make an Interpositive from the original cut negative, and an Internegative from the Interpositive. That Internegative, or "IN," is the final template from which the Release Prints are made.

31-06 Check Prints

It takes two Check Prints to test that IN, and make sure it is absolutely perfect.

31-07 Release Print

The Release Print is made from the IN and the sound source, the Optical Sound Track. (We'll continue the sound track process starting in 33-00 Music.) That print will be projected at the film's premiere at Sundance. Depending on how well it does, the studio will order more. The Executive Producer hopes they'll order many, many more.

32-00 Optical Effects

32-01 Fades, Dissolves, Titles, etc.

There are 50 effects in this film, including compositing text over picture for the opening titles, 20 dissolves, 5 slow motion effects, 5 fades, and a repositioning (one of the wranglers hats blew into a corner of the frame and no one noticed).

32-02 Shoot Interpositives

To create each effect, an IP is made from the original negative, using the marked Work Print from the Editor as a guide. Setup and color timing charges are not part of the deal (32-04). The Editor/Post Production Supervisor negotiates a $1,500 charge for about 30 color timings.

33-00 Music

33-01 Composer
The Executive Producer made a package deal with the Composer to supply all the music. So now it's the Composer's job to write the music—with the approval of the Director and the Executive Producer, of course—and have it performed. All that for $85,000. (The recording and mixing are part of the Post Sound process. See 34-00.)

34-00 Post Production Sound

34-01 Spotting for Music and Sound Effects
This is a fun, "blue sky" kind of session in which all sorts of ideas are put out. (In the sequence of things, on the picture side, the Negative Cutter and the Opticals House are into their respective endeavors.) The Director, Music and Sound Editors, Composer, Post Production Supervisor (our friend the Editor), and the Executive Producer sit down and "spot" the approved Work Print, dreaming up music. A separate session without the Composer is held for the sound effects.

(To get a jump on the process, the Composer has been meeting with the Director and the Music Editor for about two weeks, watching the Work Print as it gets closer to the final cut, and assembling musical ideas.)

The Composer returns a few days later with some concrete ideas he's recorded from his synthesizer to his DAT (Digital Audio Tape) machine. With some minor changes, everyone loves it, and he goes away again to compose the rest of the score.

34-02 Music Scoring Stage
The music is composed in about 2 weeks. Then it takes 2 weeks for the Arranger and the Copyist to prepare it for the orchestra to play. Finally, with the film projected and the orchestra cued up, the scoring session begins. Over 4 days, the Composer, working with the

Music Editor and the Recording Mixer, records the music to 24-track tape.

34-03 Music Mix Down

Over the next 2 days, the Composer, Music Editor, and Recording Engineer mix the multitrack down to three stereo tracks on a digital 8-track machine.

34-04 ADR & Foley

The need for ADR (Automatic Dialogue Replacement) isn't bad at all compared to what the Editor/Post Production Supervisor has seen on other projects. He does 2 days' worth of looping with the two actors playing "Frances" and "Skylark" (luckily they were both in L.A. at the time), and 5 days of Foley sound effects spread across the whole picture.

34-06 Laydown

As soon as the Work Print is locked, the Editor/Post Production Supervisor goes to the post sound facility and has the production sound, which is on Mag tape, laid down to one track of a multitrack tape. Time code is put to another track for reference during the Edit phase.

34-08 Sound Editing (Digital Work Station)

Now the Sound Editor and the Dialogue Editor show their prowess. The Sound Editor takes all the recorded sound from Foley, production sound, and sound effects, and syncs them to the picture at all the right places, and for the right lengths. The Dialogue Editor takes all the production dialogue, and the ADR, and prepares the dialogue track. The sound effects take 90 hours total, over about 3 weeks. The dialogue takes 60 hours over 3 weeks. (They work concurrently.) When they are finished, they have a 24-track reel that contains the effects, dialogue, and ADR playback reel during the final mix. But first, he does a Pre-Dub.

34-09 Pre-Dub

Over another 5 days, the Director, Mixers, and Sound Editor watch a projected picture and listen to how the effects levels work with the dialogue and music. They make adjustments that will save time during the final mix.

34-10 Final Dub
It's Dub Day. The Director, Executive Producer, Music Editor, Sound Editor, and Editor/Post Production Supervisor gather in a comfortable mixing stage, and start mixing. The final sound track is created on digital audio tape.

34-11 Printmaster
The Mixers take the new final mix and have it processed through a Dolby encoder to create a stereo mix with surround channel. The result is the Print master.

34-12 Optical Sound Transfer
The Editor/Post Production Supervisor takes the Print master to the optical house, where they shoot an optical negative. The optical neg is the sound track for the Internegative (31-05).

To make the Release Print, the optical neg and the IN—sound and picture—are combined. It's the last step. It's done. The movie is finished. The Executive Producer heaves a great sigh of relief, and treats himself to a massage.

But we have two more budget categories to go through.

37-00 Insurance

37-01 Producers Entertainment Package
The insurance for this film wasn't a big problem because there really wasn't anything extraordinary about the production.

37-02 - 37-06 General Liability, Hired Auto, Cast Insurance, Workers' Compensation, E&O.
The stunts were not life-threatening, all the cast showed up healthy and sober, and since it was an original story, there wasn't anyone to sue the studio or the production company because they were libeled. The 3% of below-the-line formula was applied for insurance.

38-00 General and Administrative Expenses

38-02 Legal
The $45,000 allowance is based on a rule-of-thumb applying about 1% to 1.5% of the budget total, above- and below-the-line. For this picture, it does the trick, because everything went fairly smoothly. The attorney prepared standard contracts for the Director, star talent, and department heads, as well as location, and production/distribution agreements.

38-03 Accounting Fees
After the show is wrapped, and the production auditors have gone on to other projects, there will be accounting to do, not only for unfinished stuff that trickles in, but for tax preparation as well. This is an allowance for that time.

38-05 Telephone and Fax
This line item covers phone bills for the home base production office in L.A., and therefore includes all the calls during development of the project, and during post-production. Calls during production came from the line item in the Location Expenses category.

38-11 Computer Rental
The Line Producer, 1st AD, Coordinator, and Accountant all brought their laptops to the party, and were compensated at $125 per week. The office computer and printers were budgeted as rentals, but the Line Producer suggested that for the same money they could own the equipment. The Executive Producer agreed, and that's what they did.

38-12 Software
This allowance permits the production team to buy several copies of a computerized budgeting and scheduling program for use on location and at the home office.

38-19 Wrap Party
Requires no explanation. A good time was had by all.

DOCUMENTARY
TAPE
BUDGET

Fringe assumptions:		Production:			
Payroll Tax	18%	Length:	30 min.		
Overtime	10%	Format:	Video (Beta SP)		
		Prep:	4 weeks		
		Shoot:	7 days		
		Post:	9 weeks		
		Unions:	None		

SUMMARY BUDGET

02-00 Script			4,505	
03-00 Producers Unit			18,700	
04-00 Direction			11,800	
05-00 Cast			531	
	TOTAL ABOVE-THE-LINE			35,536
10-00 Production Staff			12,980	
15-00 Set Operations			3,310	
21-00 Electrical			4,705	
22-00 Camera			8,089	
23-00 Sound			3,830	
24-00 Transportation			495	
25-00 Location Expenses			1,092	
27-00 Stock - Production			1,350	
	TOTAL PRODUCTION			35,850
30-00 Editorial			31,910	
33-00 Music			3,000	
34-00 Post Production Sound			4,475	
35-00 Titles & Graphics			3,900	
	TOTAL POST-PRODUCTION			43,285
37-00 Insurance			8,200	
38-00 General & Administrative			7,675	
	TOTAL OTHER			15,875
Total Above-The-Line				35,536
Total Below-The-Line				95,010
Total Above and Below-the-Line				130,546
Contingency @ 10 %				13,055

	GRAND TOTAL						$143,601
	ABOVE-THE-LINE						
		Amount	Units	x	Rate	Sub-Total	Total
02-00	**Script**						
02-01	Writer Salaries (non-union)	1	Flat	1	3,500	3,500	3,500
02-03	Title Registration	1	Allow	1	375	375	375
	Payroll				3,500	630	630
					Total for 02-00		4,505
03-00	**Producers Unit**						
03-02	Producer	1	Flat	1	15,000	15,000	15,000
03-06	Consultants	1	Allow	1	1,000	1,000	1,000
	Payroll				15,000	2,700	2,700
					Total for 03-00		18,700
04-00	**Direction**						
04-01	Director (non-union)	1	Flat	1	10,000	10,000	10,000
	Payroll				10,000	1,800	1,800
					Total for 04-00		11,800
05-00	**Cast**						
05-08	Narrator (non-union)	1	Day	1	450	450	450
	Payroll				450	81	81
					Total for 05-00		531
	BELOW-THE-LINE						
10-00	**Production Staff**						
10-01	Unit Production Manager	6	Weeks	1	800	4,800	4,800
Prep: 4 weeks							
Shoot: 1 week							
Wrap: 1 week							
10-08	Production Assistant	10	Weeks	1	550	5,500	5,500
Prep: 4 weeks							
Shoot: 1 week							
Wrap: 5 weeks							
	Runner	7	Days	14	$7.14	700	700

	Payroll					11,000	1,980	1,980	
						Total for 10-00			**12,980**

15-00 Set Operations
15-01 First Grip

	Shoot	7	Days	14	25	2,450	
	Overtime				2,450	245	2,695

15-05 Craft Service (PA)

Purchases		7	Days	1	30	30	30
Rentals		1	Allow	1	100	100	100
	Payroll				2,695	485	485
					Total for 15-00		**3,310**

21-00 Electrical
21-01 Gaffer

	Prep	1	Day	10	25	250	
	Shoot (10 hrs.)	7	Days	14	25	2,450	
	Overtime				2,700	270	2,970

21-06 Equip. Rental

	Light/Grip Pckg	7	Days	1	100	700	700
	Extra Package	1	Day	1	500	500	500
	Payroll				2,970	535	535
					Total for 21-00		**4,705**

22-00 Camera
22-01 Director of Photography/Op.

	Scout	1	Day	12	$32.14	386	
	Shoot (10 hrs.)	7	Days	14	$32.14	3,150	
	Overtime				3,535	354	3,889
22-07 Camera Pckg Rentals (Video)		5	Days	1	700	3,500	3,500
	Payroll				3,889	700	700
					Total for 22-00		**8,089**

23-00 Sound

23-01 Mixer	Shoot (10 hrs.)	7	Days	1	350	2,450	
	Overtime				2,450	245	2,695
23-03 Expendables (Batteries, etc)		1	Allow	1	150	150	150
23-06 Radio Mics		5	Days	2	50	500	500
	Payroll				2,695	485	485

						Total for 23-00		3,830

24-00 Transportation

24-03 Production Van	9	Days	1	55	495	495	
					Total for 24-00		**495**

25-00 Location Expenses

25-06 Catering Service

Crew Meals (8 crew + 4 guests)	7	Lunches	12	13	1,092	1,092	
					Total for 25-00		**1,092**

27-00 Stock - Production

28-03 Videotape Stock - Production	50	Tapes	1	27	1,350	1,350	
(Allow seven 30's/day)					Total for 27-00		**1,350**

30-00 Editorial

30-08 Off-Line Editor	8	Weeks	1	1,500	12,000	12,000
30-09 Off-Line Edit System (3/4")	8	Weeks	1	750	6,000	6,000
30-10 On-Line System & Editor	24	Hours	1	300	7,200	7,200
30-11 On-Line Effects	5	Hours	1	300	1,500	1,500
30-12 Videotape Dubs/Stock & Transfers						
3/4" Off-Line Dubs	50	Tapes	1	20	1,000	
Off-Line Misc. dubs	1	Allow	1	250	250	
On-Line Misc. dubs	1	Allow	1	750	750	2,000
30-13 VHS Screening Copies	20	Tapes	1	35	700	700
30-14 Video Masters/Safeties/Textless					0	0
D2 Master (30 min.)	1	Tape	1	175	175	175
D2 Protection	1	Tape	1	175	175	175
Payroll				12,000	2,160	2,160
					Total for 30-00	**31,910**

33-00 Music

33-01 Composer	1	Allow	1	3,000	3,000	3,000
(All-In Package includes: Arrangers, Copyists,					0	0
...Musicians, Instruments, Studio,					0	0
Engineers, Stock, etc)					0	0
					Total for 33-00	**3,000**

34-00 Post Production Sound						
34-01 Spotting for Music/Sound Efx	3	Hours	1	150	450	450
34-05 Narration Record	1	Hour	1	175	175	175
34-14 Laydown	1	Hour	1	175	175	175
34-15 Pre-Lay	6	Hours	1	150	900	900
34-16 Mix	10	Hours	1	200	2,000	2,000
34-17 Layback	1	Hour	1	375	375	375
34-18 Stock/Dubs/Transfers (Video)	1	Allow	1	400	400	400
				Total for 34-00		4,475
35-00 Titles & Graphics						
35-01 Graphic Design & Workstation	1	Allow	1	3,500	3,500	3,500
35-02 Stocks and Dubs	1	Allow	1	400	400	400
				Total for 35-00		3,900
37-00 Insurance						
37-01 Producers Entertainment Pckg	1	Allow	1	3,000	3,000	3,000
Negative					0	0
Faulty Stock					0	0
Equipment					0	0
Props/Sets					0	0
Extra Expense					0	0
3rd Party Property Damage					0	0
Office Contents					0	0
37-02 General Liability	1	Allow	1	2,500	2,500	2,500
37-03 Hired Auto					0	0
37-04 Cast Insurance					0	0
37-05 Workers Compensation	1	Allow	1	1,200	1,200	1,200
37-06 Errors & Omissions	1	Allow	1	1,500	1,500	1,500
				Total for 37-00		8,200
					0	
38-00 General & Administrative Expenses					0	
38-02 Legal	1	Allow	1	1,500	1,500	1,500
38-03 Accounting fees	1	Allow	1	1,000	1,000	1,000
38-05 Telephone/FAX	1	Allow	1	1,000	1,000	1,000
38-06 Copying	1	Allow	1	200	200	200
38-07 Postage & Freight	1	Allow	1	500	500	500
38-08 Office Space Rental				0	0	0
38-09 Ofice Furniture				0	0	0

38-10 Office Equipment & Supplies	1	Allow	1	350	350	350	
38-11 Computer Rental	1	Allow	1	0	0	0	
38-13 Transcription (5 hrs x 3)	15	Hours	1	25	375	375	
38-14 Messenger/Overnight	1	Allow	1	200	200	200	
38-15 Parking	1	Allow	1	250	250	250	
38-16 Storage	1	Allow	1	500	500	500	
38-17 Still Photographer	1	Allow	1	1,000	1,000	1,000	
Equip./Supplies/Film/Processing	1	Allow	1	300	300	300	
38-18 Publicity	1	Allow	1	0	0	0	
38-20 Hospitality	1	Allow	1	500	500	500	
38-21 Production Fee	1	Allow	1	0	0	0	
					Total for 38-00		7,675
Contingency @ 10%						13,055	13,055
GRAND TOTAL							$143,601
Total Above-The-Line							35,536
Total Below-The-Line							95,010
Total Above and Below-the-Line							130,546
					Check budget totals	143,601	143,601

DOCUMENTARY—TAPE

Overview:
This is a 30-minute documentary program shot locally on BetaSP videotape. It has interviews, "B-Roll," and a narrator that holds it all together. "B-Roll" refers to footage that plays over an interview (the "A Roll") and ideally illustrates what the person is talking about.

Pre-Production:	4 weeks
Shoot:	7 days
Post-Production:	9 weeks

02-00 Script

02-01 Writer's Salaries
The writer is actually the producer paying himself a little extra money, but putting it in another category to make it look better.

The "script" is the narration, which will be written in its final draft form only when the off-line editing is finishing up.

Does this mean the producer has no idea where he is heading? No. He has spent much time even before pre-production figuring what the program is about (in research), what its flow will be, and what ideas will hold it together.

During off-line editing, he will record himself reading the first draft narration copy in a "scratch track." As editing proceeds, the producer/writer will see and hear how the copy works, and make changes as the show evolves. When it's just right, he'll have a professional narrator come in to make it sound wonderful.

02-03 Title Registration
Since the producer wants this to air on a broadcast or cable network, he wants to make sure its title hasn't been used before. The investment here will protect him from having to pay more to change the title later on. His attorney will recommend a title clearance house.

03-00 Producer's Unit

03-02 Producer

The producer is paying himself a flat for 14 weeks of work, not even counting all the time he put in writing the proposal, doing research, and pitching the project. It's a low rate, even throwing in the writing fee, but what can he say—this is his first big project, it's a labor of love, and he's got to hold costs down.

03-06 Consultants

Several people have kindly spent a lot of time helping the producer shape his ideas for the show, and this is a modest payback. Since it's going out in five different checks at $200 each, he's decided not to count it as payroll.

04-00 Direction

04-01 Director

You may be wondering why a straightforward documentary needs a Director. Couldn't the Director of Photography/Camera Operator set up the lighting and handle the creative aspects of the Director's job? In this case, probably so. But the Producer has made a strategic decision to hire an experienced Director anyway because:

(a) It's his first big project and he figures he'll be busy enough handling production, writing, and listening to the content of the interviews undistracted by how it all looks.

(b) He wants the B-Roll to be visually exciting, and he doesn't think he has enough experience to shoot it the way he imagines it.

(c) His deal with the Director includes sitting in on some of the off-line editing and all of the on-line editing. In on-line, he'll use the Director's experience to help create some visually interesting transitions.

05-00 Cast

05-01 Narrator

The Producer has found a Narrator who is a member of a union but has agreed to work non-union for this show.

10-00 **Production Staff**

10-01 **Production Manager**
The Producer wants to concentrate on the content of the show, and on what the Director is doing, to make sure everything lives up to the vision he had in mind. That's why he's hired a Production Manager to help guide the project through pre-production, and shooting. The Producer can give orders, and leave all the details to the PM and the Production Assistant. The PM is hired on a weekly flat that includes the 7 days of shooting as one week.

On the scout for the shoot, the PM considers practicalities like where the nearest bathroom is at each camera setup, where the nearest power source is, crew parking, whether the carts carrying the gear will be able to get from point A to B, where the nearest grocery and hardware stores are, nearest telephones, fax machines, and so forth. Always thinking ahead.

The PM is on for a week after shooting to pay all the bills, make sure all equipment gets returned, and all other production details are neatly put to bed. This way, the Producer can get to work on the "paper cut" right away.

10-07 **Production Assistant**
The PA is on for the same pre-production period as the PM, and will assist the PM during that phase. Additionally, the PA will stay for five weeks after shooting to help clean up, and assist the Producer in getting the off-line process rolling. The Producer wants to keep the PA on for the entire post process, mainly to hold the fort at the office, but can't afford it. The PA is on a weekly flat, which includes the 7 straight days of shooting as one week.

A Runner is hired for the 7 days of shooting. Runners, also known as "go-fers," are the lowest rung on the ladder . They are usually bright, young people looking to get a start in the business. Typically underpaid, they are nonetheless indispensable. The Runner is paid $7.14 per hour, which comes out at $100 per day for 14 pay hours/12 work hours.

15-00 Set Operations

15-01 First Grip

A lot of the shooting will be exterior, and the Grip will be needed to set up silks to cut the direct sunlight, and handle shiny boards to reflect sunlight onto subjects.

Remember that the number in the multiplication ("x") column, in this case 14, refers to *pay hours*. Fourteen pay hours translates into 12 hours of work. See Chapter 2, Pre-Production, for a discussion on why using pay hours is more accurate, and less prone to confusion, than the often used shorthand of "$350 per day."

15-05 Craft Service

The PA and the Runner, along with their other duties, have the responsibility of keeping the crew lubricated and energized with plenty of water, juice, and munchies for the long days outdoors. Even with a crew as relatively small as nine (Producer, Director, Production Manager, Camera Operator, Sound, Gaffer, Grip, PA, and Runner, plus interview subjects), they'll easily go through a bag of groceries a day. Since they'll be moving around, they put the cooler on a cart, so all anyone has to do is wheel the craft service to the next setup.

21-00 Electrical

21-01 Gaffer

The prep day for a Gaffer is unusual for a relatively simple documentary like this, but there is a reason. One of the shoot days includes a night scene that requires pulling together some extra lights. Thus the prep day. The Gaffer is paid at the same rate as the Grip, since both are experienced people who usually work bigger shows. (In cases where the Grip is less experienced, he or she can be paid less than the Gaffer.)

21-06 Light Package

The package used everyday includes a standard Omni kit, plus three pieces of 4x8 foam core, a hard/soft gold shiny board, a hard/soft silver shiny board, a 4x4 silk, 6 C-stands, and an assortment of sandbags, apple boxes, and so on.

For the night shoot, the Director, DP, and the Gaffer assemble a package that is delivered to the site. It includes one 2K, six 1K's, a 12x12 silk, two hi-roller stands, and an assortment of sandbags, cable, apple boxes, and quad boxes. Since they'll be shooting near a swimming pool, they throw in four ground fault receptacles, which automatically shut off all power if a light hits the water. Nobody fries on this shoot.

22-00 Camera

22-01 Director of Photography

The DP/Camera Operator scouts the locations with the Director, Producer, and Production Manager. They consider how the sunlight will be at different times of day, how the sound ambience may affect them, and generally try to get the best angles on what they plan to shoot.

He is paid an hourly rate that adds up to about $450 for 12 hours worked—a pretty good deal for the Producer.

22-07 Camera Rentals

The camera is a BetaCam with on-board record deck, one of the newer models that shoots well in low-light conditions. The package includes a tripod, a set of filters, batteries and charger, plus a shotgun mike, two hard wire lavelier microphones, fishpole, and mixer. Radio mikes (wireless) are extra (see 23-00 Sound).

The package is rented by the day, but since the shoot goes for 7 days straight, the rental house does not charge for the weekend.

23-00 Sound

The Mixer gets the best sound he can by properly placing mikes, and by listening carefully during shooting for any sound pollution. Passing airplanes, trucks, passionate conversationalists, air conditioning units, and cats and dogs all qualify. It's one of the joys of exterior shooting. The Mixer also labels each tape as it comes out of the machine, and pops the little red button on the cassette so it cannot be recorded upon again. His rate of pay is the same as the Gaffer's and Grip's.

23-06 Radio Mikes

Some of the shooting will be done on people walking at some distance from the camera, so wireless mikes are needed. They are rented at the same "7 days for 5" rate as the camera package.

25-00 Equipment Rental

25-02 Production Van

A mini-van with the back seats removed carries the camera package, the daily light package, the cooler (up front in case of spillage), and sundries.

26-00 Location Expenses

26-06 Catering Service

One of the things the PM did on the scout was pick up menus from nearby restaurants that deliver. A couple hours before lunch, everyone agrees on one restaurant, and the PA gets orders.

28-00 Stock—Production

28-03 Videotape Stock

The Director and the Producer estimate that they'll shoot about fice 30-minute cassettes per day, so they order seven just in case. It's fairly cheap insurance against the delay and embarrassment of running out of stock.

31-00 Editorial

31-08 Off-Line Editor
The off-line editing takes 8 weeks. The Editor is experienced in documentary work, meaning he looks for interesting coverage for talking heads as well as good "natural sound" sequences where the camera has captured people in action and we see it unfold.

The Editor is working off a "paper cut" created by the Producer. (See Chapter 3 Line Items, 31-00 Editorial, for a note about paper cuts.)

He is paid on a weekly flat.

31-09 Off-Line Edit System
Everyone wanted to go non-linear for the off-line, screaming that there would be much more flexibility in placing shots quickly. The Producer agreed, but reasoned that since he was taking the time to create a tight paper cut, he could save a lot of money by cutting on a 3/4" system ($750 per week for the 3/4" versus $2,200 per week for the non-linear).

31-10 On-Line System and Editor
31-11 On-Line Effects
With all the creative decisions made in the off-line cut, a clean EDL (edit list), and only a few simple wipes for effects, the Producer and Editor estimate a total of 24 hours to assemble the show on-line. They are so confident that they will assemble in A-Mode. (See Chapter 3 Line Items, 31-00 Editorial, for a discussion of A and B mode Assembly.)

31-12 Videotape Dubs/Stock/Transfers
The Producer has had all the BetaSP's transferred to 3/4" with a burned-in time code window. One 30-minute 3/4" for each 30-minute BetaSP. He chose 3/4" because that is the system the Editor uses to edit the show. The disadvantage of not using VHS to do this is that he has to have a 3/4" playback deck to do the paper cut instead of his home VHS unit. Luckily, he was able to borrow an old 3/4" clunker from a friend.

The other items in this line, miscellaneous stock and dubs for off- and on-line, is a catch-all. The Producer knows that money can be eaten in great gulps by various editing needs for stock. He allows accordingly.

31-13 VHS Screening Copies
When all is said and done, the Producer has twenty VHS copies made—nineteen to show to potential distributors, and one for his mom.

31-14 Video Masters
The on-line will be in a Beta to D2 edit bay, so the final master can be on D2, a preferred format for many home video and broadcast/cable companies. A protection master is made as well.

34-00 Music

34-01 Composer
Once the on-line cut is completed, that does it for the picture side of the equation. Music and sound effects are next.

The Producer finds a Composer with a sophisticated home studio, and makes a flat deal. The money is so-so for a 30-minute score, so the Composer wants to do it entirely on his synthesizer. The Producer persuades the Composer to bring in some friends to play some acoustic instruments over the synth bed, to liven up the music. Seeing possible future business with this Producer, the Composer agrees. They sit down together to spot the show. Two days later the Composer has some musical ideas ready for playback.

A week later, the Composer turns in a DAT cassette with the score, all synced to the on-line cut and ready for mixing with the sound effects and production sound (dialogue and natural sounds).

35-00 Post Production Sound

The Producer calls around to a few audio post facilities. Some are busy. Some are expensive. He finds one with a good reputation, willing to do the show for the budget.

35-01 Spotting for Music/Sound Effects

The music part has already happened, so the Producer sits with a Sound Editor and spots for effects. It's only a half-hour documentary, and the effects are not complicated, so this session lasts only 3 hours.

35-05 Narration Record

The Producer knows from the off-line scratch narration exactly how long each piece of narration must be. He makes a deal with a voice-over artist to do the track. They set up in an announce booth at the post audio house and lay it down, careful to stay within the timings now dictated by the final cut.

35-14 Laydown

The D2 Master is brought to the audio post house, where the production audio is stripped off to tape.

35-15 Pre-Lay

The Sound Editor takes all the sound effects and narration, and places them at the right points in the show onto another piece of tape.

35-16 Mix

The playback sources (production sound, music, sound effects, and narration) are now mixed together into what will be the final stereo sound track of the show. The Producer, Director, and Mixer spend one long day mixing the whole show.

35-17 Layback

The mixed audio is now laid back to the original D2 Master, and the show is complete. Finito. The Producer heaves a great sigh of relief, and is first in line the next day at the unemployment office.

36-00 Titles and Graphics
(This is kind of an anti-climax, because graphics actually take place during the off-line and/or on-line process.)

36-01 Graphic Design and Workstation
The Producer and the Director want a simple but nice opening title sequence for the show, some transition graphics that will serve as the visual equivalent of chapter headings, and some bumpers to get into and out of commercial breaks.

The Producer wants to work with a Graphic Designer, a freelancer, who will work out of the graphics room at the on-line facility. The Producer, Director, Designer, and Sales person from the on-line house meet to discuss the graphics package. A design plan is worked out that can be done for the money.

When the graphics are done, they are dropped into the off-line edit to be included in the EDL. The only part that is not included is the opening title sequence, which will be assembled in the on-line first, and then edited into the show.

38-00 General and Administrative Expenses
Most of the G&A lines are self-explanatory. They cover the running of the production office. Only three require any review:

38-02 Legal
The only legal activity so far is reviewing contracts sand deal memos for cast and crew. The Producer hopes to have a little bit left in this line to apply to a review of his first distribution contract.

39-00 Insurance
The Producer has contact with a broker who handles all kinds of entertainment insurance packages, from movies to home videos. This is a simple shoot, no crazy stunts, no travel, no star cast to worry about not showing up. Even the E&O is simple because no previously published or produced materials are being used, so no one can be libeled.

40-03 Accounting

The Producer has found a bookkeeper who keeps track of all accounts, pays all bills and payroll, and prepares end-of-the-year tax forms for all employees.

40-17 Still Photographer

The Producer bites the bullet on this one. A still photographer is an expensive line for this show, but since some of the interview subjects may not be available after the show is finished, he decides to bring in the photographer for some publicity stills that will help stir up excitement later.

LIVE
MUSIC
CONCERT

Fringe assumptions:		Production:				
Payroll Tax	18.00%	Length:	1 hour			
AFM - see 05-00 Musicians		Format:	Video (Beta SP)			
Overtime	10%	Prep:	3 weeks			
		Shoot:	1 Day			
		Post:	2 weeks			
		Unions:	AFM/DGA			
SUMMARY BUDGET						
03-00 Producers Unit					55,106	
04-00 Direction					4,067	
05-00 Musicians					20,049	
07-00 Travel & Living- Musicians					4,700	
		TOTAL ABOVE-THE-LINE				83,923
10-00 Production Staff					5,989	
12-00 Sound Stage					9,950	
13-00 Production Design					3,835	
14-00 Set Construction					3,500	
15-00 Set Operations					5,304	
18-00 Property					1,750	
20-00 Make-Up and Hairdressing					1,063	
21-00 Electrical					15,272	
22-00 Camera					19,349	
23-00 Sound					688	
24-00 Transportation					240	
25-00 Location Expenses					3,428	
27-00 Film & Lab					701	
		TOTAL PRODUCTION				71,070
30-00 Editorial					17,077	
34-00 Post Production Sound					1,100	
35-00 Titles & Graphics					4,000	
		TOTAL POST-PRODUCTION				22,177
37-00 Insurance					6,800	
38-00 General & Administrative					15,225	
		TOTAL OTHER				22,025
Total Above-The-Line						83,923
Total Below-The-Line						115,272

	Amount	Units	x	Rate	Sub-Total	Total	
Total Above and Below-the-Line							199,195
Contingency @ 10 %							19,920
GRAND TOTAL							**$219,115**
ABOVE-THE-LINE							
	Amount	Units	x	Rate	Sub-Total	Total	
03-00 Producers Unit							
03-01 Executive Producer (Leader)	1	Allow	1	30,000	30,000	30,000	
03-02 Producer	5	Weeks	1	2,500	12,500	12,500	
3 weeks prep/1 day shoot/2 weeks post							
03-03 Associate Producer	3	Weeks	1	1,400	4,200	4,200	
Payroll				46,700	8,406	8,406	
				Total for 03-00			**55,106**
04-00 Direction							
04-01 Director	5	Days	1	579	2,895	2,895	
(1 Hr. Non-network variety special)							
Payroll				2,895	521	521	
DGA @ 12.50%				2,895	362	362	
Agency fee @ 10%				2,895	290	290	
				Total for 04-00			**4,067**
05-00 Musicians							
05-01 Leader Rehearsal	4	Hrs.	1	110	440		
Shoot (5 hrs.)	1	Day	1	632	632	1,072	
05-02 Sidemen							
Rehearsal	4	Hours	11	55	2,427		
Shoot	1	Day	11	316	3,476	5,903	
05-20 Arranger (Leader)	1	Allow	1	3,500	3,500	3,500	
Allow at 50% of musicians' payroll.							
05-21 Copyist		Incl			0	0	
(Included in Arranger allowance.)							
05-22 Cartage	5	Players	1	6	30	30	
Outside service	2	Players	1	275	550	550	
05-23 2nd Reuse fees @ 75% scale	1	Allow	1	5,250	5,250	5,250	
05-24 Multiple-Sponsorship bump	1	Bump	12	7	84	84	

	Payroll					10,475	1,885	1,885	
	AFM Pension/Retirement @ 9%					15,725	1,415	1,415	
	H/W @$9/person/day	20	People	1	18	360	360	
					Total for 05-00				20,049

07-00 Travel & Living-Musicians

07-01 Airfares - Leader - NY-LA	1	1st	1	2,200	2,200	2,200	
07-02 Hotels	7	Nights	1	250	1,750	1,750	
07-03 Taxi	1	Allow	1	250	250	250	
07-07 Phone	1	Allow	1	500	500	500	
			Total for 07-00				4,700

BELOW-THE-LINE

10-00 Production Staff

10-02 Assistant Directors	3	Days	1	471	1,413		
Production fee (DGA)	1	Day	1	13	13	1,426	
10-03 Stage Manager	1	Day	1	437	437		
Production fee (DGA)	1	Allow	1	13	13	450	
10-08 Production Assistants							
Office	2	Weeks	1	750	1,500	1,500	
Set	3	Days	4	125	1,500	1,500	
Payroll				4,877	878	878	
DGA @ 12.5%				1,877	235	235	
			Total for 10-00				5,989

12-00 Sound Stage (Recording Studio)

12-01 Studio Rental							
Load-In/Set	6	Hours	1	150	900	900	
Light	14	Hours	1	150	2,100	2,100	
Shoot (13 hrs)	1	Day	1	2,400	2,400	2,400	
First Engineer	10	Hours	1	150	1,500	1,500	
Audio Tape stock	1	Allow	1	2,000	2,000	2,000	
Strike	5	Hours	1	150	750	750	
Includes:							
Assist. Engineer							
24 Track analog machine							
Mics +1 hr. set up							

	Time-Link time code						
	from truck to multi-track.						
12-02 Power		Incl.			0	0	
12-03 Production Office		Incl.			0	0	
12-04 Telephone		Incl.			0	0	
12-05 Lounge		Incl.			0	0	
12-06 Make-Up		Incl.			0	0	
12-07 Wardrobe		Incl.			0	0	
12-08 Storage		Incl.			0	0	
12-09 Green Room (Shoot Day)	6	Hours	1	50	300	300	
12-10 Parking		Incl.			0	0	
				Total for 12-00			9,950
13-00 Production Design							
13-01 Production Designer	1	Week	1	2,000	2,000	2,000	
13-03 Assistants	1	Week	1	1,000	1,000	1,000	
13-09 Car Expense	1	Allow	1	250	250	250	
	Fringe @ 18%				3,250	585	585
				Total for 13-00			3,835
14-00 Set Construction							
14-01 Set Construction Package	1	Flat	1	3,500	3,500	3,500	
(Includes materials, labor, trucking, set, strike)							
				Total for 14-00			3,500
15-00 Set Operations							
15-01 Key Grip	2	Days	14	30	840	840	
15-02 Second Grip (Best Boy)	2	Days	14	25	700	700	
15-03 Other Grips							
	Grip #1 Prep	1	Days	14	22	308	308
	Grip #2 Prep	1	Days	14	22	308	308
15-04 Boom/Dolly Grips							
	Dolly Grip #1	1	Day	14	28	392	392
	Dolly Grip #2	1	Day	14	28	392	392
15-05 Craft Service Person							
	Prep	1	Allow	1	150	150	150
	Shoot	1	Day	15	13	188	188
Purchases		2	Days	1	150	300	300
Rentals		2	Days	1	25	50	50

15-06 Grip Rentals							
	Jib Arm	1	Day	1	425	425	425	
	Panther Dolly	1	Day	1	225	225	225	
	Cartage	1	Allow	1	150	150	150	
15-08 Box Rentals								
	Key Grip	2	Days	1	30	60	60	
	Payroll				2,718	489	489	
	Overtime	1	Allow	1	3,278	328	328	
			Total for 15-00					5,304
18-00 Property (Band Equipment Rentals)								
18-02 Piano Tuner			Incl.			0	0	
18-04 Rentals		1	Allow	1	1,000	1,000	1,000	
	Piano		Incl.					
	Cartage	1	Allow	1	250	250	250	
18-05 Loss & Damage		1	Allow	1	500	500	500	
			Total for 18-00					1,750
20-00 Make-Up and Hairdressing								
20-01 Key Make-Up Artist		1	Day	14	32	450	450	
20-02 Assistant Make-Up Artist		1	Day	14	29	400	400	
20-07 Box Rentals		1	Day	2	30	60	60	
	Payroll				850	153	153	
			Total for 20-00					1,063
21-00 Electrical								
21-01 Gaffer								
	Prep	2	Days	12	30	720		
	Shoot	1	Day	14	30	420	1,140	
21-02 Best Boy								
	Prep	1	Day	12	25	300		
	Shoot	1	Day	14	25	350	650	
21-03 Electrics								
	Electric #1							
	Prep	1	Day	12	22	264		
	Shoot	1	Day	14	22	308	572	
	Electric #2							
	Prep	1	Day	12	22	264		

	Shoot	1	Day	14	22	308	572	
21-04 Additional Labor								
Board Op.								
	Prep	1	Day	12	22	264		
	Shoot	1	Day	14	22	308	572	
Strike Crew		10	Hrs.	4	20	800	800	
21-06 Equip. Rentals								
	Light/Grip Pckg	1	Allow	1	7,500	7,500	7,500	
21-08 Generator 1200 Amp		2	Days	1	650	1,300	1,300	
Driver	(N/C)					0	0	
Fuel		200	Gals.	1	2	400	400	
21-09 Loss & Damage		1	Allow	1	250	250	250	
21-10 Box Rentals - Gaffer		2	Days	1	30	60	60	
21-11 Trucking		1	Allow	1	250	250	250	
	Payroll				4,306	775	775	
	Overtime				4,306	431	431	
					Total for 21-00			15,272
22-00 Camera								
22-01 Lighting Director		3	Days	1	650	1,950	1,950	
22-05 Still Photographer		1	Day	1	500	500	500	
	Film/Process	1	Allow	1	200	200	200	
22-06 Expendables		1	Allow	1	750	750	750	
22-08 Video Truck		1	Day	1	7,500	7,500	7,500	
	6 Cameras							
	2 Peds							
	6 BetaSP Record decks							
	Quad split unit							
	Wireless PL							
	10" color monitor							
	19" color monitor							
	Basic Audio Pckge.							
	Maint. Engineer	1	Day	16	27	429	429	
	Utility	1	Day	16	21	343	343	
22-09 Video Truck Crew								
Camera Operators								
	Camera Op. #1	1	Day	14	32	450	450	
	Camera Op. #2	1	Day	14	32	450	450	

Camera Op. #3	1	Day	14	32	450	450	
Camera Op. #4	1	Day	14	32	450	450	
Camera Op. #5	1	Day	14	32	450	450	
Camera Op. #6	1	Day	14	32	450	450	
Utilities	1	Day	14	23	325	325	
Video Control	1	Day	14	27	375	375	
Video Tape Operator	1	Day	14	25	350	350	
Technical Director	1	Day	14	32	450	450	
22-17 Maintenance/Loss & Damage	1	Allow	1	350	350	350	
Payroll				7,421	1,336	1,336	
Invoice Fee @ 25% (Video crew)				4,200	1,050	1,050	
Overtime				7,421	742	742	
Total for 22-00							**19,349**

23-00 Sound

23-01 Mixer	1	Day	14	32	450	450	
Payroll				450	81	81	
Invoice Fee @ 25% (Sound Crew)				450	112	112	
Overtime				450	45	45	
Total for 23-00							**688**

24-00 Transportation

24-03 Production Van	4	Days	1	35	140	140	
24-04 Gas & Oil	1	Allow	1	100	100	100	
Total for 24-00							**240**

25-00 Location Expenses
25-09 Catering Service
Crew Meals

Prep Day lunch	35	Meals	1	12	420	420	
Shoot Day lunch	45	Meals	1	12	540	540	
Guest Meal Shoot Day lunch	50	Meals	1	12	600	600	
2nd Meal Shoot Day	45	Meals	1	8	360	360	
Sales Tax				1,920	158	158	
Tables/Chairs	1	Allow	1	150	150	150	
25-20 Large Screen TV	1	Day	1	950	950	950	
Trucking/Set-up	1	Allow	1	250	250	250	
Total for 26-00							**3,428**

27-00 Videotape Stock - Production						
27-03 Videotape Stock - Production						
BetaSP	18	Hours	1	36	648	648
Sales Tax @ .0825%				648	53	53
				Total for 27-00		**701**
30-00 Editorial						
30-08 Off-Line Editor						
Edit	7	Days	1	450	3,150	3,150
30-09 Off-Line Edit System (3/4")	7	Days	1	175	1,225	1,225
30-10 On-Line System & Editor	24	Hours	1	350	8,400	8,400
30-11 On-Line Effects	5	Hours	1	400	2,000	2,000
30-12 Tape Dubs/Stock/Transfers	1	Allow	1	1,500	1,500	1,500
(BSP to 3/4" and VHS)						
30-13 Screening Copies	10	VHS	1	10	100	100
30-14 Masters/Safeties/Textless	2	D2	1	300	600	600
Payroll				567	102	102
				Total for 30-00		**17,077**
34-00 Post Production Sound (Music Mix)						
34-17 Layback to D2	3	Hours	1	200	600	600
34-18 Stock/Dubs/Transfers	1	Allow	1	500	500	500
				Total for 34-00		**1,100**
35-00 Titles & Graphics						
35-01 Designer & Workstation	1	Allow	1	3,500	3,500	3,500
35-02 Stocks and Dubs	1	Allow	1	500	500	500
				Total for 35-00		**4,000**
37-00 Insurance						
37-01 Producers Entertainment Pckg	1	Allow	1	2,000	2,000	2,000
Negative						
Faulty Stock						
Equipment						
Props/Sets						
Extra Expense						
3rd Party Property Damage						
Office Contents						
37-02 General Liability	1	Allow	1	1,800	1,800	1,800

37-03 Hired Auto					0	0
37-04 Cast Insurance					0	0
37-05 Workers Compensation	1	Allow	1	1,500	1,500	1,500
37-06 Errors & Omissions	1	Allow	1	1,500	1,500	1,500
				Total for 37-00		6,800
38-00 General & Administrative Expenses						
38-02 Legal	1	Allow	1	7,500	7,500	7,500
38-03 Accounting fees	1	Allow	1	2,500	2,500	2,500
38-05 Telephone/FAX	2	Months	1	350	700	700
38-06 Copying	1	Allow	1	250	250	250
38-07 Postage & Freight	1	Allow	1	500	500	500
38-08 Office Space Rental	5	Weeks	1	225	1,125	1,125
38-09 Office Furniture	5	Weeks	1	50	250	250
38-10 Office Equipment & Supplies	5	Weeks	1	50	250	250
38-11 Computer Rental	5	Weeks	1	50	250	250
38-14 Messenger/Overnight	1	Allow	1	500	500	500
38-15 Parking	5	Weeks	4	20	400	400
38-16 Storage	1	Allow	1	500	500	500
38-20 Hospitality	1	Allow	1	500	500	500
				Total for 38-00		15,225
Contingency @ 10%					19,920	19,920
GRAND TOTAL						$219,115
Total Above-The-Line						83,923
Total Below-The-Line						115,272
Total Above and Below-the-Line						199,195
				Check budget totals	219,115	219,115

LIVE MUSIC CONCERT

Overview:

A top jazz player and eleven of his almost equally famous friends are recording an album in a sound studio. The top guy, in musical terminology, the Leader, wants to videotape the recording session and release it as a concert show for cable and home video. It is a straight one-hour concert, with no other footage, shot locally on BetaSP with a video truck and multicameras.

Pre-Production: 3 weeks
Shoot: 1 day
Post-Production: 2 weeks

03-00 Producer's Unit

03-01 Executive Producer

The Band Leader appoints himself as the Executive Producer. This is his privilege since he dreamed up the idea and sold it to the record company, which is providing the money. He pays himself $30,000, which seems in scale to the whole budget, although a handsome sum for a few phone calls and meetings. But he can afford it, he's famous.

03-02 Producer

Somebody has to actually get the concert shot, so the Executive Producer hires a Line Producer experienced in taping music. The Producer prepares the budget, allotting 3 weeks for prep, 1 day to shoot, and 3 weeks for post. Part of his deal, however, is that all the contracts, payroll, vendor payments, and official paperwork go through the Executive Producer's company. When the post is finished, he walks.

03-03 Associate Producer

The Producer could probably handle all the production chores on this shoot, but the music is going to be really good, and he doesn't want to miss it putting out fires on shoot day. So he hires a cracker-jack Associate Producer to help. Actually, having the AP on board helps everything run smoothly on shoot day, which is guaranteed to be completely nuts. Since they only have one shot at this, it's good insurance. She agrees to a weekly flat, and will leave after shoot day.

04-00 Direction

04-01 Director

A Director with experience in multicamera concert shows is hired. She comes on 4 days before the shoot, although she was involved at a few pre-production meetings and a survey of the sound studio, all of which she threw into her deal for free. She will direct the show, and walk away, leaving all the post in the hands of the Producer.

During the 4 days of prep, she checks in on the Production Designer to see how the set is going, makes changes in the seating arrangement for the musicians, confers with the Producer about camera placement, attends the 4 hours of rehearsal, and most important, goes over all the music, spotting for solos and other musical exchanges that will make for good camera moments. During the 2 days before the shoot, an Assistant Director, who also reads music, comes on board to attend the rehearsal and help plan all the shots.

During the shoot, the Director and the AD sit next to each other in the video truck. The Director keeps her eyes on the camera monitors, and directs the camera moves and the switching between cameras. At the same time, the AD tracks the sheet music, alerting the Director about what's coming next, and also telling the six camera operators what to do to get ready for their next shot. It's quite a show inside the truck.

Her deal is straight DGA for a one hour non-network variety special. (The Executive Producer wants to release the concert on cable.)

05-00 Musicians

<u>A note about paying musicians:</u>
The labor of union (AFM) musicians is heavy-laden with rules and regulations. If you are not experienced in this line, contract with a music payroll service to handle the paperwork, and show you the ropes. You'll shout hooray from the rooftops—guaranteed! There are good ones all over; one we like in L.A. is Half Note Music Payroll.

05-01 Leader
The Leader is paid at AFM (American Federation of Musicians) scale, which is double the hourly for "sidemen." The plan is to rehearse for 4 hours two days before shoot day. Then come in on shoot day and play for 5 hours, going through the whole set twice.

05-02 Sidemen
The eleven sidemen are all local players who play in each other's bands and at recording dates. They've also played a lot with the Leader, so this is old home week for them. One observation the Leader makes about players of this caliber: "If you rehearse these guys too much, they get bored, and then they start getting squirrely on you, trying all sorts of different things. The trick is to rehearse them just enough so that on shoot day, they still have to pay attention."

By the way, the Leader has made a blanket royalty arrangement with all of these people on the release of the album.

05-20 Arranger
This is the Leader, who has done all the arrangements on the songs. The AFM rule of thumb is to make an allowance that is 50% of the total musician's payroll.

05-21 Copyist
The person who copies out all the different parts for each musician gets paid on a per page basis out of the Arranger's allowance.

05-22 Cartage
There is an AFM requirement that certain players with large instruments get paid for having to haul them to the site. Some players, like drummers and percussionists, get an outside trucking service to do the hauling for them, and charge the show.

05-23 2nd Re-use Fees
For additional play dates on television within the first year of release, the AFM stipulates a 75% of scale payment to the musicians. The Executive Producer wanted to include this as part of the production budget to make a TV sale easier.

05-24 Multiple Sponsorship Bump
This a weird one. The AFM requires an additional $7 per player payment if there are multiple sponsors of the television release. We have no idea why.

07-00 Travel and Living—Musicians

The Leader/Executive Producer lives in New York, so his air fare and living expenses while in L.A. are covered here.

10-00 Production Staff

10-02 Assistant Director
The AD comes on 2 days prior to shoot day to watch the rehearsal with the music in hand, and prepare shots and shot lists with the Director. On shoot day, he sits with the Director in the truck (see 04-01 Director). The AD gets DGA scale, plus the "production fee," a DGA bump for each camera day worked.

10-03 Stage Manager
The SM arrives on shoot day. It is her job to relay the Director's orders to the Musicians, Grips, Electrics, Production Designer, and others on the floor, and to prepare the floor for cameras to roll. (The camera operators are all connected by headset directly to the Director.)

The SM is another DGA position, who also gets a "production fee" bump.

10-08 Production Assistants
The Office PA works with the Producer to help set up the show, answer phones, run errands, and perform other duties. On shoot day he is at the set, reporting to the Producer.

The $150 per day rate is a raise from the last time he worked for this Producer, who paid $125 at the time.

The Set PA comes on board one day before the shoot, works the shoot, and stays on for one day of returns. She gets the introductory rate of $125 per day.

12-00 Sound Stage (Recording Studio)

12-01 Studio Rental
Here's the overall setup. The Recording Studio is a large room with an "elephant" door at one end providing good access for the lighting trusses and simple set. A generator for the lights is parked in the alley. The video truck parks in an alley off another entrance, and runs cable in for the cameras.

There is another large room in the complex that holds 50 invited guests and a large screen TV that plays the concert live. That way, the guests enjoy the show, and can mingle with the musicians before and after, but are kept out of the way during the shoot.

The Studio starts the clock on Day One, which begins at 6 P.M. with the Load-in of the lighting trusses, lighting instruments, and set. The trusses and set go up in 6 hours that night. Trusses, by the way, are portable metal grids to which the lights are attached. In this case they bolt onto collapsible stanchions that can be raised and lowered to specific heights. They have been used here because there is no lighting grid as you might find in a sound stage set up for shooting.

The following morning, Day 2, the Gaffer, Best Boy, and two

Electrics, plus the Key Grip, Best Boy Grip, and two Grips, come in to hang the lights on the trusses, wire them, and focus them on the set. It takes them 10 hours.

Day 3 is shoot day. The video truck arrives at 6 A.M., and runs cable and cameras into the Studio. By 8 A.M., the First Engineer and his Assistant set up to record the music in the Recording Studio Mixing Room.

The music is being recorded to a 24-track analog machine in the Studio Mixing Room, while the picture is being recorded by 6 BetaSP decks in the video truck. To make sure the music syncs up with the picture frame for frame, they are locked by a Time-Link system that connects the two recording entities.

By 10 A.M. the musicians arrive and take their places for camera blocking. Here the Director sees for the first time what it all looks like—set, lights, and talent. The camera operators get familiar with the shot lists.

By noon, the guests arrive for the first run-through. They take their places, and cameras and tape machines roll. It's a pretty good taping musically, but the Director sees several shots that are missed. At 1 P.M., everyone breaks for lunch. The Director reviews the problem areas with the AD.

It's two o'clock as the band gets back into place. Everyone is fighting the after-lunch glooms, but as cameras roll and the music starts, the energy builds. They shoot until 3:30 P.M. and then spend a final half-hour doing pickups of smaller shots that were missed.

By 4 P.M., the musicians and guests go home, and strike begins. The video truck strikes first to get the cameras and dollies out of the way. The Production Designer and the Set Construction crew simultaneously work on dismantling the set. Once the floor is clear, the lighting strike begins.

By 7:30 P.M., the video truck is loaded and pulls out. The set pulls out in another truck. By 8 P.M., the lighting and trusses are stacked in another truck, and the big elephant doors slide shut.

Looking back, the whole thing seemed to happen so fast ... and the music was so fine ... the Producer wonders if it was a dream.

13-00 Production Design

13-01 Production Designer

The Producer brings in a Production Designer with instructions to build something very simple (the construction budget is only $3,500). Simple it is: Wooden platforms for the band, painted black and nicely arranged so some are higher than others, and a black duvatene backdrop. (Duvatene is a drapery cloth often used in TV and film work because it doesn't reflect light.) Since there is nothing in the Studio to build onto, a frame must be constructed to hold the sheets of duvatene.

The Production Designer is hired on a weekly flat.

14-00 Set Construction

The Production Designer hires the carpenters, buys and/or rents all the materials, rents the trucks, and so on, to make the above happen.

15-00 Set Operations

15-01 Key Grip

The Key Grip comes on for one prep day to help with the pre-light. On shoot day he and his team build the dolly track.

15-02 Best Boy Grip

The Best Boy has the same schedule as the Key.

15-03 Grips

Two Grips are on for the prep day only. They help with the pre-light, which is a big job. They are not needed for the shoot day because by then everything is up and running. Ordinarily, they might return for the strike, but in this case, a separate Strike Crew has been hired through the Lighting Designer.

15-04 Boom/Dolly Grips

There is one dolly on the set which makes a long run across the entire front of the band, and curves around behind the piano player (the Leader). The Dolly Grip assists with the track, and actually sets up and operates the dolly. Dolly Grips earn a bit more per hour than regular Grips.

15-05 Craft Service

Since the prep day is a long, hard day, and the crew needs to be kept energized, craft service is on for both prep and shoot days. It is not available to the 50 guests, who have their own nibbles set up in the Green Room. A few more groceries are needed for shoot day because more crew is present, and the musicians get hungry too.

15-06 Grip Rentals

The Director orders a Panther dolly, a personal favorite, and a jib arm. The dolly will run on the track described above. The camera at the end of the jib arm will be able to get about 15 feet high, for some great shots of the piano player and drummer, and some high wide shots. It can also lower itself and shoot straight on like a camera on an ordinary pedestal.

18-00 Property (Band Equipment Rentals)

This is an allowance category in case the Leader decides to bring in extra instruments. As it turns out, he doesn't.

20-00 Make-Up and Hairdressing

20-01 Key Make-Up Artist
Since the Director plans some close ups of the band as they play, a Key and Assistant Make-Up artist come in. They have 2 hours to Make-Up 12 performers.

21-00 Electrical

We described the set and lighting plan in 12-00 Sound Stage, but here's a quick review.

21-01 Gaffer
The Gaffer preps one extra day because he comes by for a survey with the Director and the Lighting Director, and prepares the lighting order.

21-02/ 21-03/ 21-04 Best Boy/Electrics/Board Op/Additional Labor
On prep day and shoot day, the Electric team consists of the Lighting Director (see 22-00 Camera) Gaffer, Best Boy (who, among other things, checks the lighting inventory coming in and when it's returned to make sure the production company is charged correctly), and two Electrics. The Board Operator runs the dimmers and controls all lighting cues.

The Set/Strike crew comes on for 6 hours during prep day, and 4 hours during strike the following day.

21-06 Equipment Rentals
The Director and the Lighting Director worked out a fairly simple lighting plan that called for several changes of overall color on the musicians, effected by the Board Operator. The package came to $7,500.

21-08 Generator

Since the Studio does not have enough power to run both the video truck and the lights, a 120 amp genny is brought in on prep day. It is a tow genny, set up by the Genny Driver, and left with 20 gallons of gas to run it during the two days. The Gaffer is in charge of it during the shoot. It is picked up early the day after the shoot.

22-00 Camera

22-01 Lighting Director

In television studio work, a Lighting Director usually replaces the Director of Photography category. An LD specializes in the lighting of large set areas on a stage. He generously shows up for a free survey when the Producer is selecting Sound Studios to lend his expertise. Since lighting must be built from scratch in this case, his input is important.

Once the place is selected, he surveys it again with the Director, and works out a lighting plot. He supervises the setup on prep day, and is on hand during the shoot to make sure it all works as ordered.

22-05 Still Photographer

The Producer brings on a Still Photographer for the shoot, to get publicity shots of the band and some of the VIP guests.

22-08 Video Truck

This is obviously an important piece of gear. A representative of the company visits the sound stage for a survey with the Producer, Director, and a representative of the stage. They inspect the parking area for the truck, power sources, the access for cameras and cable.

The Director wants six cameras. Two on regular pedestals, one for the dolly, one for the jib, and two hand-held. This gives a nice range of movement.

There will be six Beta record machines. Five of them are isolated ("iso-ed") or dedicated to their own cameras, and one is a "line cut," meaning it will record whatever shots the Director calls out during the concert. The line cut becomes the basis for the final cut of the show.

In addition, there will be a 3/4 inch machine recording a *5-way split* (five windows on one screen, with time code in the 6th window). This is important because later on in editing he can view all five of the iso-ed cameras at one time, and immediately see what shot he wants to use at any given moment.

The package also includes a wireless PL, or headset system from everyone in the truck to all Camera Operators, the Board Operator, and the Stage Manager.

Inside the truck the Audio person records the music onto the BetaSP's even though it later will be mixed from the superior Recording Studio sound. In editing, the Producer will obviously need to hear the music.

The Video Control person makes sure that all the cameras are balanced and registered, and that the overall image quality from each camera is up to snuff.

The Videotape Operator keeps all the tape machines running smoothly, and changes and labels tapes.

The Technical Director is charged with the overall running of the truck. He also switches the cameras according to the Director's orders to create the line cut.

A Maintenance Engineer is on hand in case anything breaks, and a Utility is on hand to help lay cable and assist where needed.

With the exception of the Maintenance Engineer and the Utility, all of the Camera Operators and other video crew are free-lance. What's more, they are all union people working non-union for this gig.

What's more, they are all top-of-the-line people, meaning they are always called for the big shows and wanted by the Executive Producer. But there's a price, and it comes in the form of an "invoice fee." Since it's a non-union shoot, the crew asks the production company to pay them what they would have received in union benefits. The pay comes in the form of extra cash based on 25% of their gross pay.

23-00 Sound

23-01 Mixer
This is the Audio person in the video truck, as mentioned above. He takes his sound from a patch to the Recording Studio's Mixing Room.

24-00 Transportation

24-03 Production Van
A van driven by one of the PA's is on hand for errand running, light hauling, and to help the Production Designer with some pickups and returns.

25-00 Location Expenses

25-09 Catering Service
A service is hired to prepare lunches for the crew on prep and shoot days, and for the guests on shoot day, at $12 per head.

A second meal on shoot day is not catered. Pizzas are brought in for the strike crew to eat as a "working meal."

25-20 Large Screen TV
This unit is contracted with a company specializing in the setup of these monsters. It is patched to the line cut in the truck. Audio is piped in from the Mixing Room.

27-00 Videotape Stock
Six machines run 6 one-hour tapes for two shows, plus pickups. A total of 18 one-hour BetaSP cassettes.

30-00 Editorial
The Producer now has about 3 hours of material on six cameras to watch and assemble into a one-hour show. Because he had a *5-way split* of the five iso-ed cameras put onto a 3/4 inch cassette with time code, he can screen all five shots at once and pick which one he wants at any given moment. It's a tremendous time-saver.

He has the 5-way split reel, and the line cut reel transferred with a time code window to VHS so he can make edit decisions on paper. The only disadvantage of the 5-way split, is that he needs to borrow a 27-inch screen monitor from a friend so he can see all five shots.

He takes the VHS cassettes home, brews up a strong pot of coffee, and watches it all on television for about 5 days, making notes as to which shots go where in a paper cut.

Then he has 3/4 inch copies made of the Betas for Off-Line.

30-08 Off-Line Editor
With a pretty tight paper cut, the Off-Line edit comes together in 7 days. The tricky part was that some of the songs had to be shortened for time, and cutting music is a knack.

30-09 Off-Line Edit System
A 3/4 inch system of two playbacks and one record machine is rented for one week from a company that delivers the whole package to the Producer's office.

30-10 On-Line System and Editor
With a tight, clean Edit List from the 3/4 inch system, the On-Line goes together in three 8-hour sessions. About 4 hours is used up assembling a long, complicated opening titles montage.

30-11 On-Line Effects
The opening titles montage takes up most of the effects budget. Character generated credits take up the rest.

30-12 Tape Dubs/Stock/Transfers
The BetaSP to VHS for the paper cut runs $19/hour x 3 hours x 2 record machines (the line cut and the 5-way split). The total is $114 and that includes stock.

The BetaSP to 3/4 inch for the Off-Line runs $40/hour x 3 hours x 6 record machines. The total is $720, which includes stock. In addition, the Producer allows another $600 for various pieces of stock and transfer costs.

30-13 Screening Copies
Ten VHS copies are struck, one for the Producer, and nine for the Executive Producer to send to VIP's.

30-15 Masters/Safeties/Textless
After the Post-Production Sound process, the producer returns to the On-Line facility to make dubs. In addition to the Edited Master on D2, two other D2 clones are made, one for the cable company, and one for the home video distribution company. Since there are no English language titles except the opening title and the names of the players, there is no need for a textless master. Any foreign sale will make dubs from the original Edited Master. The Executive Producer has it stored in a vault at the on-line facility.

34-00 Post Production Sound

34-17 Layback
The music was mixed on the record company's nickel in the days following the session. It exists on 24 track. Since there is no dialogue, and no other sound elements other than the music, there is no need for "audio post" in the traditional sense. All that's needed is a Layback from the 24-track to the D2 master. This is done at the On-Line facility with their 24-track machine.

35-00 Titles and Graphics

The opening titles montage consists of footage from the show in quick cuts over a piece of opening music. In the middle of the montage, the opening title sequence appears. It is a 20-second piece of layered video with the text of the title. It took the Graphic Designer a day to put it together at a $400 per hour digital graphics workstation, and it looks great.

37-00 Insurance

The cost of the standard package is reduced somewhat because the shoot is only one day.

38-00 General and Administrative

38-02 Legal

The Executive Producer's attorney prepared all the musicians' contracts between the players and the Leader's music company. The attorney also handled the production personnel contracts, and the negotiations and contracts with the cable company and the home video company.

38-03 Accounting

The Executive Producer's accountant handles all payroll for the production personnel, pays all the vendors, and prepares tax forms at the end of the year. (The musicians are paid through the music payroll service.)

DOCUMENTARY
FILM
BUDGET

Fringe assumptions:				FILM DOCUMENTARY			
Payroll Tax	18%			Shoot Days:	20 total		
Overtime	10%			Location:	Local		
				Unions:	None		
				Production:	16mm film		
				Off Line:	Non-Linear		
				Finish:	16mm film		
SUMMARY BUDGET							
03-00 Producers Unit						35,400	
06-00 Travel & Living – Producers						2,500	
			TOTAL ABOVE-THE-LINE				37,900
10-00 Production Staff						17,110	
21-00 Electrical						11,088	
22-00 Camera						33,061	
23-00 Sound						12,781	
25-00 Location Expenses						1,500	
27-00 Film & Lab						136,514	
			TOTAL PRODUCTION				212,054
30-00 Editorial						31,130	
31-00 Post-Prod. Videotape/Film & Lab						17,544	
33-00 Music						5,000	
34-00 Post Production Sound						23,750	
			TOTAL POST-PRODUCTION				78,278
37-00 Insurance						8,400	
38-00 General & Administrative						10,425	
			TOTAL OTHER				18,825
Total Above-The-Line							37,900
Total Below-The-Line							309,157
Total Above and Below-the-Line							347,057
Contingency @ 10 %							34,706
	GRAND TOTAL						$381,762

ABOVE-THE-LINE						
03-00 Producers Unit	Amount	Units	x	Rate	Sub-Total	Total
03-02 Producer/Writer/Director						
Payroll @ 18%	1	Flat	1	30,000	30,000	30,000
					30,000	5,400
			Total for 03-00			**35,400**
06-00 Travel & Living – Producer/Director						
06-01 Airfares/Hotels						
	1	Allow	1	2,500	2,500	2,500
			Total for 06-00			**2,500**
BELOW-THE-LINE						
10-00 Production Staff						
10-04 Production Coordinator	1	Flat	1	10,000	10,000	10,000
10-08 Production Assistants						
Set PA	30	Days	1	100	3,000	3,000
Edit PA (logger)	3	Weeks	1	500	1,500	1,500
Payroll	1	Allow	1	14,500	2,610	2,610
			Total for 10-00			**17,110**
21-00 Electrical						
21-01 Gaffer	20	Days	12	25	6,000	
Overtime	1	Allow	1	6,000	600	6,600
21-05 Expendables (Gels etc.)	1	Allow	1	500	500	500
21-06 Equip. Rental						
Light/Grip Package	20	Days	1	100	2,000	2,000
21-09 Loss & Damage	1	Allow	1	200	200	200
21-10 Box Rentals						
Gaffer	20	Days	1	30	600	600
Payroll				6,600	1,188	1,188
			Total for 21-00			**11,088**
22-00 Camera						
22-01 Director of Photography/OP	20	Days	12	$28.57	6,857	
Overtime	1	Allow	1	6,857	686	7,542

Acct	Description	Amount	Units	X	Rate	Sub-Total	Total
22-03	1st Asst. Camera Operator	20	Days	12	$23.21	5,570	
	Overtime	1	Allow	1	5,570	557	6,127
22-05	Still Photographer	1	Week	1	1,000	1,000	1,000
22-06	Expendables	1	Allow	1	500	500	500
22-07	Camera Package Rental	15	Days	1	1,000	15,000	15,000
	Arri SR3 w/time code						
22-17	Loss & Damage	1	Allow	1	250	250	250
	Payroll				14,670	2,641	2,641
					Total for 22-00		**33,061**
23-00	**Sound**						
23-01	Mixer	20	Days	12	25	6,000	
	Overtime	1	Allow	1	6,000	600	6,600
23-02	Boom Operator						
	Shoot	5	Days	12	$14.29	857	
	Overtime	1	Allow	1	857	86	943
23-03	Expendables (Batteries, etc)	1	Allow	1	450	450	450
23-04	Sound Pckg (w/time code)	15	Days	1	150	2,250	2,250
23-05	Audio Stock (1/4") (30:00)	120	Reels	1	$7.75	930	930
23-10	Loss & Damage	1	Allow	1	250	250	250
	Payroll				7,543	1,358	1,358
					Total for 23-00		**12,781**
25-00	**Location Expenses**						
25-09	Crew meals	20	Days	5	10	1,000	1,000
25-20	Miscellaneous Expenses						
	Mileage	1	Allow	1	500	500	500
					Total for 25-00		**1,500**
27-00	**Film & Lab - Production**						
27-01	Raw Stock (Film-Production)	144,000	Ft.	1	$0.38	54,720	
	Sales Tax	1	Allow	1	4,514	4,514	59,234
27-02	Lab-Negative Prep & Process	144,000	Ft.	1	$0.12	17,280	17,280
27-04	Prep/Clean Neg for Telecine	120	Rolls	1	20	2,400	2,400
	(120 1200' rolls @ $20/roll)						
27-08	Telecine (Video Dailies) (4:1)	240	Hrs.	1	230	55,200	55,200
27-09	3/4" stock (recycled)	240	Hrs.	1	10	2,400	2,400
					Total for 27-00		**136,514**

30-00 Editorial							
30-08 Off-Line Editor		8	Weeks	1	2,000	16,000	16,000	
30-09 Off-Line Editing System		8	Weeks	1	1,500	12,000	12,000	
	Extra Memory	1	Included	1		0	0	
	3/4" deck (paper cut)	1	N/C	1		0	0	
30-12 Dubs/Transfers		1	Allow	1	250	250	250	
	Payroll				16,000	2,880	2,880	
				Total for 30-00				31,130

31-00 Post-Prod. Film & Lab/Videotape							
31-02 Negative Cutter								
	Breakdown xtra charge	1	Allow	1	400	400	400	
	Cut/Splice	60	Min.	1	85	5,100	5,100	
	Supplies	1	Allow	1	275	275	275	
31-04 Answer Prints (2)		2,500	Ft.	2	$0.93	4,650	4,650	
	Titles burn	2,500	Ft.	1	$0.04	100	100	
31-05 Internegative/Interpositive								
	Interpositive	2,500	Ft.	1	$0.73	1,825	1,825	
	Internegative	2,500	Ft.	1	$0.62	1,550	1,550	
31-06 Check Prints (2)		2,500	Ft.	2	0.18	900	900	
31-07 Release Prints		2,500	Ft.	2	$0.24	1,200	1,200	
31-10 Cassette Duplication		50	Cass.	1	10	500	500	
31-11 Telecine (Interpositive to D2)		3	Hours	1	270	810	810	
	D2 stock	1	Hour	1	234	234	234	
				Total for 31-00				17,544

33-00 Music							
33-01 Composer		1	Allow	1	5,000	5,000	5,000	
(All-In Package includes: Arrangers, Copyists,								
...Musicians, Instruments, Studio,								
Engineers, Stock, etc)								
				Total for 33-00				5,000

34-00 Post Production Sound							
Supervising Sound Editor		1	Allow	1	2,300	2,300	2,300	
Equipment fee/spotting/overhead		1	Allow	1	8,000	8,000	8,000	
34-01 Spotting for Music/Sound efx		1	Incl.	1	0	0	0	
34-06 Laydown					0	0	0	

34-07 Conform Dialogue	1	Incl.	1	0	0	0	
34-08 Sound Edit							
	Dialogue edit	1	Allow	1	4,700	4,700	4,700
	Sound Efx edit	1	Allow	1	2,300	2,300	2,300
34-10 Final Dub (Mix)	10	Hours	1	450	4,500	4,500	
34-12 Optical Sound Transfer	2500	Ft.	1	$0.42	1,050	1,050	
34-13 Stock/Dubs/Transfers	1	Allow	1	500	500	500	
34-17 Layback to D2	2	Hours	1	200	400	400	
				Total for 34-00			23,750
35-00 Titles & Graphics							
35-01 Graphic Artist	1	Allow	1	250	250	250	
35-02 Graphics shoot/process pckg							
	Art supplies	1	Allow	1	100	100	100
	Arri 16 SR2 rental	1	Day	1	300	300	300
	Hi-con reversal stock	400	Ft.	1	$0.38	152	152
	Lab prep/process	400	Ft.	1	$0.13	52	52
				Total for 35-00			854
37-00 Insurance							
37-01 Producers Entertainment Pckg	1	Allow	1	2,400	2,400	2,400	
Negative					0	0	
Faulty Stock					0	0	
Equipment					0	0	
Props/Sets					0	0	
Extra Expense					0	0	
3rd Party Property Damage					0	0	
Office Contents					0	0	
37-02 General Liability	1	Allow	1	2,400	2,400	2,400	
37-03 Hired Auto					0	0	
37-04 Cast Insurance					0	0	
37-05 Workers Compensation	1	Allow	1	1,200	1,200	1,200	
37-06 Errors & Omissions	1	Allow	1	2,400	2,400	2,400	
				Total for 37-00			8,400
38-00 General & Administrative Expenses							
38-02 Legal	1	Allow	1	5,000	5,000	5,000	
38-03 Accounting fees	1	Allow	1	1,000	1,000	1,000	
38-05 Telephone/FAX	1	Allow	1	1,000	1,000	1,000	

38-06 Copying		1	Allow	1	150	150	150	
38-07 Postage & Freight		1	Allow	1	500	500	500	
38-08 Office Space Rental		1	Allow	1	0	0	0	
38-09 Office Furniture		1	Allow	1	350	350	350	
38-10 Office Equipment & Supplies		1	Allow	1	250	250	250	
38-11 Computer Rental								
	Producer/Director	1	Allow	1	0	0	0	
38-12 Software		1	Allow	1	0	0	0	
38-13 Transcription (17 hrs. x 3)		51	Hours	1	25	1,275	1,275	
38-14 Messenger/Overnight		1	Allow	1	300	300	300	
38-15 Parking		1	Allow	1	150	150	150	
38-18 Publicity		1	Allow	1	0	0	0	
38-20 Hospitality		1	Allow	1	450	450	450	
					Total for 38-00			10,425
Contingency @ 10%							34,706	34,706
	GRAND TOTAL							$381,762
Total Above-The-Line								37,900
Total Below-The-Line								309,157
Total Above and Below-the-Line								347,057
					Check budget totals		381,762	381,762

DOCUMENTARY—FILM

Overview:

This is a one-hour documentary film following the stories of three people across several months. There are interviews with the three primary subjects, and with people who know them, but the Producer wants to stay off "talking heads" as much as possible. Instead, she uses footage with natural sound up, and B-Roll under voices. There are also lyrical passages featuring long, slow shots with music up.

The show is shot on 16mm. film, transferred to tape, and edited on a non-linear system, then finished on film. It is a local shoot, estimated at 20 days across several months.

Pre-Production:	6 weeks
Shoot:	20 days (across several months)
Post-Production:	16 weeks

03-00 Producer's Unit

03-02 Producer/Director

This is the Producer's vision, a labor of love. The Producer/Director ends up working for almost a year on this project, mostly because the shooting span is deliberately extended to allow for developments in her subjects' lives.

She figures she can live on $30,000 for the year by pinching pennies, and she wants to put as much money as possible onto the screen.

As Producer she interviews many prospective subjects and selects the final three. She handles the overall coordination of the production and the budget.

There is no narration to write but the Producer shapes the story in editing, trying to craft the most dramatic story arc she can, remaining true to her subjects' lives.

As Director, she is responsible for the overall look and style of the shooting, the lighting, and the editing.

06-00 Travel and Living—Producer/Director

06-01 Air Fares/Hotels
She provides for a travel and living allowance because she needs to fly to other cities, pick up a stringer crew (included in 22-00), and shoot interviews and action with people who have influenced her subjects' lives.

10-00 Production Staff

10-04 Production Coordinator
The Coordinator is a close friend who agrees to take on the position, even though she has to juggle other duties as a part-time illustrator, and mother of two young children. As Coordinator, she books and schedules the crew, books equipment rentals, handles the lab processing and transfer of the film to tape, and pays bills. A bookkeeper comes in once or twice a month to reconcile accounts, and take care of payroll and taxes (38-03).

For her services, the friend will take a flat fee of $10,000, and see the project through to the bitter end.

10-08 Production Assistants
The Set PA is actually several college film/TV students who work on shoot days as available. The deal is a flat $100 per day, and meals, no matter how long it takes.

The Edit PA, or Logger, is one person hired for 3 weeks to screen the video dailies on 3/4 inch, and log each and every shot and piece of dialogue. The interviews, about 17 hours' worth, are sent to a transcriber. (See Chapter 3 Line Items, 31-00 Editorial, for a note about logs and paper cuts.)

21-00 Electrical

21-01 Gaffer
The decision to hire a Gaffer was a difficult one for the Producer. She figured she could use the money on opticals, music, or even

mortgage payments. In the end, however, she wants the look of the film to be as good as she can afford, and since much of her shooting is in interiors, where another hand and eye can really help, she includes a Gaffer.

She knew her erratic shooting schedule might preclude having one Gaffer for the whole time, so she interviews several during pre-production, creating a pool from which she can draw.

21-06 Equipment Rental

The lighting package consists of two portable kits which she obtains for $100 a day. She saves a little whenever she works weekends by getting two days for one.

22-00 Camera

22-01 Director of Photography

The Producer faces the same problem here as with the Gaffer—she may never get the same DP twice. The DP position, however, is even more critical, since not only the lighting but the shooting style may differ with each shooter. So the Producer takes great pains to meet with several DP's during pre-production, see their work, and show samples of the kind of look she wants. When she has five whom she likes, she's got her DP pool. For the out-of-town shoots, she gets recommendations from friends and local producers, interviews several DP's by phone, and asks for sample reels.

22-03 1st Assistant Camera

Similarly, a pool of 1st ACs are on hand to shoot on a day's notice. The Producer could do this job herself in a pinch, but doesn't want to think about baby-sitting the camera, lenses, and film magazines when she must focus on her subjects.

22-05 Still Photographer

As a favor, a friend who is a professional still photographer agrees to shoot 5 to 10 days for a flat feeof $1,000, which includes film and processing. Out of these pictures, the Producer hopes to get some striking publicity shots which she'll use to create a poster she can distribute at film festivals.

22-07 Camera Package Rental

The Producer and her DP's, agree on an Arriflex SR-3 camera with the capability of putting time code on the film, right along with the edge numbers. Since she is editing on videotape, where time code is king, this will prove very handy. The package incudes a 10:100 mm. zoom lens, a 60 mm. prime lens, filters, tripod, an assortment of shades, batteries, a matte box, and three 400 foot magazines, one on the camera, one always loaded, and one for backup.

The rate is $1,000 per day, and because the Producer knows that some of those will be two-for-one weekend days, she budgets 15 separate days.

23-00 Sound

23-01 Mixer

The Producer has also interviewed several Mixers for the project, and lined up half a dozen for her pool.

23-02 Boom Operator

On most shoot days, the Mixer handles the job of mixing sound and miking the subjects, either with a lavelier mike pinned to clothing, or with a shotgun mike on a fishpole. For what she expects to be 5 days, however, she budgets for a Boom Op. to help mike some dinner scenes in which six or so people gather in one room.

23-04 Sound Package

The edit plan is to transfer all the footage to 3/4 inch tape, and edit the rough cut on video. A Nagra recorder with time code is therefore needed to stripe the 1/4 inch audio tape with time code. Again, the producer budgets for 15 separate days.

The Producer could use a non-time code Nagra with a 60 cycle "pilot tone," but then special care would have to be taken to lock up the time code in the telecine process (see this budget at 27-09 Film and Lab Production).

23-05 Audio Stock
The Producer is allowing for an average of 3 hours of shooting per day. With 30 minute reels of 1/4 inch audio stock, that's six reels per day, or 120 reels for the whole shoot.

25-00 Location Expenses

25-09 Crew Meals
This expense covers lunches plus snacks and an occasional breakfast or dinner for the shooting crew.

25-20 Miscellaneous
Crew members who use their own cars to travel to and from the location get 30 cents/mile reimbursed.

27-00 Film and Lab—Production

27-01 Raw Stock
The Producer and the DP's figure that budgeting 3 hours a day of shooting is ample. That's about 10 minutes for every 400-foot magazine of film, amounting to about 7,200 feet per day times 20 days or 144,000 feet.

27-02 Lab Negative Prep and Process
The lab quotes her 12 cents a foot, which she hopes to get down by some persuasive arm-twisting—something along the lines of "This is your opportunity to contribute to a profoundly serious social issue." It's a good line which also happens to be true.

27-04 Prep and Clean Neg for Telecine
The lab cleans the negative, and spools it onto 1,200-foot reels in preparation for telecine transfer to tape.

27-09 (Telecine) Video Dailies
The plan is for the film to be edited off-line, and then the EDL (edit list) is given to the Negative Cutter to conform to the negative. The video dailies, therefore, need only be "one lights," which is a

non-color-corrected duplicate of the film. Color correcting is done later as part of the Answer Print process.

Even though it's a "one-light," the transfer time takes 4 hours for every one hour of film shot. That's because for each shot, the Colorist needs to check the time code and key code numbers, and make sure the audio is correctly synced.

The 3/4 inch stock is not included in the Telecine rate.

Post-Production Audio Note: When the film is transferred to tape, the audio is synced up at the top, and the time code from the 1/4 inch audio is transferred to the video as the edit reference. But remember, that's for Off-Line only, and it's therefore only a temporary audio track.

If a non-time code Nagra was used in production, the telecine house can adjust the 60-cycle "pilot tone" from the original 1/4 inch audio to lock it with the time code on the film and tape. Most people like to use a time code Nagra, however, to make sure there will be no problems with time code later on. It can be a nightmare in audio post.

30-00 Editorial

30-08 Off-Line Editor
This is a critical function on any project, but for a documentary with 60 hours of material, an editor with a strong sense of the purpose of the film and the way it should be cut is essential. No switching around of personnel here. The Producer interviews several editors, sees their work, and discusses the project in depth before selecting one. They agree that 8 weeks of editing should do it, provided the Producer shows up with complete logs, and a rough "paper cut" that gets the material down to about 15 hours. (See Chapter 3 Line Items, 30-00 Editorial, for a note about logs and paper cuts.)

The Producer gets a 3/4 inch playback deck and monitor, and hires an editing PA to work full time for 3 weeks to log the footage (see this budget 10-08). Since about 17 hours of the footage is sit-down interview, the Producer sends that material off to a transcriber (see 38-13).

Once everything has been logged, the Producer sits down for a long visit with the material, about 5 weeks in fact, to sift through every moment of footage and construct a rough narrative. When she has it down to about 15 hours, Off-Line begins.

30-09 Off-Line Editing System
She rents a D-Vision non-linear system, and has it delivered to her office. (The D-Vision is cheaper to rent than an AVID, and has more storage capacity for the money.)

The system rents for a weekly flat of $850, which includes three gigabytes of memory, not nearly enough for her 15 hours of material. She now has a choice. She can edit at medium resolution or low resolution. The medium looks better but takes up more memory. Since she has no finicky client from whom she must get off-line approval, and since she has spent the last five weeks memorizing every shot, she figures the low resolution will do just fine.

At low resolution, each gig holds about 90 minutes. (At medium resolution, each gig holds about 35-50 minutes.) She needs 10 gigs, and makes a deal for a weekly flat of $1,500, which includes the system, and all 10 gigs. The dealer even throws in the 3/4 inch playback deck and 13 inch monitor (for the paper cut), which otherwise would have cost her $250 per week for 8 weeks, or $2,000.

At the beginning of the Off-Line process, the Producer makes sure the Editor and the Negative Cutter talk to each other to get all the details of the Edit List (EDL) squared away. The final Edit List contains not only the time code, but the key code numbers from the original 16mm film, which the Negative Cutter needs to conform to the negative.

Sometimes the non-linear editing computer needs special software to work with key code numbers. Also, the computer will have to spit out a "Nagra cut list" of audio cuts for the Post-Production Sound Editor.

30-12 Dubs and Transfers

This is a slop category for the various dubs and whatnot that always have to happen in editing. In this case, it helps cover some shooting of some snapshots of her subjects.

31-00 Post-Production Film and Lab/Videotape

31-02 Negative Cutter

After the 8 weeks of Off-Line Editing, the picture is finally locked, and ready to go to the Negative Cutter. The Negative Cutter gets all 60 hours of original negative, the EDL with the film key code numbers, a copy of the 3/4 inch locked cut for visual reference, plus all the 3/4 inch video dailies to check that the key code numbers match the original negative.

The first thing the Negative Cutter does is cut that 60 hours of original negative down to size. He "breaks down" the material, pulling only what will be used. The process takes about 50 hours, and is normally included in his fee, although this time he charges an extra $400 because there is so much original negative.

The Producer saves a little money here by having the Off-Line Editor create an Edit List identifying what rolls of the original are used in the cut. Sure enough, there are several rolls not used at all, and they are not delivered to the Negative Cutter, thus lessening his load and his charges.

The Negative Cutter charges $85 per finished minute, plus an allowance for supplies. He delivers A&B rolls of the cut negative, with all dissolves and fades built right in (see this commentary at 32-00 Opticals). (Normally, a feature has about 100 cuts in a given 10 minutes of running time. Documentaries often have fewer cuts.) After the 50 hours of breakdown, it takes the Negative Cutter 8 days to cut and splice the negative.

(For what the producer does for titles, see this budget at 35-00 Titles And Graphics.)

The off-line cut has all the dissolves and wipes that will appear in the final cut, so while the Negative Cutter is conforming, 3/4 inch copies of the Off-Line cut go to the Composer for the score (33-00 Music), and to the Audio Post facility (34-00 Post Production Sound).

31-04 Answer Prints
The finished cut negative is now ready to be viewed and color corrected. A first trial Answer Print comes out pretty well, but one more will be needed to get the color correction right. The making of the second AP is put on hold, however, until the sound is ready. Meanwhile, a one-light telecine transfer of the 1st AP is made to 3/4 inch (see Telecine 31-11) to give to the Post-Production Sound facility to make sure the picture and sound are in sync.

The 2nd AP is matched up with the Optical Sound Negative containing the fully mixed sound track (see this budget at 34-12 Optical Sound Transfer) so the film picture can now be seen with sound.

31-05 Internegative/Interpositive
The color timing formula that made the Answer Print perfect is now applied to make the Interpositive from the original cut negative, and then an Internegative from the Interpositive. The Internegative is the final template from which Release Prints are made.

31-06 Check Prints
The Producer allows for two Check Prints to make sure that the IN has no dirt, scratches, or other problems.

31-07 Release Prints
The Producer makes one Release Print for now, to show at film festivals.

31-10 Cassette Duplication
From the final D2 master, the Producer makes 50 VHS cassettes to send to distributors, film festivals, and broadcasters in hopes of making deals. The D2 will also serve as her broadcast master (see 31-11).

31-11 Telecine
The transfer of the 1st AP to 3/4 inch is a one-light at 2:1 ratio.

The Producer wants to make a broadcast television master, so a D2 copy of the Interpositive is made in a telecine bay. However, it is made with picture only, because the sound quality from 16mm optical is not great for TV (See Post-Production Sound 34-17).

32-00 Optical Effects
This item is not in the budget because the Producer finds a way to save money avoiding an opticals house. In the film, there are only titles to insert, and no tricky wipes or other fancy opticals, so the Negative Cutter creates all the fades and dissolves right on the A&B rolls. They are then printed along with everything else as part of the Answer Print.

The Producer also finds a way to save money on opening and closing titles and lower third identifiers (see 35-00 Titles and Graphics).

33-00 Music

33-01 Composer
A Composer with a small synthesizer studio agrees to score the film. The music is not "wall-to-wall," but of the 58 minutes running time, 35 minutes gets music. Most of it is built on the synthesizer as a bed, and three musicians come in to play acoustic instruments over the bed to add depth and feeling to the score. The Composer delivers the music on DAT, ready to be mixed into the final sound track.

34-00 Post-Production Sound
Most Post-Production Sound facilities put out a flat bid on the whole project, after assessing what's involved. In this case, the Producer takes the 3/4 inch Off-Line cut to the sound house, and sits with the Sound Supervisor to work out the bid. The total comes

to about $23,000 for the one-hour documentary. This show could be done for less than that, say around $15,000, but the Producer wants to enhance the total effect with a fairly elaborate sound design. The costs add up this way:

Dialogue Editing:	$ 4,700
Sound Effects Editing:	$ 2,300
Spotting/Overhead/Equip. fee	$ 8,000
Mix	$ 4,275
Optical Negative (sound lab)	$ 1,500
Supervising Sound Editor	$ 2,300
Package price:	$23,075 grand total.

These are the steps of the process:

34-01 Spotting for Sound Effects
The Producer and a Sound Editor use the 3/4 inch off-line cut to spot for sound effects. A few dozen places are selected where the impact of the film is enhanced considerably with some sound design.

34-06 Laydown
For this project, there is no laydown per se, because the Producer is showing up with a 3/4 inch Off-Line cut and 60 hours of original 1/4 inch audio tape.

34-07 Edit (Conform) Dialogue
The D-Vision puts out an Edit List (EDL) called a "Nagra cut list," which tells the Sound Editor exactly what audio from the original 1/4 inch is to be used. He then digitizes the selected cuts on the 1/4 inch into the DWS, and assembles a clean audio track. The charge for this is included in the general overhead and equipment fee of $8,000.

34-08 Sound Editing
Since the dialogue on the production sound track has been recorded in all sorts of different ambiences, it needs to be smoothed out and balanced in a process called Dialogue Assembly. This is also done in a Digital Work Station (DWS). Any ambience to make the dialogue

track smoother is added here. The process is the most complicated of all the sound editing, and takes a couple of weeks. When he is done, all the dialogue is at the right place in the show, and it's all balanced and smoothed out. It is on 24-track, and ready to be mixed. The dialogue edit portion of the process costs about $4,700.

At the same time as the Dialogue Editor is working, the Sound Effects Editor is pulling the effects, and editing them onto 24-track. The charge for this portion is about $2,700.

The Producer has opted for no ADR (looping) or Foley work, preferring instead to stick with the original sound, warts and all. It creates a more realistic sound.

34-10 Final Dub (Mix)
The Producer sits in with the two Mixers and the Sound Supervisor and away they go, adjusting all the levels of the various sound elements until everything is just right. They mix to 24-track tape. It takes one 9 hour day.

34-12 Optical Sound Transfer
The Producer takes the 24-track to a sound optical house, where they shoot an optical negative of it. That optical negative is the soundtrack for the Answer Print and/or Internegative (31-05).

34-17 Layback
The Producer makes a D2 broadcast master of the show, but the sound quality from a 16mm optical track is not the best source. Since she has gone to the trouble of mixing the show to 24-track (and it sounds great!), she decides to spend the extra money and do a layback from the mixed 24-track to the D2 copy of the film. She now has a D2 broadcast master with good quality stereo sound on Channels 1 and 2. It costs $400.

35-00 Titles and Graphics

35-01 Graphic Artist
The Producer wants to save money on the opening titles, closing credits, and several lower third identifiers. This can run up quite a

bill at an opticals house, so to avoid that, she has a graphic artist friend create the titles as white letters on black art cards.

35-02 Graphics Shoot/Process/Package
She rents a camera for a day, and shoots the titles in their correct positions in the frame. She uses a Hi-con (high contrast) reversal stock. The lab processes this, and she gets the negative to the Negative Cutter to cut into a dupe. In the Answer Print stage, the lab makes a separate pass and literally burns in the titles where the producer wants them.

It's a bit more work on her part, but it saves her from going to an opticals house and spending more money. The drawback is that this only works with white letters, which happens to be fine with her for this project.

37-00 Insurance

37-01 Producer's Entertainment Package
Standard package.

37-02 General Liability
This film is pretty tame stuff from an insurance company's point of view. No big budget hits here.

37-05 Workers' Compensation
Another standard package.

37-06 Errors and Omissions
The insurance company was most interested in this one, since three people's stories are told, and many others are interviewed. They wanted to insure that no one would sue the Producer for libel. The Producer had to create an explicit and complete Release Form for each person to sign. The form was written by her attorney.

38-00 General and Administrative Expenses

38-02 Legal
The Release Form was written by the attorney, as well as basic crew contracts. The remainder of the money is budgeted for the attorney to review hoped for distribution agreements.

38-03 Accounting
The Bookkeeper comes in once or twice a month to check the Coordinator's bill paying prowess, balance the books, and handle payroll and taxes.

38-08 Office Space Rental
The Producer's spare bedroom, and she got it for free. Ditto office furniture, and computer rental.

38-13 Transcription
All the interviews were transcribed and sent by modem to the producer's computer. From there, she could simply pull them off one file directly into the paper cut, and also on the computer.

38-20 Hospitality
This line is for the moment of truth at the moderately expensive lunches she has with distributors, agents, and TV programming executives. She can offer to pick up the check and at least know the money is there.

'NO BUDGET'
DOCUMENTARY

NO BUDGET' DOCUMENTARY

Fringe assumptions:							
Payroll Tax	0%			Shoot Days:	12		
WGA	0%			Location:	N.Y.C.		
DGA	0%			Unions:	None		
SAG	0%			Production:	Hi-8		
AFTRA	0%			Off-Line:	3/4 inch videotape		
Agency Fees	0%			Finish:	3/4 inch SP videotape		

LOW BUDGET DOCUMENTARY

SUMMARY BUDGET

02-00	Script			0	
03-00	Producers Unit			0	
04-00	Direction			0	
05-00	Cast			400	
06-00	Travel & Living - Producers/Director			1,200	
		TOTAL ABOVE-THE-LINE			1,600
10-00	Production Staff			600	
13-00	Production Design			100	
22-00	Camera			2,900	
23-00	Sound			0	
24-00	Transportation			500	
25-00	Location Expenses			300	
27-00	Film & Lab			455	
		TOTAL PRODUCTION			4,855
30-00	Editorial			990	
33-00	Music			0	
34-00	Post Production Sound			0	
35-00	Titles & Graphics			0	
		TOTAL POST-PRODUCTION			990
37-00	Insurance			0	
38-00	General & Administrative			0	
		TOTAL OTHER			0
Total	Above-The-Line				1,600

		Amt.	Units	x	Rate	Sub-ttl	Total	
Total Below-The-Line								5,845
Total Above and Below-the-Line								7,445
Contingency @ 10 %								0
	GRAND TOTAL							$7,445
	ABOVE-THE-LINE							
		Amt.	Units	x	Rate	Sub-ttl	Total	
02-00 Script								
02-01 Writer's Salaries		2	Weeks	1		0		
					Total for 02-00			0
03-00 Producers Unit								
03-01 Executive Producer						0	0	
03-02 Producer						0	0	
	Prep	1	Week	2		0		
	Shoot	12	Days	2		0		
	Post	4	Weeks	1		0		
					Total for 03-00			0
04-00 Direction								
04-01 Director								
	Prep	1	Week	1		0	0	
	Shoot	12	Days	1		0	0	
	Edit	1	Week	1		0	0	
					Total for 04-00			0
05-00 Cast								
05-01 Lead Actors								
	Re-enactment scene	1	Day	1		200	200	
	Sleight-of-hand man	1	Day	1		200	200	
05-08 Narrator		1	Day	1		0	0	
					Total for 05-00			400
06-00 Travel & Living - Producers/Director								
06-02 Living expenses (N.Y.C.)		1	Allow	1	1,200	1,200	1,200	
					Total for 06-00			1,200

BELOW-THE-LINE						
10-00 Production Staff						
10-08 Production Assistants	12	Days	2	25	600	600
				Total for 10-00		600
13-00 Production Design						
13-02 Art Director						
Prep	1	Day	1		100	100
Shoot	1	Day	1		0	0
				Total for 13-00		100
22-00 Camera						
22-01 Director of Photography/Op. (Director)						
Prep	1	Week	1		0	0
Shoot	12	Days	1		0	0
22-02 Camera Operator (2nd Cam)	2	Days	1		0	0
22-07 Camera Package (Purchase)						
Hi-8	1	Allow	1		1,400	1,400
Spy cam/record deck	1	Allow	1		1,500	1,500
				Total for 22-00		2,900
24-00 Transportation						
24-03 Equipment Rental						
Personal cars					0	0
24-04 Gas & Oil	1	Allow	1	500	500	500
				Total for 24-00		500
25-00 Location Expenses						
25-07 Permits						
25-09 Catering Service					0	0
Crew Meals (brown bags)	1	Allow	1	300	300	300
25-17 Location Site Rental					0	0
				Total for 25-00		300
27-00 Film & Lab - Production						
27-03 Videotape Stock (Hi-8)	30	Hours	1	7	210	

	Super VHS	10	Hours	1	5	50	
Sales Tax		1	Allow	1	21	21	281
27-08 Telecine							
	Transfer to 3/4"SP	24	Hours	1	0	0	0
	Duplicate set 3/4"	5	Hours	1	0	0	0
27-09 Telecine Tape Stock							
	3/4" b&c (recycled)	5	Hours	1	10	50	50
	3/4" SP b&c	5	Hours	1	22	110	110
	Sales tax				160	13	13
				Total for 27-00			455
30-00 Editorial							
30-08 Off-Line Editor (Producer)		4	Weeks	1		0	0
30-09 Off-Line Edit System (3/4")		4	Weeks	1		0	0
30-10 On-Line System & Editor		2	Days	1		0	0
30-11 On-Line Effects (Slo-mo)		6	Hours	1	100	600	600
30-12 Videotape Dubs/Stock & Trans		1	Allow	1	50	50	50
30-13 Screening Copies		25	Cass.	1	12	300	300
30-14 Video Master/Safety (3/4"SP		2	Reels	1	20	40	40
				Total for 30-00			990
33-00 Music							
33-01 Composer		1	Allow	1		0	0
All-In Package includes: Composer,						0	0
Musicians, Instruments, Synth Studio.						0	0
				Total for 33-00			0
34-00 Post Production Sound							
				Total for 34-00			0
35-00 Titles & Graphics							
35-01 Grfx Designer/Workstation		10	Hours	1		0	0
35-02 Stocks and Dubs		1	Allow	1	0	0	0
				Total for 35-00			0
37-00 Insurance							
37-01 Producers Entertainment Package						0	0
				Total for 37-00			0
						0	

38-00 General & Administrative Expenses					0		
				Total for 38-00			0
	GRAND TOTAL						$7,445
Total Above-The-Line							1,600
Total Below-The-Line							5,845
Total Above and Below-the-Line							7,445
				Check budget totals		7,445	7,445

'NO BUDGET' DOCUMENTARY

The Grifters of New York is a half-hour documentary produced by professional filmmakers on a low, low budget (about $7,400). For that reason, (and because it's a compelling film to watch), it's worth showcasing as a sample budget.

It's about the street grifters of New York—the people who run the Three-Card Monte, the shell games, and the other con acts that swindle passersby out of their cash. With hidden cameras, the filmmakers posed as street people and recorded the tricks the con artists play—tricks that range from sleight of hand to outright intimidation.

The two producers and one director/camera operator own their own production companies in Maryland and New York. They teamed up, and worked for nothing more than living expenses to make this film. *Fast Game Fast Money: The Grifters of New York* has won several awards in film festivals, including a Cine Golden Eagle, and, the director's personal favorite, Best Documentary at the Social Outcast Festival in Atlanta.

Producer/Editor:Ed Bishop, ColorCast Productions, Inc., Severna Park, Maryland.
Producer: Lisa De Lucia, Odd Sprocket Films, N.Y.C.
Director/Camera Operator/Writer: Pericles Lewnes

02-00 Script

02-01 Writer's Salaries
The Director wrote and recorded the narration in Off-Line editing. The creative approach is like sharing a personal journal with the viewer, giving a blow-by-blow account of the filmmakers' adventures among the street hustlers.

03-00 Producer's Unit

03-01 Producers
The show was shot in 12 days over about 2 months. The team would gather in New York for a few days of shooting, usually on weekends, and then return to their paying work in between.

Lisa was the New York Producer. She provided the home base in the city, hosting the production team in her apartment, and researching the best locations where the grifters operate.

Ed and Pericles drove up from Maryland. Ed got an arts grant from the Maryland Arts Council for $1,000, and helped get a $6,400 loan from a friend who doesn't expect his money back anytime soon.

The prep period began with many conversations talking down the idea, and getting the money. Then the team spent a week in New York checking out the street scenes.

04-00 Direction

04-01 Director
Pericles' schedule was the same as Ed's and Lisa's during prep and shoot. The editing was Ed's job, but Pericles put in about a week's worth of time over the month of editing, to help shape the show and write the narration.

05-00 Cast

05-01 Lead Actors
The first person hired was a man to re-enact a scene in which he meets with Pericles to talk about where a person gets an education in grifting (mostly in prison).

The second scene was with a sleight-of-hand expert, a former grifter who agreed to demonstrate, in slow motion, exactly how the experts cheat. (Ed and Pericles met him at a baseball festival doing card tricks with baseball cards.)

The third "cast member" was the narrator, Pericles, telling the story of how the film gets made.

06-00 Travel and Living - Producers/Director

06-02 Living Expenses—N.Y.C.
About $1,200 covered the groceries and subway fare for the team while shooting in New York.

10-00 Production Staff

10-08 Production Assistants
Two friends of Lisa's agreed to be PA's on shoot days.

13-00 Production Design

13-02 Art Director
An Art Director was hired to design the dreamlike opening title sequence—a "hustler," out of focus, his mouth working but silent, pitching us his street rap. He stands amidst an array of playing cards floating in space (hanging by fishing lines from the ceiling) against a drapery background, lit in red and gold, and shot in soft focus.

22-00 Camera

22-01 Director of Photography/Operator
The Director also operated the camera.

22-02 Camera Operator/2nd Camera

Lisa got a second camera operator for two days to shoot different angles on the action.

22-07 Camera Package

The team checked out rentals on Hi-8 cameras, and realized that buying one made the most sense. They needed one that gave sharp pictures, yet was small enough to fit inside the cardboard box that disguised it. They decided on a Canon S1.

The second camera operator brought his own camera, a Super VHS with a 50:1 zoom lens.

The third camera was a bona fide "spy" or micro camera, basically a lens on a circuit board. It was hidden inside a hat, and connected to a Hi-8 record deck in a knapsack.

24-00 Transportation

24-03 Equipment Rental

Personal cars did the trick.

25-00 Location Expenses

25-07 Permits

Permits? Since everything was hidden camera anyway, the Producers figured why bother.

25-09 Catering

Brown bag lunches and hot dogs from the Sabrett wagons.

25-17 Location Site Rental

Again, the Producers were working on the street, and so low key they decided to take the risk.

27-00 Film and Lab

27-03 Videotape Stock
They bought about 30 hours of Hi-8 stock, plus about 10 hours of SVHS stock for the second camera.

27-08 Telecine
Hi-8 is a fragile stock. If you play it back in the camera, sometimes even once, the likelihood of dropouts goes way up. When Ed and Pericles got back to the office in Maryland, where they have a 3/4 inch edit system, they transferred the Hi-8 selected footage (selecting and transferring in one or two passes) to 3/4 inch SP. These 3/4 inch SP's now became their new masters. For editing purposes, they made a duplicate set on 3/4 inch recycled stock.

30-00 Editorial

30-08 Off-Line Editor
Ed now switched hats and became the Editor. The process took about four weeks.

30-09 Off-Line Edit System
Fortunately, Ed's company owns a 3/4 inch editing system, so they saved money here too.

30-10 On-Line System and Editor
This is Ed again, and the same 3/4 inch system he used to cut the Off-Line.

30-11 On-Line Effects
To achieve the slow motion effects used sparingly throughout the show, they did have to go out to a larger post facility. They created the effects on 3/4 inch SP, then took the new cassettes back to the edit system and laid them in.

30-13 Screening Copies

These were needed to submit to potential distributors and film festivals.

33-00 Music

33-01 Composer

The old institution of barter is coming back, and Ed used it here. He found a composer with a decent small studio. It turned out the composer wanted to have a music video produced, so a deal was struck: one music video in exchange for one original score. It worked out well, and the music is terrific.

34-00 Post Production Sound

There was no audio post in the budget, so all the smoothing out of production sound, the few sound effects, and the music were all cut in the On-Line process.

35-00 Titles and Graphics

35-01 Graphics Designer and Workstation

Opening titles, closing credits, and a few internal text graphics were achieved with the company's Video Toaster, which has a character generator.

37-00 Insurance

Ed's company carries standard liability insurance, but beyond that, no other insurance was affordable.

38-00 General and Administrative Expenses

There were no line items in the budget for any legal, accounting, or office expenses. It was just make-do.

INDUSTRIAL
BUDGET

Fringe assumptions:				INDUSTRIAL BUDGET		
Payroll Tax	18%			Shoot Days:	2	
WGA	13%			Location:	Local	
DGA	13%			Unions:	AFTRA	
SAG	13%			Production:	35mm film	
AFTRA	13%				BetaSP	
Agency Fees	10%			Off-Line:	Non-linear - 5 days	
				On-Line	D2 - 12 hrs.	
SUMMARY BUDGET						
02-00 Script					2,360	
03-00 Producers Unit					7,700	
04-00 Direction					0	
05-00 Cast					1,371	
		TOTAL ABOVE-THE-LINE				**11,431**
10-00 Production Staff					1,593	
13-00 Production Design					2,729	
14-00 Set Construction					2,000	
15-00 Set Operations					4,199	
16-00 Special Effects					750	
19-00 Wardrobe					1,962	
20-00 Make-Up and Hairdressing					443	
21-00 Electrical					3,593	
22-00 Camera					9,147	
23-00 Sound					604	
24-00 Transportation					660	
25-00 Location Expenses					2,700	
27-00 Film & Lab					4,077	
		TOTAL PRODUCTION				**34,458**
30-00 Editorial					11,660	
33-00 Music					3,500	
34-00 Post Production Sound					3,175	
35-00 Titles & Graphics					2,500	
36-00 Stock Footage					2,700	
		TOTAL POST-PRODUCTION				**23,535**
37-00 Insurance					0	
38-00 General & Administrative					0	
		TOTAL OTHER				**0**

		Amount	Units	x	Rate	Sub-Total	Total	
Total Above-The-Line								11,431
Total Below-The-Line								57,993
Total Above and Below-the-Line								69,424
Contingency @ 10 %								6,942
	GRAND TOTAL							$76,366
ABOVE-THE-LINE								
		Amount	Units	x	Rate	Sub-Total	Total	
02-00 Script								
02-01 Writer's Salaries		5	Days	1	400	2,000	2,000	
	Payroll				2,000	360	360	
					Total for 02-00			2,360
03-00 Producers Unit								
03-02 Producer		14	Days	1	500	7,000	7,000	
	Payroll				7,000	700	700	
					Total for 03-00			7,700
04-00 Direction								
04-01 Director						0	0	
					Total for 04-00			0
05-00 Cast								
05-01 Lead Actors								
	Basketball star					0	0	
	Scientist	1	Day	1	380	380	380	
	Narrator (2x scale)	1	Hour	1	622	622	622	
	Agency fee @ 10%	1	Allow	1	622	62	62	
	Payroll				1,002	180	180	
	AFTRA				1,002	127	127	
					Total for 05-00			1,371

BELOW-THE-LINE						
10-00 Production Staff						
10-08 Production Assistants						
	Set PA	8 Days	1	150	1,200	1,200	
	PA/Script	1 Day	1	150	150	150	
	Payroll			1,350	243	243	
				Total for 10-00			**1,593**
13-00 Production Design						
13-02 Art Director						
	Prep	3 Days	1	325	975	
	Shoot	2 Days	1	325	650	1,625
13-03 Assistant						
	Prep	3 Days	1	125	375	
	Shoot	2 Days	1	125	250	
	Wrap	0.5 Day	1	125	63	688
	Payroll			2,313	416	416
				Total for 13-00			**2,729**
14-00 Set Construction						
14-06 Purchases (Bld. materials)		1 Allow	1	1,000	1,000	1,000
14-07 Rentals (Greens/drapery etc.)		1 Allow	1	1,000	1,000	1,000
				Total for 14-00			**2,000**
15-00 Set Operations						
15-01 First Grip						
	Prod. shot Shoot	1 Day	12	25	300	
	Talent Shoot	1 Day	12	25	300	600
15-02 Second Grip (Best Boy)						
	Prod. shot Shoot	1 Day	12	22	264	
	Talent Shoot	1 Day	12	22	264	528
15-04 Dolly Grip						
	Prod. shot Shoot	1 Day	12	22	264	
	Talent Shoot	1 Day	12	22	264	528
15-05 Craft Service						
	Prep	1 Day	6	13	78	
	Shoot	2 Days	12	13	312	390

Purchases		2	Days	1	100	200	200
15-06 Grip Rentals							
	Package	2	Days	1	250	500	500
	Dolly	2	Days	1	250	500	500
	Cartage	1	Allow	1	75	75	75
	Smoke cracker	1	Day	1	200	200	200
15-07 Grip Expendables		1	Allow	1	200	200	200
15-08 Box Rentals						0	0
Key Grip		2	Days	1	30	60	60
Craft Service		2	Days	1	25	50	50
	Payroll				2,046	368	368
					Total for 15-00		**4,199**
16-00 Special Effects							
16-05 Special Effects-Squishy Shoe		1	Allow	1	750	750	750
					Total for 16-00		**750**
19-00 Wardrobe							
19-01 Stylist							
	Prep (shoes/wrdrobe)	2	Days	1	350	700	
	Shoot	2	Days	1	350	700	1,400
19-04 Expendables		1	Allow	1	50	50	50
19-05 Purchases		1	Allow	1	100	100	100
19-10 Box Rentals		2	Days	1	30	60	160
	Payroll				1,400	252	252
					Total for 19-00		**1,962**
20-00 Make-Up and Hairdressing							
20-01 Key Make-Up Artist		1	Day	1	350	350	350
20-07 Box Rentals		1	Day	1	30	30	30
	Payroll				350	63	63
					Total for 20-00		**443**
21-00 Electrical							
21-01 Gaffer							

	Prod. shot Shoot	1	Day	12	25	300		
	Talent Shoot	1	Day	12	25	300	600	
21-02 Best Boy								
	Prod. shot Shoot	1	Day	12	22	264		
	Talent Shoot/Wrap	1	Day	14	22	308	572	
21-05 Purchases		1	Allow	1	350	350	350	
21-06 Equipment Rentals		2	Days	1	900	1,800	1,800	
21-10 Box Rentals								
	Gaffer	2	Days	1	30	60	60	
	Payroll				1,172	211	211	
					Total for 21-00			3,593
22-00 Camera								
22-01 Director/DP/Op								
Prod. Shot:	Prep	1	Day	1	1,000	1,000		
	Shoot	1	Day	1	2,000	2,000		
	Invoice fee @ 10%	1	Allow	1	300	300	3,300	
Talent Shoot:	DP/Op							
	Prep	1	Day	1	450	450		
	Shoot	1	Day	1	750	750	1,200	
22-03 1st Asst. Camera								
	Prep	1	Day	6	30	180		
	Shoot	1	Day	12	30	360	540	
22-06 Expendables		1	Allow	1	250	250	250	
22-07 Camera Package Rental								
Prod. Shot:	Arri 35-3PL (MOS)	1	Day	1	300	300		
	Prime lense set	1	Day	1	250	250		
	Cam. accessories	1	Day	1	450	450	1,000	
Talent shoot:	BetaCam Pckge.	1	Day	1	700	700	700	
22-12 Teleprompter/Operator		1	Day	1	450	450	450	
22-13 Video Assist/Operator		1	Day	1	800	800	800	
	Payroll				5,040	907	907	
					Total for 22-00			9,147
23-00 Sound								
23-01 Mixer								
	Talent Shoot:	1	Day	12	25	300	300	
23-03 Expendables (Batteries, etc)		1	Allow	1	100	100	100	

23-04 Sound Pckg (Incl. w/cam pckg)					0	0
23-06 Radio Mikes	1	Allow	1	150	150	150
Payroll				300	54	54
			Total for 23-00			604
24-00 Transportation						
24-03 Equipment Rental						
Production Van	4	Days	1	65	260	260
Set Dressing	4	Days	1	75	300	300
24-04 Gas & Oil	1	Allow	1	100	100	100
			Total for 24-00			660
25-00 Location Expenses						
25-09 Catering Service						
Crew Meals (2 days)	25	Meals	2	12	600	600
Tent/Tables/Chairs	1	Allow	1	100	100	100
25-17 Location Site Rental						
Gym	2	Days	1	1,000	2,000	2,000
			Total for 25-00			2,700
27-00 Film & Lab - Production						
27-01 Raw Stock (Film-Production)	3200	Feet	1	$0.46	1,472	
Sales Tax	1	Allow	1	1,472	121	1,593
27-02 Lab-Negative Prep & Proc.	3200	Feet	1	$0.19	608	608
27-03 Videotape Stock - Production						
BetaSP (20 min.)	8	Cass.	1	22	176	176
27-08 Telecine (sc. to sc.-circled takes @ 5:1)						
	4	Hours	1	350	1,400	1,400
27-09 D2 Tape Stock (1 hr.)	1	Allow	1	300	300	300
			Total for 27-00			4,077
30-00 Editorial						
30-08 Off-Line Editor	5	Days	1	450	2,250	2,250
30-09 Off-Line Editing System						
Non-linear	5	Days	1	400	2,000	2,000
30-10 On-Line System & Editor	12	Hours	1	450	5,400	5,400
D2 Record/D2+BSP playback						

30-11 On-Line Effects		4	Hours	1	300	1,200	1,200
30-12 Videotape Dubs/Stock & Transfers							
Prod. shot:	D2 to BetaSP	1	Allow	1	70	70	70
	Misc.	1	Allow	1	450	450	450
30-13 Screening Copies (VHS)		10	Cass.	1	12	120	120
30-14 Video Masters/Safeties/Textless							
	D2 Edit Master-10:00	1	Cass.	1	85	85	85
	D2 Safety (textless)	1	Cass.	1	85	85	85
				Total for 30-00			**11,660**
33-00 Music							
33-01 Composer		1	Allow	1	3,500	3,500	3,500
(All-In Package includes: Arrangers, Copyists,						0	0
...Musicians, Instruments, Studio,						0	0
Engineers, Stock, etc)						0	0
				Total for 33-00			**3,500**
34-00 Post Production Sound							
34-01 Spotting for Music/Sound Efx		3	Hours	1	150	450	450
34-05 Narration Record		1	Hour	1	200	200	200
34-14 Laydown		0.5	Hour	1	250	125	125
34-15 Pre-Lay		6	Hours	1	150	900	900
34-16 Mix		5	Hours	1	250	1,250	1,250
34-17 Layback		0.5	Hour	1	200	100	100
34-18 Stock/Dubs/Transfers (Video)		1	Allow	1	150	150	150
				Total for 34-00			**3,175**
35-00 Titles & Graphics							
35-01 Graphic Designer & Workstation							
	Package	1	Allow	1	2,500	2,500	2,500
				Total for 35-00			**2,500**
36-00 Stock Footage							
36-01 Film and Tape Clips Licensing		60	Seconds	1	45	2,700	2,700
				Total for 36-00			**2,700**
37-00 Insurance							
37-01 Producers Entertainment Package						0	0
Negative						0	0
Faulty Stock						0	0

Equipment			0	0
Props/Sets			0	0
Extra Expense			0	0
3rd Party Property Damage			0	0
Office Contents			0	0
37-02 General Liability			0	0
37-03 Hired Auto			0	0
37-04 Cast Insurance			0	0
37-05 Workers Compensation			0	0
37-06 Errors & Omissions			0	0
		Total for 37-00		0
			0	
38-00 General & Administrative Expenses			0	
38-02 Legal			0	0
38-03 Accounting fees			0	0
38-05 Telephone/FAX			0	0
38-06 Copying			0	0
38-07 Postage & Freight			0	0
38-08 Office Space Rental			0	0
38-09 Ofice Furniture			0	0
38-10 Office Equipment & Supplies			0	0
38-11 Computer Rental			0	0
38-12 Software			0	0
38-14 Messenger/Overnight			0	0
38-15 Parking			0	0
		Total for 38-00		0
Contingency @ 10%			6,942	6,942
GRAND TOTAL				$76,366
Total Above-The-Line				11,431
Total Below-The-Line				57,993
Total Above and Below-the-Line				69,424
		Check budget totals	76,366	76,366

INDUSTRIAL

Overview:

Industrial films and videos can be the sorriest little projects you ever laid eyes on. Or they can be artistic, interesting, and even well budgeted. Some are for training (<u>Service, Maintenance, and Assembly of Rear-Axle Components</u>). Others are for sales or promotions to the public (<u>BeautiControl - Cosmetics for your everyday</u>).

Whatever the project, the producer must ask the client, "What's the point?" Or, put a bit more delicately, "Who are we trying to reach, and what do we want to have happen?" Surprisingly, many companies are fuzzy on this, and you as the expert communicator get to help clarify and focus.

If the client's first question to you is, "How much for a 15-minute video?" you know you're dealing with a neophyte. It's like asking an architect, "How much for a house?"

Since a 15-minute video can be a talking head, shot in real time, and unedited (a few hundred bucks), or an extravaganza of live action, computer graphics, and original score (many thousands), it's a good idea to agree beforehand on the general amount of money a company wants to spend. You wouldn't want to be like the architect who spends weeks designing a mansion for a client who can only afford a tree house.

Once you know what the point of the piece is, and roughly how much the client wants to spend, you can finalize your deal on paper and start scripting.

This sample industrial budget is for an athletic shoe company that will introduce a new line of basketball shoes. The 8-minute video will be shown on funky old VHS players in the back rooms of retail shoe stores. The audience is salespeople, mostly young men in their twenties, who want to be entertained as they learn three or four key selling points they can use on customers.

02-00 Script

02-01 Writer's Salary

The Writer/Producer is hired to take the company's existing research and sales materials, and conjure up a concept that will drive the sales points home to the audience. He negotiates a day rate, which is smart, because several people in different departments must approve the script, and there may be twists and turns, even reversals, in the conceptual approach.

The approved script calls for 2 days of shooting. The first day is the product shot, in which the shoe is shot on 35 mm film in a number of situations in a gym. The second day is a comic scene between a basketball star under contract with the company, and an actor playing a scientist. This is shot on BetaSP video. There is also stock footage, and graphics intercut.

03-00 Producer's Unit

03-02 Producer

The Producer negotiates a flat day rate here as well. He estimates 4 days of prep, 2 shoot days, 5 days of off-line editing, 2 days of on-line, and 1 day of audio post. In truth, some of the prep time overlaps into his writing time.

His flat rate means he gets that rate no matter how many hours he may work in a day beyond a minimum of 8 to 10. It also means he'll be directing the one day of talent shooting for no extra money.

04-00 Direction

As mentioned, the Producer directs the talent day shoot. The product shot is directed by the Director of Photography.

05-00 Cast

05-01 Lead Actors
The basketball star is under contract with the company to appear in a specified number of promotionals and commercials, so his salary does not appear in this budget.

The actor playing the scientist is an AFTRA member (this is the only guild to which this company is signatory), and he receives day scale for non-broadcast.

The Producer finds him by calling a number of agents and asking for auditions. The auditions are taped on a VHS camera, so company officials may approve the casting.

10-00 Production Staff

10-08 Production Assistants
It would be helpful to have a Unit Production Manager or Associate Producer for a few days to help pull everything together, especially on the talent shoot day when the producer will be busy directing. But the company gets kind of cheap when it comes to staff.

They insist on hiring a PA who knows their operation, and can almost do the work of a UPM for a PA's pay. This person, the Set PA, is hired for 8 days (5 days prep, 2 days shoot, 1 day wrap).

A Script PA is hired for the talent shoot day to be a Script Supervisor. She takes time code notes, tracks all takes with the script, and watches for continuity. Had it been a more complicated shoot, the Producer would have insisted on a professional Script Supervisor, but he figures he can scrape by with a competent PA.

13-00 Production Design

13-02 Art Director
An Art Director is hired to make both the product shot and the talent shoot look great. The location for both is a gymnasium at a local

private school, chosen because it has one wall of gracefully arched windows that will look good in the background.

The Art Director meets with the Director of Photography and the Producer to discuss both shoot days.

The product shot is easier because it's all in close-sup, meaning everything in the background is out of focus. They agree on a plan to place an 8x10 panel of translucent material, a shoji screen of rice paper on a wood lattice, about 30 feet back from the shoe, and light it from behind. A smoke machine gives atmosphere to the scene, and other lights create shafts of light through the smoke and illuminate the shoe.

A second product shot places the shoe on a Greek style pedestal, with drapery in the background.

The talent shoot is tougher because these two guys, one of whom is almost 7 feet tall, are having a conversation in this huge, empty gymnasium, and the company doesn't want to light the whole place. In the scene, the scientist interrupts the star's practice by wheeling in a teacher's desk, a student's desk/chair, and a blackboard for an unlikely science lesson.

The set and lighting problem is solved by using several translucent "wild walls" placed at strategic points in the background and lit from behind. The arched windows are lit from outside (since the sun refuses to stay in one place during the shoot). Careful camera placement and lens selection lets the team get the best of the gymnasium setting without having to light the whole room.

It's a good example of how collaboration between Writer, Director, Art Director, and Director of Photography can get a great look for not a whole lot of money.

13-03 Assistant
The Art Director's Assistant helps throughout the prep and shoot, and is assigned the half day wrap (returning rented materials), on his lower rate.

14-00 Set Construction

14-06 Purchases
The wild walls need to be built, plus sundries purchased. The Art Director and Assistant do the labor.

14-07 Rentals
The greens, pedestals, drapery, and classroom furniture are rental items. They would ordinarily go into a Set Dressing budget, but to keep the Art Department's expenses in one category, they are placed here.

15-00 Set Operations

15-01 First Grip and 15-02 Second Grip
Key and Best Boy Grips show up on shoot days to help with lighting setups, dolly setup, and assist the Art Department. The "12" refers to the number of *pay hours*. Twelve pay hours is equal to 10 hours actually worked. Lunch is one half-hour, catered, and off the clock.

15-04 Dolly Grip
A dolly is used each shoot day for tracking shots. The Dolly Grip sets up and operates the dolly.

15-05 Craft Service
The Craft Service person preps for a half day, buying groceries, and works for 2 days. The grocery bill is $100 per day.

15-06 Grip Rentals
The Grip Package includes all the C-stands, camera flags, sand bags, and Hi-Roller stands that the Electric Department needs to position and focus lights both inside and outside the building.

The smoke machine also comes out of this budget.

The dolly is a Fisher 10 that is picked up and delivered by the dolly company.

15-07 Grip Expendables

This is the tape, black wrap and other items purchased by the Grip Department for the shoot. Some producers make it a habit to claim what's left over at the end of the shoot for the production company, since it is technically owned by the company. If you've got the storage space, it's a good idea, since the stuff adds up.

16-00 Special Effects

16-05 Special Effects Package

A special prop is needed for the talent shoot. A competitor's shoe (the brand name is masked) is rigged so that a vile green jelly will squish out from the heel when the basketball star squeezes it. A special effects company charges $750 to rig up two shoes that can be refilled for multiple takes.

19-00 Wardrobe

19-01 Stylist

A Costume Designer is replaced by a Stylist for this shoot. She gathers the wardrobe together for the basketball star, and the white lab coat for the scientist.

Most importantly, however, she coordinates with the company about the shoes. The shoe, after all, is the "hero." This is why the product shot is also known as the "hero shot" - glorified with all the lighting, touch-up, and attention given to a hero. The right shoe must be confirmed (left or right), in the right size, in the right colors, with the right laces tied the right way. Various paints and sprays are on hand should the hero need a touch-up of any kind. The pampering is endless, and were it not for the money involved, quite ridiculous.

There are company people, ad agency people, plus stylist, grip and lighting people, camera crew, and Director, all hovering over a dumb shoe. But everyone takes it quite seriously. It is, after all, a living.

20-00 Make-Up and Hairdressing

20-01 Key Make-Up Artist
For the talent day, make-up is needed for the basketball star and the scientist.

21-00 Electrical

21-01 Gaffer and 21-02 Best Boy
The Gaffer and Best Boy Electric come on for the two shoot days. The Best Boy is allowed 14 pay hours (12 work hours) on the second day to check inventory on the lighting package and return it to the rental company.

21-06 Equipment Rentals
The Director of Photography (for the product shot), the Director of Photography (for the video shoot of the talent), and the Producer/Director meet days before the shoot at the gymnasium to work out the lighting needs. The Producer gives the list to the lighting equipment company. On the first day of shooting, the Best Boy checks all the equipment for inventory and breakage, and drives the lighting truck to the location. On the last day, he returns all the gear, again checking inventory and breakage to make sure the production company is not charged for anything undue.

22-00 Camera

22-01 Director/Director of Photography/Operator (Film)
For the product shot, the DP is also the Director and the camera operator. The prep day includes the site survey, a meeting with the

company marketing executive about the look of the shoe, and planning for the shoot.

He is in a union, but since he works this job on a non-union basis, he agrees to a 10% invoice fee that will make up a portion of what he would have been paid for health and pension.

22-01 Director of Photography/Operator (Video)

The talent shoot is on BetaSP video. The entire job is not shot on 35 mm film because of expense. Also, the product shot, in addition to being used in the promotional, will be used in a commercial.

The difference between the film and video look is deliberate, and in fact will be enhanced in post when some of the video is played in black and white. It's a stylistic choice.

22-03 1st Assistant Camera

For the product shot, this person checks out the camera package on prep day, and on shoot day, loads the magazines, labels the film cans, checks focus, and helps the DP around the camera. There is no 2nd AC on this shoot.

22-07 Camera Package Rental

For the 35mm product shot, an Arri 35-3PL camera is rented. No sound is needed. A set of prime lenses and various camera accessories are also rented.

For the talent shoot, a Betacam package that includes a camera, tripod, sound mixer, fish pole, and shotgun mike, plus various accessories is rented.

22-12 Teleprompter

For the talent shoot, there are several pages of dialogue that both characters speak to camera. For the dialogue to each other, two monitors are placed just off the set, so each person can look over the other's shoulder and see the words. It looks as though they speak to each other, as long as they maintain eye contact with the monitors.

Eventually, they learn the lines anyway, and actually look at each other when they speak. It's better that way.

22-13 Video Assist/Operator
For the product shot, a video tap is attached to the 35mm camera and run to two monitors, one for the Director/DP, and one for the company and agency people. This allows everyone to see a semblance of the shot while it's happening, and hopefully prevents misunderstandings and expensive reshoots.

23-00 Sound

23-01 Mixer
For the talent shoot, a Mixer is on hand for the production audio.

23-06 Radio Mikes
Two radio mikes are rented for the talent.

24-00 Transportation

24-03 Equipment Rental
Two trucks are needed for this shoot—a production van to carry camera equipment and sundries, and a cube truck for the Art Department to carry furniture, lumber, drapery, etc. The lighting/grip truck is included in the package (21-06).

25-00 Location Expenses

25-09 Catering Service
Approximately 25 people per day eat lunch on the set for the 2 days.

25-17 Location Site Rental
The Producer makes a deal with the private school to rent the gymnasium for the 2 days, and throw in all the electricity, for a flat feeof $1,000 per day. That includes parking, access to bathrooms, a place for the meals, an office doubling as a dressing and make-up room,

and access to a telephone for local calls. The school is not in session, and is inside a gated area, so security is not needed.

27-00 Film and Lab—Production

27-01 Raw Stock (Film-production)
Here, 3,200 feet of 35mm film is brought. About 2,200 feet is shot at normal motion of 24 frames per second. That's about 24 minutes of actual shooting. The other 1,000 feet will be shot at 64 frames per second for a slow-motion effect. That's about 4 minutes worth of shooting.

27-02 Lab-Negative Prep and Processing
The 3,200 feet is cleaned and processed at .19 per foot.

27-03 Videotape Stock - Production
Eight 20-minute loads of BetaSP stock is used for the talent shoot.

27-08 Telecine
The 35mm film for the product shot is transferred to D2 videotape for editing and finishing. The process takes about 4 hours at a 5 to 1 ratio, since this is the final look for the hero shoe. The DP supervises the session (as part of his deal) with the Producer and a representative from the company.

30-00 Editorial

30-08 Off-Line Editor
It is critical that the Editor be experienced in cutting comedy, since timing of the cuts is often what provokes the laugh.

30-09 Off-Line Editing System
An AVID non-linear system is rented for the 5 days of editing, and a Beta playback machine is thrown into the package. Since there are 9 gigabytes of storage in the AVID package, no extra memory is required. (Each gig stores about 35-45 minutes of video and audio at medium resolution.)

In the Off-Line sessions, the Producer and the Editor follow the script, laying in the circled takes and building the show. The Producer records a narration scratch track that will be replaced by the real Narrator in the final Off-Line session. When it's done, it's laid off to VHS for approvals. After a few minor fixes, the Producer sends a copy of the show to the Composer for the score, and proceeds to On-Line.

30-10 On-Line System and Editor
This is a straightforward assembly of a clean EDL from Off-Line, so the Producer and Editor agree on the less expensive, more efficient A-Mode assembly procedure (See Chapter 3, Editorial 30-00). They are editing onto a D2 Edited Master from two sources, the D2 product shot reel, and the BetaSP source reels, BetaSP stock footage, and BetaSP with the narration audio.

30-11 On-Line Effects
An allowance of 4 hours is made for credits, laying in of title elements, and a few transition effects in On-Line.

30-12 Videotape Dubs/Stock/Transfers
A BetaSP dub, on recycled stock, is made from the D2 product shot for Off-Line editing. The Producer logs the takes, marking the appropriate time code. Similarly, he screens and logs the circled takes from the talent shoot.

The Producer has already selected the stock footage by screening it on VHS window dubs. The stock house transfers it to BetaSP, with about 10 seconds on the head and tail of each shot for editing handles.

30-14 Video Masters
A D2 Edited Master is created in On-Line. The D2 Protection Copy of the edited master is textless, just in case someone decides to use portions of the show for something else, or in case they decide to change the text. Without the textless master, the show would have to be rebuilt in On-Line to accommodate changes.

33-00 Music

33-01 Composer
Two guys with a garage studio (albeit a good one) are hired to compose the rock and roll score. They sit with the Producer and spot for music from the off-line cut. Then they compose from the off-line cut to get started, and finally, from the on-line cut to match all the music cues frame accurately. The score is a synthesizer bed with some acoustic work and live voices laid in on top.

34-00 Post-Production Sound

34-01 Spotting
After the Off-Line cut is complete, the producer sits with a Sound Editor at the audio post facility to spot for sound effects. There are a dozen effects, mainly to accent the stock footage, give authoritative sound design to the hero shot, and hit the comic moments from the talent shoot.

34-05 Narration Record
A voice-over actor is hired to narrate. He's in demand, and although the Producer tries to get him for AFTRA non-broadcast scale of $311, the agent insists on double scale plus a 10% agency fee.

The narration is recorded to BetaSP at the audio post house, after the Off-Line cut is approved except for minor fixes. The narration is then digitized and laid into the Off-Line cut. For On-Line, it becomes a source reel.

34-14 Laydown
The Edited D2 Master is brought to the audio post facility, where the production sound and narration are laid down to separate tracks on a multitrack tape.

34-15 Pre-Lay
In this editing session, the sound effects and music are edited onto separate tracks at the right places.

34-16 Mix
Now the levels of production sound, narration, music, and effects are balanced.

34-17 Layback
The fully mixed audio is now laid back onto the D2 Edited Master. Channels 1 and 2 have a full stereo mix of music, effects, dialogue, narration, the works. Music is also recorded onto Channel 3, and effects onto Channel 4. This way, if an executive decides later on to change the narrator's copy, and he probably will, it will only cost an arm to go in and remix. Without the separate M&E (music and effects), everything is married, and the producer would have to return to the Pre-Lay stage to rebuild the tracks.

35-00 Titles and Graphics

35-01 Graphic Designer and Workstation
There are only a few graphics in the piece, mostly text points that reiterate the narrator's main points about the shoes. Even so, they must be designed with panache, and created as separate elements to be rolled in the On-Line session. In an expensive session, the graphics would be recorded to D1, a component tape format ideal for high resolution and true colors. But cost is a factor here, so the text graphics are recorded to BetaSP, which will do.

36-00 Stock Footage

36-01 Film/Tape Clips Licensing
The Producer selects a total of 60 seconds of footage from old silent films to use as comedic punctuation. For non-broadcast use, the license fee is negotiated at $45 per second. The prep fee for selecting potential shots and transferring them to VHS window dubs for viewing is waived.

37-00 Insurance

Everything is covered under the shoe company's blanket production insurance policy. One less thing to worry about.

38-00 General and Administrative Expenses

These are part of the company's standard operating expenses.

MUSIC
VIDEO
BUDGET

Fringe assumptions:				MUSIC VIDEO		
Payroll Tax	18%			Shoot Days:	2	
WGA	13%			Location:	Local	
DGA	13%			Unions:	None	
SAG	13%			Production:	16mm film	
AFTRA	12%			Off-Line:	3/4 inch video	
Agency Fees	10%			Finish:	D2 video	
SUMMARY BUDGET						
02-00 Script					0	
03-00 Producers Unit					2,277	
04-00 Direction					4,556	
05-00 Cast					0	
			TOTAL ABOVE-THE-LINE			6,833
10-00 Production Staff					3,776	
11-00 Extra Talent					990	
15-00 Set Operations					2,714	
18-00 Property					200	
19-00 Wardrobe					400	
20-00 Make-Up and Hairdressing					1,003	
21-00 Electrical					4,347	
22-00 Camera					3,863	
23-00 Sound					1,314	
24-00 Transportation					400	
25-00 Location Expenses					1,950	
27-00 Film & Lab					5,129	
			TOTAL PRODUCTION			26,085
30-00 Editorial					8,600	
			TOTAL POST-PRODUCTION			8,600
37-00 Insurance					3,450	
38-00 General & Administrative					8,197	
			TOTAL OTHER			11,647
Total Above-The-Line						
Total Below-The-Line						6,833
Total Above and Below-the-Line						53,166
Contingency @ 10 %						0
	GRAND TOTAL					$53,166

	Amt.	Units	x	Rate	Sub-ttl	Total
ABOVE-THE-LINE						
02-00 Script						
02-01 Writer's Salaries					0	
				Total for 02-00		0
03-00 Producers Unit						
03-02 Producer	1	Allow	1	1,930	1,930	1,930
Prep: 5 Days						
Shoot: 2 Days						
Post: 10 Days						
Payroll	1	Allow	1	1,930	347	347
				Total for 03-00		2,277
04-00 Direction						
04-01 Director	1	Allow	1	3,861	3,861	3,861
Prep: 5 Days						
Shoot: 2 Days						
Post: 10 Days						
Payroll	1	Allow	1	3,861	695	695
				Total for 04-00		4,556
05-00 Cast						
05-01 Band members					0	0
				Total for 05-00		0
BELOW-THE-LINE						
10-00 Production Staff						
10-01 Unit Production Manager						
Prep:	5	Days	1	150	750	
Shoot:	2	Days	1	150	300	
Wrap:	1	Day	1	150	150	1,200
10-08 Production Assistants						
Prep:	5	Days	2	125	1,250	
Shoot:	2	Days	2	125	500	

	Wrap:	1	Day	2	125	250	2,000	
	Payroll	1	Allow	1	3,200	576	576	
					Total for 10-00			3,776
11-00 - Extra Talent								
11-02 Extras		12	Extras	1	75	900	900	
	Payroll	1	Allow	1	900	90	90	
					Total for 11-00			990
15-00 Set Operations								
15-01 First Grip		2	Days	1	450	900	900	
15-02 Second Grip (Best Boy)		2	Days	1	375	750	750	
15-03 Other Grips		2	Days	1	150	300	300	
15-06 Grip Rentals (Dolly)		1	Day	1	250	250	250	
Cartage						0	0	
15-07 Grip Expendables		1	Allow	1	100	100	100	
	Payroll	1	Allow	1	2,300	414	414	
					Total for 15-00			2,714
18-00 Property								
18-03 Purchases		1	Allow	1	200	200	200	
					Total for 18-00			200
19-00 Wardrobe								
19-02 Costumer						0	0	
19-05 Purchases		1	Allow	1	400	400	400	
					Total for 19-00			400
20-00 Make-Up and Hairdressing								
20-01 Key Make-Up Artist		2	Days	1	400	800	800	
20-07 Box Rentals		2	Days	1	25	50	50	
	Payroll	1	Allow	1	850	153	153	
					Total for 20-00			1,003
21-00 Electrical								

21-01 Gaffer	2	Days	1	450	900	900	
21-02 Best Boy	2	Days	1	375	750	750	
21-05 Purchases (Expendables)	1	Allow	1	200	200	200	
21-06 Equipment Rentals	1	Allow	1	1,750	1,750	1,750	
21-08 Generator	1	Allow	1	250	250	250	
Driver					0	0	
Fuel	1	Allow	1	50	50	50	
21-09 Loss & Damage	1	Allow	1	150	150	150	
Payroll	1	Allow	1	1,650	297	297	
				Total for 21-00			4,347
22-00 Camera							
22-01 Director of Photography (Director)					0	0	
22-02 Camera Operators (Director)					0	0	
22-03 1st Asst. Camera							
Prep	0.5	Day	1	450	225	225	
Shoot	2	Days	1	450	900	900	
22-04 2nd Asst. Camera	2	Days	1	375	750	750	
22-06 Expendables	1	Allow	1	250	250	250	
22-07 Camera Pckg Rental (Wknd)	1	Day	1	1,200	1,200	1,200	
Scoopic rental	1	Day	1	50	50	50	
22-17 Maintenance/Loss & Damage	1	Allow	1	150	150	150	
Payroll	1	Allow	1	1,875	338	338	
				Total for 22-00			3,863
23-00 Sound							
23-01 Playback	2	Days	1	300	600	600	
23-03 Expendables (Batteries, etc)	1	Allow	1	100	100	100	
23-04 Sound Package (Wknd)	1	Day	1	300	300	300	
23-05 Walkie Talkies (Wknd)	8	Units	1	12	96	96	
23-09 Sound Stock	1	Allow	1	10	10	10	
23-10 Misc./Loss & Damage	1	Allow	1	100	100	100	
Payroll	1	Allow	1	600	108	108	
				Total for 23-00			1,314
24-00 Transportation							
24-03 Equipment Rental							

Cube Truck		4	Days	1	75	300	300	
24-04 Gas & Oil		1	Allow	1	100	100	100	
					Total for 24-00			400
25-00 Location Expenses								
25-07 Permits		1	Allow	1	400	400	400	
25-08 Parking		1	Allow	1	100	100	100	
25-09 Catering Service								
	Lunches	30	Meals	1	10	300	300	
	2nd Meals (working)	30	Meals	1	5	150	150	
25-17 Location Site Rental		1	Allow	1	1,000	1,000	1,000	
					Total for 25-00			1,950
27-00 Film & Lab - Production								
27-01 Raw Stock (Film-Production)		5800	Feet	1	$0.32	1,856	1,856	
Incl. 200' Scoopic								
	Sales Tax	1	Allow	1	153	153	153	
27-02 Lab-Negative Prep & Proc.		5800	Feet	1	$0.15	841	841	
27-08 Telecine (16mm to BSP)(3:1)		6	Hours	1	350	2,100	2,100	
27-09 Video Tape Stock		3	Hours	1	55	165	165	
Sales Tax		1	Allow	1	14	14	14	
					Total for 27-00			5,129
30-00 Editorial								
30-08 Off-Line Editor		10	Days	1	400	4,000	4,000	
30-09 Off-Line Editing System		10	Days	1	100	1,000	1,000	
	Dissolve session	0.5	Day	1	700	350	350	
30-10 On-Line System & Editor		5	Hours	1	350	1,750	1,750	
30-11 On-Line Effects		1	Hour	1	300	300	300	
30-12 Videotape Dubs/Stock & Transfers								
	Audio Transfers	1	Allow	1	450	450	450	
	3/4" to BSP	3	Hours	1	40	120	120	
	3/4 inch edit stock	3	Hours	1	10	30	30	
	On-Line Misc.	1	Allow	1	450	450	450	
30-14 Safety Master		1	D2	1	150	150	150	
					Total for 30-00			8,600
37-00 Insurance								

37-01 Producers Entertainment Pckg	1	Allow	1	1,750	1,750	1,750
Negative					0	0
Faulty Stock					0	0
Equipment					0	0
Props/Sets					0	0
Extra Expense					0	0
3rd Party Property Damage					0	0
Office Contents					0	0
37-02 General Liability	1	Allow	1	1,700	1,700	1,700
37-05 Workers Compensation (payroll svce)					0	0
				Total for 37-00		3,450
38-00 General & Administrative Expenses						
38-05 Telephone/FAX	1	Allow	1	250	250	250
38-06 Copying	1	Allow	1	25	25	25
38-07 Postage & Freight	1	Allow	1	100	100	100
38-08 Office Space Rental	1	Allow	1	0	0	0
38-14 Messenger/Overnight	1	Allow	1	100	100	100
38-21 Production Fee (20%)	1	Allow	1	38,610	7,722	7,722
				Total for 38-00		8,197
Contingency @ 10%					0	0
GRAND TOTAL						$53,166
Total Above-The-Line						6,833
Total Below-The-Line						46,332
Total Above and Below-the-Line						53,166
				Check budget tot:	53,166	53,166

MUSIC VIDEO

Current Styles
Things have changed from the days of taking a song at its word and telling a story or doing a strict performance piece. The graphic image, the strong visual, even the surrealistic approach are popular today. Many directors rely on in-camera effects and filtration as well as the telecine process (Ursa as opposed to Rank) to bring out a more impressionistic look. Texture is big—anything to affect the image as it comes into the camera, such as putting Plexiglass in front of the lens and running sheets of water down, or flashing lightening, or using lots of reflective plastic sheeting in the background. People are having fun dreaming up ways to paint the image.

Markets
MTV is no longer the only game in town. There's Black Entertainment Television, The Box (request video), VH-1, and local affiliates running their own shows. In addition, there's the long form market, a sell-through video category of one-hour or so programs with inside interviews with the band, performance footage, back stage, and behind-the-scenes, and whatever other hodgepodge they can throw in.

Average Budgets
Music video budgets range all over the place. It is expected that an artist like Madonna will spend a million dollars. A smaller label will call in favors and produce a piece for $20,000 to $40,000. It's even possible to get something on the air for $5,000 or $10,000.

Guerrilla production tactics are common for the low-end projects (waiving insurance, nabbing locations without fees, permits, or clearances). Risky business. And record labels often want personal and location releases so they won't get sued.

Who Pays?
The record label cuts the checks to the production company, but the cost of production often comes as an advance against record sales.

Thus, the artist really pays for it—and the artists rarely gets paid for the shoot.

The Bidding Process
In commercials the producer gets a storyboard from an ad agency that represents the concept of the ad. You consult with your Director, do a budget (on the AICP form), and submit it as your bid. If you get the job, you get a fixed fee, and you are expected to come in on budget, unless they change concept on you in mid-stream.

In music videos, a record label may come to you and say, "We've got $30,000 in our marketing budget for this video, submit a treatment." You go to your Director and together work out the idea (usually one to five pages and maybe storyboards). Be careful here, since Directors in their zeal may design a concept way out of line with the budget. As the Producer, you need to bring the treatment and the budget into alignment. If you don't, you either go over budget to please the label, or you deliver a product that disappoints everyone. It's wiser to promise a smaller, more focused vision, and deliver a product that exceeds expectations. Have frank discussions with the record label, and the Director, to see eye-to-eye on concept and budget.

A *production fee* is usually entered in the budget as your company's profit. This can be as low as 10% and as high as 35% of the bottom line, but averages 15% to 20%. Since the label gives you a fixed fee, and most do not audit, you might be able to pad the budget a bit. What you don't spend is additional profit. Labels usually pay 50% up front, 25% upon completion of shooting, and 25% on delivery.

Do Record Co. Execs Visit the Shoot/Editing?
Yes, the head of the video department will probably show up. According to some of the producers with whom we spoke, some are a pain in the butt, and some are a pleasure.

Negotiating with Crews
There is a shifting rate for crew in music videos, meaning the same Gaffer, for example, might get $450 for 10 hours worked in a commercial, but expect $450 for 12 hours worked in a music video.

Typical are 14- to 16-hour days. Unions are rare in music videos, and rates are usually based on straight time for 10 hours worked, with time and a half from then on.

What Formats?
35mm film is not the only choice; in fact, many producers and directors prefer other formats. For example, 16mm is cheaper, and since the end medium is the small screen, the quality difference between 16mm and 35mm is not noticed by the average viewer. When budget won't allow even 16mm or Super 16mm (bigger film plane/cleaner image), there are still many alternatives, including Betacam (SP or oxide), 3/4 inch, Hi-8 video, Super 8 film, and even the Fisher-Price toy pixel camera for kids.

One producer with whom we spoke owns an old Canon "Scoopic" 16mm camera (also rentable at about $50/day). The Scoopic is a fixed lens news camera, no longer made. It is not a sync sound camera, but most shots for music videos are less than 30-seconds, and the Scoopic will hold sync for just about that long before it starts to drift. The editor can sync up the sound by matching lip sync or drum beat, or some obvious visual reference.

These days, it seems it matters less what you shoot on, it's what you shoot. Everything is feasible, even multiple format (mixing different films and tapes together in one piece). It's based more on the concept, and the budget.

Average Number of Shoot Days/Edit Days
For low budgets usually a day with the artist and maybe another day on other shots. If the Director wants to go out alone with a Bolex (16mm field camera) or Hi-8, fine. More days than that depend on the budget.

Music Playback
Most music videos do not record much, if any, dialogue or other production sound. On the contrary, they require music played back as the camera rolls, so musicians can lip-sync, and dancers can move to the right beat.

To make sure the music always plays back at the same speed, take after take, most producers like to use a Time Code Nagra and Smartslate. The music is then synced in Telecine and forever locked to picture through the edit process.

Budgets are not always there for Nagras, however, so producers use older, non-time code Nagras, or even CD players, and get adequate results. Some even use cassettes played on boom boxes, but cassettes tend to drift.

The record label provides the music source before the shoot, often on a CD. The producer then has the CD transferred to 1/4 inch for the Nagra playback, to 3/4 inch for Off-Line editing, and to D2 as the record tape, or Edited Master for On-Line editing.

Audio Post
The only time a producer would go to an audio post house is when there is other production sound, such as dialogue or effects, that needs extensive mixing. Most times, the music is the sole audio, and it has already been recorded to the D2 Edited Master from the fully mixed CD provided by the record label.

Telecine
The film to tape transfer is a vital element in music videos, since it is often here that texture and color are changed, sometimes to a radical degree. A 2: 1 or 3:1 ratio (3 hours of transfer time for every 1 hour of film being transferred) is considered standard. Allow more if highly opinionated record company executives are present.

Editing
Usually, producers skip the paper cut process, and go right into Off-Line editing. They present a rough cut for approval from the artist and the label. If there are important On-Line effects involved, the producer may include some of them, roughly done, in the approval cut.

Producers warn that Post (including Telecine) is every bit as important as shooting, and should be budgeted as amply as possible.

If the artist and/or label demands changes that are not part of the original concept, then the producer may want to renegotiate the terms.

Sample Budget
The sample budget is a moderate one in the $50,000 range. The group is a critically acclaimed band that has not broken out yet, which is why the record company is only laying out moderate dollars.

02-00 Script

02-01 Writer's Salary
The script, or concept, has been written by the Director, several times in fact. To his relief, it was finally given a green light by the record company. He gets no writing fee, it's all figured into his flat Director's fee.

03-00 Producer's Unit

03-02 Producer
Prior to the prep week, the Producer works with the Director to make sure the treatment can be shot for the money they guess the record company will pony up. He therefore starts budgeting the concept in its earliest phases. Once the treatment is approved, a budget is submitted. After the requisite amount of haggling, it is approved, and production is given a green light.

The Producer gets a flat 5% of the bottom line, which is low, but since he also is a partner in the production company, he gets a piece of the production fee, in this case, 20% of the bottom line (see 38-21).

The Producer sees the project through from prep to post and delivery.

04-00 Direction

04-01 Director
The Director's flat fee is based on 10% of the bottom line. He is responsible for the creative vision of the video, from concept to shooting to post. In this concept, the five-member band eats a huge breakfast together before playing a party at a surrealistic trailer park. The party guests emerging from the trailers are dressed as vagabonds and beatniks.

05-00 Cast

05-01 Band Members
The band members are the unpaid stars of the music video. It helps that they are enthusiastic about the concept.

10-00 Production Unit

10-01 Unit Production Manager
The UPM preps for 5 days, assisting the Producer in getting the location secured, the paperwork completed, the permit paid up on time, booking crew, organizing the casting session for the extras, and booking equipment. During the one-day wrap, he checks all the time cards for the payroll service and completes any other paperwork. He also supervises the Production Assistants during the wrap day as they return equipment.

10-08 Production Assistants
Two ace PA's are hired for prep, shoot, and one day of wrap to help the UPM and the Producer.

11-00 Extra Talent

11-02 Extras
The Party Extras are 12 actors hired on a non-union basis through an ad in the local *Dramalogue* (an actor's newsletter with casting

notices). The ad brings in about 50 candidates. The final 12 are selected for their ability to move to a beat, and their overall look. They are paid a flat $75 for a day's work, plus lunch.

15-00 Set Operations

15-01 First Grip, 15-02 Best Boy, 15-03 Other Grips
The three Grips, plus the Gaffer and Best Boy Electric, make up the five person crew. The Producer judged that this number would suffice for the two interior locations (the breakfast scene, and the trailer interiors), and the exterior party scene at the trailer park. There is a dolly and track to set up, and a modest lighting package.

15-06 Grip Rentals
The Fisher 10 dolly and track is picked up by a PA in the cube truck on the Friday afternoon before the first day of shooting, thus getting a two for one bonus by shooting on a weekend.

18-00 Property

18-03 Purchases
Various props are needed, including a statue of a Buddha, a small trampoline, a Ouija board, and an assortment of large paper hoops that party guests crash through in slow motion. Don't ask.

19-00 Wardrobe

19-02 Costumer
The wife of one of the band members pitches in to help select the thrift shop wardrobe for the party guests.

19-05 Purchases
There is $400 allowance for party clothes purchases.

20-00 Make-Up and Hairdressing

20-01 Key Make-Up Artist
A Make-up artist is hired for the two days at $400/day for 12 hours worked.

21-00 Electrical

21-01 Gaffer and 21-02 Best Boy
See discussion of crew in this budget at 15-01.

21-06 Equipment Rentals
The lighting package consists of a complement of tungsten lights, an open faced 750-watt "redhead," a 2,000-watt "blonde," several HMI 1200s, and two HMI "lightening strikes" for a lightening effect. It's a weekend deal, so they get two days for one.

21-08 Generator
The trailer park lacks sufficient power for all the lights, so a 350 amp generator is rented. The company tows it to the location Friday afternoon, and picks it up Monday morning.

22-00 Camera

22-01 Director of Photography and 22-02 Camera Operator
The Director handles both functions. He's a versatile guy.

22-03 1st Assistant Camera
The First AC preps the camera on the Friday morning before the shoot, making sure it's working properly, and that all the lenses and accessories ordered by the Director are in the package. On the shoot, he assists the Director with the camera functions.

22-04 2nd Assistant Camera
Primarily a "loader" person on this gig, the 2nd AC makes sure there is always a loaded magazine at the ready. He also changes the film, and labels all the reels.

22-07 Camera Package Rental

An Arriflex 2, with three 400' mags, a prime lens, and a zoom, plus sticks and standard accessories are in the package. It is on the weekend rate of two days for one.

The producer also rents a Canon "Scoopic," an old fixed lens news camera, and a cable release that allows the Director to go out for a couple days on his own shooting pixilated live action, like clouds racing across the sky.

23-00 Sound

23-01 Playback

The person who operates the Nagra in a music video is the playback person responsible for accurate playback of the music on every take.

23-04 Sound Package

A time code Nagra is rented on a weekend rate. With time code on the 1/4 inch audio, and code on the film, it will stay in perfect sync through telecine transfer to tape.

Some producers like to save a little money and rent a non-time code Nagra for playback. Since this 1/4 inch has no time code on it, a slate is used for each take, identifying the verse of the song. In Off-Line, the Editor then must hand-sync the action with the same verse on the 3/4 inch. It's the old-fashioned way, and it still works.

23-05 Walkie-Talkies

The extras for the party scene get wardrobe and make-up in a trailer about 300 yards from the set, and the lighting truck has to park about 75 yards away, so the eight walkies help the crew stay in contact during the shoot, and save a lot of wasted running back and forth.

23-09 Sound Stock

No recording is done during the shoot, but this line item reflects the cost of the 1/4 inch stock that is used to play back the music.

24-00 Transportation

24-03 Equipment Rental
A cube truck is rented for a day of prep (picking up the camera, dolly, wardrobe, etc.), for the 2 shoot days, and the wrap day to return everything.

25-00 Location Expenses

25-07 Permits
A city permit makes sure everything is legal and the Producer won't get hassled by an eager cop wondering what all the noise is about.

This brings out another point about shooting on location. The producer has already received permission from the residents of the trailer park, and even the residents of a nearby house, to make sure no one will be disturbed by the music and the activity of the shoot. Nasty neighbors can shut you down, so its good to douse any fires before they start.

25-09 Catering Service
The producer has contracted with a catering service to prepare food and drop it off at the set, thus saving a bit of money by not having to pay servers and setup charges. The second meal is pizza and soda.

25-17 Location Site Rental
The producer negotiates with the trailer park association and settles on a fee of $500 per day.

27-00 Film and Lab—Production

27-01 Raw Stock
Fourteen 400-foot loads of 16mm film (5,600 feet), and another 200 feet for the Scoopic.

27-02 Lab Negative Prep and Processing
The lab processes the negative and preps it for telecine.

27-08 Telecine
It takes about 6 hours to transfer the film to Beta SP in a scene to scene (color correction) session. That's a pretty good clip for almost 3 hours of film (a 2:1 ratio).

27-09 Videotape Stock
The Beta SP for the Telecine is about $55 for each of three one-hour tapes. The Director chooses BetaSP as the source reel stock because it is a component format with good color separation, making it perfectly adequate for a music video look and broadcast on TV. There really is no reason to spend extra money for a higher end stock like one inch or D2.

30-00 Editorial

30-08 Off-Line Editor
The Producer, Director, and Editor go right into Off-Line with no paper cut. It takes 8 days for a completed rough cut, and two days of fixes until approval is given by the record label and the band.

30-09 Off-Line Edit System
Since the Director knows pretty well what has been shot (he was looking through the viewfinder), they decide to save some money and rent a cuts- only 3/4 inch Off-Line system. It works fine to assemble the video, then they go to a dissolve-capable system for a half-day to create some dissolves and supers of one image over another.

30-10 On-Line System and Editor
The BetaSP's are the playback reels, and the D2 that was used to record the mixed music is now the record master. Including one hour of ADO, the 4-minute video comes together in a C-Mode assembly in about 5 hours.

30-12 Videotape Dubs/Stock/Transfers

The Audio Transfers refer to the transfer session that happened before the shoot. The Producer takes the CD with the fully mixed music and transfers it to three pieces of tape. First it goes to 1/4 inch to become the playback source for the Nagra in production. Then it goes to 3/4 inch as a playback source for Off-Line editing. Third, it goes to D2 to be used as the record master in On-Line editing. Now all three music tapes are operating off the same time code, and everything will likely stay in sync.

The BetaSP's from the Telecine session are dubbed to 3/4 inch for Off-Line. The 3/4 inch stock for Off-Line is recycled stock.

The "On-Line Miscellaneous" is a pad line for the sundry pieces of stock and dubbing that always seems to happen in On-Line. The Producer always pads liberally for this, and is always glad he did.

30-14 Safety Master

A D2 clone is made of the Edited Master as a protection.

37-00 Insurance

37-01 Producer's Entertainment Package and 37-02 General Liability

The producer's insurance broker arranges for a standard entertainment policy and liability for this size production and budget. The fact that it's a local shoot with crazy stunts keeps the cost down.

Workers' Compensation insurance is provided by the payroll service as part of its fee.

38-00 General and Administrative Expenses

A minimal amount is budgeted for general expenses like telephone and messenger. Just enough is allotted to meet these costs.

38-21 Production Fee

As its profit margin, 20% of the bottom line goes to the production company.

STUDENT
FILM
BUDGET

Fringe assumptions:				STUDENT FILM	
Payroll Tax	0%			Shoot Days:	4
WGA	0%			Location:	Local
DGA	0%			Unions:	None
SAG	0%			Production:	16mm film
AFTRA	0%			Off-Line:	3/4 inch videotape
Agency Fees	0%			Finish:	3/4 inch SP videotape

SUMMARY BUDGET			
02-00 Script			0
03-00 Producers Unit			0
04-00 Direction			0
05-00 Cast			0
	TOTAL ABOVE-THE-LINE		0
10-00 Production Staff			0
13-00 Production Design			25
15-00 Set Operations			50
17-00 Set Dressing			50
18-00 Property			100
19-00 Wardrobe			25
20-00 Make-Up and Hairdressing			25
21-00 Electrical			0
22-00 Camera			25
23-00 Sound			181
24-00 Transportation			0
25-00 Location Expenses			0
26-00 Picture Vehicle/Animals			0
27-00 Film & Lab			11,582
	TOTAL PRODUCTION		12,063
30-00 Editorial			230
33-00 Music			50
34-00 Post Production Sound			75
35-00 Titles & Graphics			25
	TOTAL POST-PRODUCTION		380
37-00 Insurance			0
38-00 General & Administrative			0
	TOTAL OTHER		0

Total Above-The-Line							0
Total Below-The-Line							12,443
Total Above and Below-the-Line							12,443
Contingency @ 10 %							0
	GRAND TOTAL						$12,443
	ABOVE-THE-LINE						
		Amt.	Units	x	Rate	Sub-ttl	Total
02-00 Script							
02-01 Writer's Salaries		6	Weeks	1		0	
					Total for 02-00		0
03-00 Producers Unit							
03-01 Executive Producer						0	0
03-02 Producer						0	0
	Prep	4	Weeks	1		0	
	Shoot	4	Days	1		0	
	Post	4	Weeks	1		0	
03-03 Associate Producer		9	Weeks	1		0	0
					Total for 03-00		0
04-00 Direction							
04-01 Director							
	Prep	2	Weeks	1		0	0
	Rehearsals	2	Weeks	1		0	0
	Shoot	4	Days	1		0	0
	Edit	4	Weeks	1		0	0
					Total for 04-00		0
05-00 Cast							
05-01 Lead Actors							
	Rehearsals	2	Weeks	4		0	0
	Shoot	4	Days	4		0	0
05-02 Supporting Cast							
	Rehearsals	1	Week	5		0	0
	Shoot	3	Days	1		0	0
05-03 Day Players (Shoot)		2	Days	10		0	0
					Total for 05-00		0

BELOW-THE-LINE							
10-00 Production Staff							
10-01 Unit Production Manager	5	Weeks	1		0	0	
10-02 Assistant Director	3	Weeks	1		0	0	
10-04 Production Coordinator	5	Weeks	1		0	0	
10-05 Script Supervisor	3	Weeks	1		0	0	
10-08 Production Assistants	4	Days	2		0	0	
				Total for 10-00			0
13-00 Production Design							
13-01 Production Designer					0	0	
Prep	4	Weeks	1		0	0	
Shoot	4	Days	1		0	0	
Wrap	2	Days	1		0	0	
13-10 Film	1	Allow	1	25	25	25	
				Total for 13-00			25
15-00 Set Operations							
15-01 First Grip							
Prep	1	Day	1		0	0	
Shoot	4	Days	1		0	0	
Wrap	1	Day	1		0	0	
15-02 Second Grip (Best Boy)					0	0	
Prep	1	Day	1		0	0	
Shoot	4	Days	1		0	0	
Wrap	1	Day	1		0	0	
15-04 Boom/Dolly Grip	4	Days	1		0	0	
15-05 Craft Service					0	0	
Purchases	1	Allow	1	0	0	0	
15-07 Grip Expendables	1	Allow	1	50	50	50	
				Total for 15-00			50
17-00 Set Dressing							
17-01 Set Decorator					0	0	
Prep	4	Weeks	1		0	0	
Shoot	4	Days	1		0	0	

	Wrap	2	Days	1		0	0	
17-05 Expendables		1	Allow	1	0	0	0	
17-07 Rentals		1	Allow	1	50	50	50	
					Total for 17-00			50
						0		
18-00 Property						0		
18-01 Property Master						0	0	
	Prep	1	Week	1		0	0	
	Shoot	4	Days	1		0	0	
	Wrap	1	Day	1		0	0	
18-03 Purchases		1	Allow	1	50	50	50	
18-04 Rentals		1	Allow	1	50	50	50	
					Total for 18-00			100
19-00 Wardrobe								
19-01 Costume Designer						0	0	
	Prep	2	Weeks	1		0	0	
	Shoot	4	Days	1		0	0	
	Wrap	2	Days	1		0	0	
19-02 Costumer						0	0	
	Prep	2	Weeks	1		0	0	
	Shoot	4	Days	1		0	0	
	Wrap	2	Days	1		0	0	
19-04 Expendables		1	Allow	1	25	25	25	
19-06 Rentals		1	Allow	1	0	0	0	
					Total for 19-00			25
20-00 Make-Up and Hairdressing								
20-01 Key Make-Up Artist								
		1	Day	1		0	0	
		4	Days	1		0	0	
20-02 Additional Make-Up Artist						0	0	
		1	Day	1		0	0	
		4	Days	1		0	0	
20-05 Purchases		1	Allow	1	25	25	25	
20-08 Film		1	Allow	1	0	0	0	
					Total for 20-00			25
21-00 Electrical								
21-01 Gaffer						0	0	

	Prep	3	Days	1		0	0	
	Shoot	4	Days	1		0	0	
	Wrap	1	Day	1		0	0	
21-02 Best Boy						0	0	
	Prep	3	Days	1		0	0	
	Shoot	4	Days	1		0	0	
	Wrap	1	Day	1		0	0	
21-03 Electrics		4	Days	2		0	0	
21-05 Purchases		1	Allow	1	0	0	0	
21-06 Equipment Rentals		1	Allow	1	0	0	0	
21-09 Loss & Damage		1	Allow	1	0	0	0	
					Total for 21-00			0
22-00 Camera								
22-01 Director of Photography								
	Prep	2	Weeks	1		0	0	
	Shoot	4	Days	1		0	0	
	Wrap (Telecine)	3	Days	1		0	0	
22-02 Camera Operator		4	Days	1		0	0	
22-03 1st Asst. Camera								
	Prep	1	Day	1				
	Shoot	4	Days	1				
22-04 2nd Asst. Camera		4	Days	1		0	0	
22-06 Expendables		1	Allow	1	25	25	25	
22-07 Camera Package Rentals		4	Days	1		0	0	
					Total for 22-00			25
23-00 Sound								
23-01 Mixer								
	Prep	1	Day	1		0	0	
	Shoot	4	Days	1		0	0	
23-02 Boom Operator		4	Days	1		0	0	
23-03 Expendables (Batteries, (		1	Allow	1	25	25	25	
23-04 Sound Package (TC Nagra)						0	0	
23-09 Sound Stock		4	Days	3	13	156	156	
					Total for 23-00			181
24-00 Transportation								
24-03 Equipment Rental								
Production Van						0	0	

24-04	Gas & Oil						0	0	
						Total for 24-00			0
25-00	**Location Expenses**								
25-07	Permits (Student waiver)								
25-09	Catering Service						0	0	
	Crew Meals (brown bags)						0	0	
25-17	Location Site Rental	2	Days	1			0	0	
						Total for 25-00			0
26-00	**Picture Vehicles/Animals**								
26-03	Picture Cars (4 student c	2	Days	4			0	0	
						Total for 26-00			0
27-00	**Film & Lab - Production**								
27-01	Raw Stock (30% off)	19,200	Feet	1	$0.26		4,992		
	Sales Tax			1	Allow	1	412	412	5,404
27-02	Lab-Negative Prep & Prod	19,200	Feet	1	$0.09		1,728	1,728	
27-04	Prep/Clean Neg for Telec	1	Allow	1	200		200	200	
27-08	Telecine (pix and sound to 3/4 inch)								
	One-light	24	Hours	1	157		3,768	3,768	
	to 3/4" @ 3:1								
	Sc. to Sc. to 3/4"S	2	Hours	1	157		314	314	
27-09	Telecine Tape Stock								
	3/4" (recycled)	8	Hours	1	10		80	80	
	3/4" SP	1	Allow	1	75		75	75	
	Sales tax				155		13	13	
						Total for 27-00			11,582
30-00	**Editorial**								
30-08	Off-Line Editor	4	Weeks	1			0	0	
30-09	Off-Line Edit System (3	4	Weeks	1			0	0	
30-10	On-Line System & Editor	2	Days	1			0	0	
30-12	Videotape Dubs/Stock & T	1	Allow	1	50		50	50	
30-13	Screening Copies	10	Cass.	1	12		120	120	
30-14	Video Master/Safety (3/4	3	Reels	1	20		60	60	
						Total for 30-00			230

33-00 Music						
33-01 Composer	1	Allow	1		0	0
(All-In Package includes: Composer,					0	0
Musicians, Instruments, Synth Studio.					0	0
Stock	1	Allow	1	50	50	50
			Total for 33-00			50
34-00 Post Production Sound						
34-01 Spotting for Music/Sound	2	Days	1		0	0
34-14 Laydown	1	Hour	1		0	0
34-15 Pre-Lay (Sound Edit)	10	Hours	1		0	0
34-16 Mix	8	Hours	1		0	0
34-17 Layback	1	Hour	1		0	0
34-18 Stock/Dubs/Transfers (V	1	Allow	1	75	75	75
			Total for 34-00			75
35-00 Titles & Graphics						
35-01 Grfx Designer/Workstatic	10	Hours	1		0	0
35-02 Stocks and Dubs	1	Allow	1	25	25	25
			Total for 35-00			25
37-00 Insurance						
37-01 Producers Entertainment Package					0	0
Negative					0	0
Faulty Stock					0	0
Equipment					0	0
Props/Sets					0	0
Extra Expense					0	0
3rd Party Property Damage					0	0
Office Contents					0	0
37-02 General Liability					0	0
37-03 Hired Auto					0	0
37-04 Cast Insurance					0	0
37-05 Workers Compensation					0	0
37-06 Errors & Omissions					0	0
			Total for 37-00			0
					0	
38-00 General & Administrative Expenses					0	
38-02 Legal					0	0
38-03 Accounting fees					0	0

38-03 Accounting fees					0	0
38-05 Telephone/FAX					0	0
38-06 Copying					0	0
38-07 Postage & Freight					0	0
38-08 Office Space Rental					0	0
38-09 Ofice Furniture					0	0
38-10 Office Equipment & Supplies					0	0
38-15 Parking					0	0
38-16 Storage (Equip./Supplies/Film/Tape)					0	0
				Total for 38-00		0
Contingency @ 10%						
GRAND TOTAL						$12,443
Total Above-The-Line						0
Total Below-The-Line						12,443
Total Above and Below-the-Line						12,443
				Check budget totals	12,443	12,443

STUDENT FILM BUDGET

Film and TV Departments across the country vary widely in their approaches to student projects. In some places, the school pays for 99% of expenses, the exception being food for cast and crew, and any sets, props, wardrobe or special equipment the school lacks. Other schools require students to put up money, sometimes as much as half the budget. Some produce half-hour films. Others go for five or ten minutes. Some crew up entirely from student ranks. Others get volunteer professional help.

Sometimes it all boils down to money. If you don't have much, design a shorter film. If you're really strapped for cash, plan long takes that don't require much internal editing. While it does lock you into a certain style, it'll save you a bundle.

Some students shoot on film and finish on film, the old fashioned way. At one school, students editing on an old linear 3/4 inch system got so sick of the degraded images (from going down a generation so many times), they went back to editing on film.

On the good side, many schools try to keep pace with technology by having equipment like time code capable cameras and sound recorders, film to tape transfer rooms, non-linear editing suites, and analog and digital post audio work stations and mixing rooms.

For the students using this book, the process of creating a budget is the same as for anyone else. It's an exercise in pre-visualizing the project, and estimating the needs. The only difference is, students get to put in more zeroes in the money columns. For that reason, students can benefit from reading other sample budgets in this chapter that may resemble their project.

In this sample Student Film budget, we have assumed the following: this is a ten minute dramatic story, shot on 16mm film, and finished on 3/4 inch SP. All the cast and crew are students, and at this hypothetical school, they follow the ants-on-a-cookie technique of ganging up on a project until the shooting is done. That way, many people get a taste of a variety of jobs.

02-00 Script

02-01 Writer
The 10-minute script tells a contemporary story of romantic intrigue. The time is the present, and the writer has been careful about writing scenes impossible for her to shoot, since she is also the Director.

03-00 Producer's Unit

03-01 Executive Producer
This is a faculty advisor overseeing the project.

03-02 Producer
Since there isn't any pitching to studios involved here, this job is mainly that of a Line Producer - someone who administrates the details of production, and makes sure the paperwork gets handled.

The entire project is completed inside one 16-week semester. The pre-production period is about four weeks. The shooting is in four days on two weekends. The post-production takes up another four weeks.

04-00 Direction

04-01 Director
If this is any one person's project, it's the Director's. She is creating the vision, the look, and feel of the film. She puts in almost as much time in pre-production as the Producer, but leaves him to final prep while she rehearses the actors for the final two weeks before shooting.

05-00 Cast

05-01 Lead Actors
Two young men and one young woman from the Theater Department are cast in lead roles. The other young woman's role is filled from an ad placed in the local professional casting weekly. The actress agrees to perform for free, plus a VHS copy of the finished film.

05-02 Supporting Cast
Two young men and two young women fill supporting roles, and to the Director's delight, a retired professional film actor agrees to play

the role of an older man just for the fun of it. Their rehearsals occur during the same two week period as the leads.

05-03 Day Players
Ten friends of the crew are recruited on the two shoot weekends to perform in bit parts and as atmosphere.

10-00 Production Staff

10-01 Unit Production Manager
For the four weeks of pre-production, and the four days of shooting, a student acts as the UPM, helping the Producer scout locations, get permissions from property owners, recruit crew members, reserve equipment, and do the budget.

10-02 Assistant Director
A student in the Directing class comes on as the AD, helping the Director during rehearsals to block scenes, and plan shooting schedules.

10-04 Production Coordinator
Many hands make light work, so this student comes on to help the UPM and the Producer handle pre-production.

10-05 Script Supervisor
This student sits in during rehearsals, because she's also in the Directing class and wants to watch. On set, she takes script notes, marks circled takes, and watches for continuity.

10-08 Production Assistants
Two good friends of the Director agree to schlep and go-for during the shoot days.

13-00 Production Design

13-01 Production Designer
There are no sets to build, but this student wants to experiment with as many colors and textures in the existing locations as possible, to create different moods that further the story. He therefore spends about four weeks in pre-production scouting locations and rustling up set dressing and props.

15-00 Set Operations

15-01 First Grip - 15-02 Best Boy (Grip) - 15-04 Dolly Grip
These three students are Cinematography majors, helping out with the grip and dolly work.

15-05 Craft Services
Everyone chips into a kitty for on set munchies.

15-07 Grip Expendables
Tape, black wrap, gels, and other grip/electric expendables are provided by the school.

17-00 Set Dressing

17-01 Set Decorator
This is a student working with the Production Designer helping out with choosing and hauling set pieces and props.

17-05 Expendables
Sundry paints, supplies, sewing machine, etc., are provided by the school.

17-07 Rentals
The school provides an allowance of $50 to help with the rental of an opulent looking dining room set for an important formal dinner scene.

18-00 Property

18-01 Property Master
This student, also a Production Design major, helps the Production Designer and the Set Decorator organize props.

18-03 Purchases
The school allows $75 toward purchases of food used as props in the formal dining scene.

18-04 Rentals
The school allows $50 toward the rental of an expensive looking silver plated dinner serving and place setting set.

19-00 Wardrobe

19-01 Costume Designer and 19-02 Costumer
These two students volunteer to coordinate wardrobe among all the actors. Actors mostly use their own clothes, but the color schemes and textures become part of the overall production design, and require attention.

19-04 Expendables
The school allows $50 toward sewing supplies and fabric, as several actors need to be draped for a dream scene.

19-06 Rentals
The school allows $50 to rent several police costumes.

20-00 Make-Up and Hairdressing

20-01 Key Make-Up Artist and 20-02 Assistant
These two students from the Theater Department volunteer for film make-up.

20-05 Purchases
Make-up supplies.

21-00 Electrical

21-01 Gaffer and 21-02 Best Boy
Two more from the Cinematography Department help out with lighting. They prep by scouting the locations and organizing the lighting package for each shoot day, per the Director of Photography's instructions.

21-03 Electrics
Two more Cinematography majors drop in for shooting days to help light the shots.

21-05 Purchases
The school supplies some money for new bulbs, and to repair some bad connections.

21-06 Equipment Rentals
The school supplies all lighting gear except for HMI lights, which must be rented at a discount over the two weekends.

22-00 Camera

22-01 Director of Photography
The DP is also from the Cinematography Department. He helps scout locations during prep, and drops in on rehearsals to see how the blocking will work for each scene.

22-02 Camera Operator
A student specializing in Cinematography comes on for the four shoot days .

22-03 1st Assistant Camera
Preps the camera to make sure everything is working, and the package is complete, then comes for the shoot.

22-04 2nd Assistant Camera
Drops in for the shot days only.

22-06 Expendables
The school supplies an allowance for tape and other camera supplies.

22-07 Camera Package
The entire package comes right out of the school equipment room. It's an Arriflex 16 SR3 16mm sound camera with time code, three 400' magazines, a set of prime lenses, tripod, and accessories. There's even a video tap which helps everyone visualize the shots as they're rolling.

23-00 Sound

23-01 Mixer
The Mixer checks out the locations on prep day, gets stock, and organizes the gear.

23-02 Boom Operator
The Boom Op signs on for the shoot days to handle the fish pole.

23-02 Expendables
Batteries etc. are provided by the school.

23-04 Sound Package
A Nagra with time code, shotgun mike, and fishpole are provided.

23-09 Sound Stock
Cash is provided for three reels of 1/4 inch stock for each of the four days.

24-00 Transportation

24-03 Equipment Rental
Two station wagons, and a borrowed pickup truck comprise the production fleet.

24-04 Gas & Oil
An allowance is provided by the school.

25-00 Location Expenses

25-07 Permits
Permits are routinely waived by the city for student projects.

25-09 Catering
A euphemism for brown bag lunches.

25-17 Location Site Rental
They luck out. One of the student's parents owns a large house and actually allows the crew in for the dining room scene. They must remove the owner's dining table, however, and replace it with the rental. All other locations are student apartments, houses, and exterior locations.

26-00 Picture Vehicles

26-03 Picture Cars
Four of the wealthier student's cars are borrowed for an exterior scene in front of the large house.

27-00 Film & Lab - Production

27-01 Raw   Stock (Production)
The Producer and Director estimate that over the four days, they

will shoot about two hours per day, using 48 four hundred foot rolls of film, for a total of 19,200 feet. The school has a standing 30% discount on raw stock and processing.

27-02 Lab - Negative Prep and Processing
The 30% discount also applies to processing.

27-04 Prep/Clean Negative for Telecine
Also discounted at 30%.

27-08 Telecine
The 16mm film and 1/4 inch audio is locked and transferred to 3/4 inch in a one-light pass. Those 3/4 inch tapes are used for the Off-Line editing.

After the Off-Line edit is done, and there is an Edit List, the Producer returns to Telecine, and transfers, with full color correction, only the final shots from the 16mm to 3/4 inch SP. Those become the source reels for both picture and sound, for the final edit.

The post-production facility takes off 30%.

27-09 Telecine Tape Stock
Recycled 3/4 inch tape stock is used for the Off-Line because it's just for editing purposes, not for the final master.

The scene to scene transfer goes to a 3/4 inch SP reel. A dub is made so two playback sources are available in On-Line.

30-00 Editorial

30-08 Off-Line Editor
A student with an emphasis in editing and post-production edits the 8 hours of material into the final 10 minutes, over an accumulated term of four weeks.

30-09 Off-Line Edit System
Next year the school is getting a non-linear system, but for now, the old 3/4 inch clunker has to do. At least it's free.

After the off-line cut is locked, a copy goes to the Composer for the score.

30-10 On-Line System and Editor
The same Editor moves into a more sophisticated edit suite with a better switcher. The playback sources are the two 3/4 inch SP reels with all the "selects," the final shots. The Edited Master is also on 3/4 inch SP. A copy of the final edit also goes to the Composer.

30-12 Videotape Dubs/Stock & Transfers
The school provides an allowance for miscellaneous dubs and stock.

30-13 Screening Copies
When the show is finished, ten VHS cassettes are made to show to faculty, and proud parents. Later, these copies will be used as calling cards to get jobs.

30-14 Video Master
The Edited Master is on 3/4 inch SP, with a safety copy, plus a third copy for the Composer as part of his deal.

33-00 Music

33-01 Composer
A struggling composer, not a student, agrees to compose the score in exchange for a stock allowance and a copy of the show on 3/4 inch SP. He delivers the music on DAT, ready for mixing.

34-00 Post Production Sound

34-01 Spotting for Sound Effects
The Producer and Director with a student Sound Editor and watch the show, picking out places for sound effects.

34-14 Laydown
The production audio from the Edited Master is stripped off and laid down to a multitrack tape.

34-15 Pre-Lay
Now the Sound Editor places the production audio, the sound effects, and the music at all the right places on the multitrack, so that sound and picture are synced.

34-16 Mix
In the Mix, the Sound Editor, with the Director and Producer, agree on the right levels for the production dialogue, sound effects, and music.

34-17 Layback
When it's done, the show is all mixed and ready to be laid back to the 3/4 inch SP Edited Master.

35-00 Titles and Graphics

35-01 Graphic Designer/Workstation
The school owns a Video Toaster capable of doing perfectly adequate effects and character generation. The Editor is also the Graphic Designer.

35-02 Stock and Dubs
An allowance is provided by the school.

37-00 Insurance
No insurance is provided.

38-00 General & Administrative Expenses
There are no allowances for offices, phones, legal or accounting services. It's up to the students.

APPENDIX

DESPERATE MEASURES
& MONEY SAVING IDEAS

1. Legal Services
To see what various contracts look like before you put your lawyer on the clock, check out <u>Film Industry Contracts</u>, written and published by John Cones ($89.95). (We make no guarantees.) Samuel French Books in Los Angeles has it (213) 876-0570. Or go to a university law library and take notes from among the volumes of entertainment industry contracts.

2. Obtaining Rights
Use your native eloquence and passion to convince a rights owner that your <u>earnest efforts</u> to get the project sold constitute sufficient consideration. Then you buy the option for a dollar (some money must change hands to make it legal). It's a perfectly valid option agreement.

3. Getting A Writer
When a writer (WGA or not) is eager to get his or her property produced, or just get some work, you can strike a "spec" deal. This means the writer:

A) becomes your partner and gets paid an agreed sum, plus a percentage of the "back end."

B) gets paid an agreed sum at an agreed time but no percentage. Or some combination of the above. What about the WGA? If a guild member chooses to work non-guild, it's not your problem. Just be up front about it.

4. Getting a Producer
Make the Producer your partner, and defer salary to "back end," or some future point. Or pay below rate and defer the balance. This approach can apply to anyone "above-the-line" on your project. It can work for "below-the-line" people as well, but they are not as used to the idea of not getting paid at the end of the day, so take it case by case.

5. Getting a Director

If the Director really wants to see the project made, or if it's a personal project, salary could be deferred until profits, if any, start rolling in. When you are starting out and producing low budget projects, you cannot afford to pay thousands of dollars to a Director (even if that's you!). DGA? Again, if a Director wants to work non-guild, it's his or her decision to make.

6. Getting Actors

• Student actors may be willing to work free.
• The American Film Institute (L.A.) has a deal with SAG, whereby its student's films can use willing SAG actors without charge.
• Use union or non-union actors and pay below scale (say $100/day). It's the actor's decision to work non-union.
• Check with SAG to see if your project qualifies for their Experimental Film Agreement. If your film is no longer than 35 minutes, and its budget is no more than $35,000, you may qualify. You may then use any willing SAG actors and defer salaries until the film is sold.

7. Getting a Dialect Coach

If you can't afford the real thing, buy a booklet and audio cassette instruction packet. Samuel French Books in L.A. (213) 876-0570, has them for about $18 in a variety of accents.

8. Getting a Choreographer

Music video producers on tight budgets often hire "choreographers" who are young people with great dance skills. Look into a local dancing school's classes. Be careful, however, since lack of experience with cameras can waste a lot of time.

9. Getting a Narrator

Narration for experimental films or "cause" projects has a cache to it. Actors often do it for love and/or recognition. Go to the biggest actor you can think of and ask if he or she will do it for minimum scale. You may be pleasantly surprised.

10. Getting a Production Assistant

When you're too broke to hire a PA, try the local college Film/TV Department and ask for volunteer "Interns," who work for the experience, and free lunch.

11. Getting Extras

For non-union projects you could pay below scale rates, or even just provide free cofee and doughnuts. Maybe throw in a free lunch. (Some people just want to be in–the movies!)

12. Getting a Sound Stage

Can't afford a sound stage? You can set up anywhere if all you need is a roof over your heads. Just run the studio checklist from Chapter 3 (12-00) on your proposed location (adding items like toilets, or honeywagons). Spend a minute standing silently — what you hear in the background is what you'll hear on your show. Is there an airport nearby? A kennel? A turkey farm?

13. Getting the Most from Your DP

Negotiate half-day rates for travel, which is pretty standard, but also ask the DP to throw in some prep or scouting at no extra charge. It's worth a try.

14. Getting Your Crew Fed

On low-budget shows, if you don't have enough people to warrant hiring a caterer, pass around the menu from a good local restaurant and have a PA take orders. Or, if it's tighter than that, say for a student film, order in a pizza.

15. Getting Film Stock

Film stock companies sometimes keep "short ends," "long ends," and "re-canned" film stock. Short ends are leftover reels with less that 400 feet per reel (they can be hard to use if they're too short). Long ends have 700 feet or more. Re-canned stock means they may have put the film in the magazine and changed their minds. Long ends and re-cans are used by productions big and small, but there are some possible snags. As mothers like to say, "Don't touch that, you don't know where it's been." Insist that the film be tested. The good stock houses do this anyway, processing a strip from each can at a lab to check for density levels, scratches, fogging, and edge damage. Testing is also the only way to verify what kind of film is in the can, since cans are often mislabled or de-labled in the field.

Also, if you are a student, some film and tape companies provide automatic discounts. If you are a member of Independent Feature Project (IFP) West or East, ask them about discounts for stock.

16. Getting Really Cheap Film Stock
Conventional wisdom says to buy decent stock no matter how broke you are. But what if even Beta oxide is too expensive? Some film and tape stock companies, or post-production houses, have re-cycled tape stock that has one or two passes on it. The tape should be checked for picture and audio drop outs, degaussed (demagnetized), and cleaned. Studio Film & Tape in Los Angeles and New York pioneered recycling tape, and markets it in all formats as ECOTAPE. If shooting with recycled stock sends shivers up your spine, you can certainly use it for Off-Line Editing.

17. Getting Composers and Musicians
Hire student composers and musicians from music schools. They may well do the job for only a sample reel and a credit, if you cover the hard costs of studios, instrument rental, cartage, tape stock etc. Yet another way is to ask the composer for any unreleased recordings you can license directly, provided the composer owns 100% of the publishing rights (sync and master rights).

18. Getting Music
If you can't afford to score with real musicians, then the composer records the score from a synthesizer. You then skip the Music Scoring Stage step, and go directly to Music Pre-Lay (see Ch. 3, Music 33-00 and Post-Production Sound 34-00).

19. Getting a Mix
If your "orchestra" is a combo of friends, and you can't afford a scoring stage, try packing into a friend's garage recording studio rigged for video projection. Remember, if you have not recorded a

synthesizer bed already locked to picture, the recording machine needs to be electronically locked to the picture, otherwise music cues may be out of sync. Consult an audio engineer at the audio sound house where you'll do your final mix.

If you did record a synthbed, and have transferred the music to a multitrack tape with time code, you are already synced to picture, and your combo can jam along to the synth — no picture or picture lock needed.

20. Getting ADR

For bare bones ADR, you need a quiet place, a film loop of each scene to be looped, or a video playback, some earphones, decent microphones, a decent recording machine such as 1/4 inch, multi-track, or video (Beta deck or better), and the ability to lock your recording machine to your picture. If you only have some small ADR to do, you could squeeze it in during the final mix. Be sure the Mixer knows all about it beforehand, and don't be too surprised if he looks at you in horror.

21. Inexpensive Narrator Recording

Some producers record the narrator with a Nagra or comparable recorder (or onto BetaSP videotape) in their shower stall, with blankets over the windows at four in the morning. A friend may also have a garage recording studio that will work.

22. Getting a Good Rate on Post

You can try to play one facility against another to get the bids down, but don't make up stories — all these people know each other, and word quickly spreads if you're faking low quotes. If the price is still too steep, sit down with the house of your choice and work out what services you can cut to fit your budget. Most houses are willing, and it they really can't do it, they may recommend a lower end house that can.

23. Getting Inexpensive Titles and Graphics

Can't afford time on a graphics work station or character generator? Art cards still work, and you can get quite creative, even wild, using simple press-on letters, paint, ink, and drawing tools. Talk over your ideas with your Editor. The art cards can be shot during your regular production period, while you're still renting your camera package, or you can shoot them during post-production on an overhead camera. The text images can be moved around on screen, and made bigger or smaller, in On-Line. We once saw an opening titles piece for a network sitcom done by a single artist painting one or two brush strokes at a time, and "clicking off" a few video frames. It was a great effect.

24. Getting a Graphic Designer for Less

If your graphics budget really is below standard for the kind of show you're producing, go to a Graphic Designer and say, "I have $2,000 (or whatever), do you want to get creative and take on the job?" If the Designer is busy, he or she will have to turn you down, but you may get back, "I'm swamped now, but in two weeks I'll have time. Can you wait?"

RESOURCES

Film/TV/Theater Bookstores

A note about production guides. Several enterprising companies publish thick, expensive books that list every conceivable local product or service a film or TV maker could wish for. They are called production guides, and they are usually worth every penny. Some of the better known are: the *LA 411 Production Guide*, the *Hollywood Reporter Blu Book*, and the *NYPG* (New York Production Guide). Other cities sometimes have their own, so check with local bookstores that carry film and TV books.

- **Larry Edmunds Books**
6644 Hollywood Blvd.
Hollywood, CA 90028
(213) 463-3273

Edmund's has a vast collection of professional books, including the above production guides. They take orders by mail.

- **Enterprise of Hollywood - Printers & Stationers**
7401 Sunset Blvd.
Hollywood, CA. 90046
(213) 876-3530
Outside CA. (800) 896-4444.

Enterprise stocks all kinds of production forms, contracts, budgets, script supplies, production boards etc. Ask for their $3.00 catalogue to order by mail.

- **Samuel French Theater and Film Bookshops**

7623 West Sunset Blvd.
Hollywood, CA 90046
(213) 876-0570

11963 Ventura Blvd.
Studio City, CA 91604
(818) 762-0535

45 W. 25 Street
N.Y., N.Y. 10010
(212) 206-8990

80 Richmond Street East
Toronto, Ontario, M5C1P1
Canada
(416) 363-3536

French's stocks a vast collection of film, television, and theater books, including the above-mentioned production guides. They also take orders by mail.

• **The Writers Computer Store**
11317 Santa Monica Blvd.
West Los Angeles, CA. 90025
(310) 479-7774

Books for producers and writers, as well as all kinds of production and scripting software.

DIRECTORIES

• Baseline, Inc.

838 Broadway
N.Y., N.Y. 10003
(212) 254-8235

8929 Wilshire Blvd.
Los Angeles, CA 90211
(310) 659-3830

Baseline is an on-line information company that provides subscribers with up to date entertainment industry news like projects in development, production, and post, budgets and grosses, production company services and personnel, release dates and distributors, and more. If you want to be included in their data bank, give them a call.

• Brooks Standard Rate Book
1460 Westwood Blvd. Suite 205
Los Angeles, CA 90024
(310) 470-2849

Contains all the daily and weekly union rates for actors, directors, writers, camera people, crew etc. as well as the contract conditions. Stanley Brooks has been publishing this book since 1958. He's got it down.

• The Industry Labor Guide
11717 Kiowa Ave., Suite 104.
Los Angeles, CA 90049
(310) 820-7601.

The Guide, like the Brooks Standard Rate Book, contains the most requested rates, rules and practices of all the major union agreements. If you're doing union projects, it's a big help.

• Hollywood Creative Directory
3000 W. Olympic Blvd.
Santa Monica, CA 90404
(310) 315-4815
Publishes the seven directories listed below. Although the name says "Hollywood," the books list companies nationwide.

The Hollywood Creative Directory: Lists all major production companies and studios, their creative executives and story development people, and each company's credits, plus addresses, phones, and fax numbers.

The Hollywood Agents and Managers Directory: Lists the agency and management names, addresses and phone numbers for performing, writing and directing talent.

The Hollywood Distributors Directory: Lists domestic and foreign distribution companies for TV and film, their sales and marketing staff, plus broadcast and cable networks.

The Hollywood Movie Music Directory: Lists composers, lyricists, music production companies, and clearance and licensing people.

The Hollywood Interactive Entertainment Directory: Lists title developers, publishers, products, released titles, platforms, new media, and key staff.

The Hollywood Financial Directory: Lists lending institutions, completion bond companies, entertainment attorneys, insurance companies and brokers, and the financial officers of studios and major production companies.

QuickPhone: A quick reference book listing just the names and phone numbers of the people in the creative, agents, and distribution directories.

TRADE PUBLICATIONS

- *Advertising Age*
6500 Wilshire Blvd., Suite 2300
Los Angeles, CA 90048
(213) 651-3710

- *American Cinetographer*
P.O. Box 2230
Hollywood, CA 90078
(213) 876-5080

- *Billboard*
5055 Wilshire Blvd., Seventh Fl.
Los Angeles, CA 90036
(213)525-2300

- *Film & Video*
8455 Beverly Blvd., Suite 508
Los Angeles, CA 90048
(213) 653-8053

- *Hollywood Reporter*
5055 Hollywood Blvd., Sixth Fl.
Los Angeles, CA 90036
(213) 525-2000

- *Location Update*
2301 Belleview Ave.
Los Angeles, CA 90026
(213) 461-8887

- *Millimeter Magazine*
5358 Melrose Ave., Suite 119W
Los Angeles, CA 90038
(213) 960-4050

- *Variety*
5700 Wilshire Blvd., Suite 120
Los Angeles, CA 90036
(213) 857-6600

MISCELLANEOUS RESOURCES

• Thomson and Thomson, a copyright search firm (800) 692-8833

• Breakdown Services
The CD (Casting Directors) Directory
1120 South Robertson Blvd., Third Fl.
Los Angeles, CA 90035
(310) 276-9166

If its open casting you want - up to hundreds of actors submitting pictures and resumes for roles in your project, call Breakdown Services. They'll tell you what to do. For a further discussion, see Chapter 2 , Pre-Production, under Casting.

• <u>The American Society of Cinematographers Manual</u>
is a portable compendium of technical information about shooting on film. It costs in the $50 range, but it's fully loaded. Ask at any of the bookstores above.

TRADE ASSOCIATIONS

• **Academy of Motion Picture Arts and Sciences**
8949 Wilshire Blvd.,
Beverly Hills CA.
(310) 247-3000
The library has Academy Players Directories (photos, names and agents for many hundreds of leading men, women, children, character actors, ingenues etc. The library is also a treasure house of film research material.

• **Academy of Television Arts and Sciences**
5220 Lankershim Blvd.
North Hollywood, CA 91601
(818) 754-2800
ATAS is primarily a professional membership and awards (the Emmy) organization, but it has a number or programs of interest to students and teachers, such as:

Student Internship Program: Students or recent grads spend a summer working as full-time, paid interns for prime time entertainment companies.

College Television Awards: Student projects in many categories compete for cash prizes.

Faculty Seminars: Annual three-day event in which film/TV teachers hob nob with heavy-hitters in prime time entertainment television.

• **American Federation of Musicians (AFM)**
1777 North Vine St., Suite 500
Hollywood, CA 90028
(213) 461-3441

• **American Federation of Television and Radio Artists (AFTRA)**
6922 Hollywood Blvd, 8th Floor
Hollywood, CA 90028
(213) 461-8111

- **American Society of Cinematographers (ASC)**
P.O. Box 2230
Hollywood, CA 90078
(213) 969-4333

- **American Society of Composers, Authors, & Publishers (ASCAP)**
7920 Sunset Blvd., Suite 300
Los Angeles, CA 90046
(213) 883-1000

- **Association of Independent Commercial Editors (AICE-West)**
c/o FilmCore
849 North Seward St.
Hollywood, CA 90038
(213) 464-7303

- **Association of Independent Commercial Producers (AICP)**
11 E. 22nd St., 4th Floor
N.Y. N.Y. 10010
(212) 475-2600

- **Association of Independent Commercial Producers (AICP-West)**
5300 Melrose Ave., Suite 104E
Hollywood, CA 90038
(213) 960-4763

- **Broadcast Music, Inc. (BMI)**
8730 Sunset Blvd., Third Floor
West Los Angeles, CA 90069
(310) 659-9109

- **Directors Guild of America, Inc.**

7920 Sunset Blvd.
Los Angeles, CA 90046
(310) 289-2000

110 W. 57th St
NY 10019
(212) 581-0370

400 N. Michigan Ave, Suite 307
Chicago, Illinois 60611
(312) 644-5050

• International Alliance of Theatrical Stage Employees (IATSE)

IATSE represents many different types of craftspeople and technicians spread across more than thirty unions. Since rates vary by geographical location, type of project, medium (film or tape), etc. we recommend contacting a reputable payroll service in your area that handles union personnel.
Los Angeles contact:
I.A.T.S.E. & M.P.M.O (AFL-CIO)
13949 Ventura Blvd.
Suite 300
Sherman Oaks, CA 91423

• International Television Association (ITVA)

6311 North O'Conner Rd., Suite 230
Irving, Texas, 75039
(214) 869-1112

For production, post, and crafts people working in corporate and industrial filmmaking. Local chapters hold seminars and meetings.

• Screen Actors Guild (SAG)

5757 Wilshire Blvd.
Los Angeles, CA 90036
(213) 954-1600

• Women In Film

6464 Sunset Blvd., Suite 530
Los Angeles, CA 90028
(213) 463-6040
A membership organization for men and women (but mostly women) with   offices in many major cities in the U.S. and Europe.

Members receive a monthly newsletter, and there are frequent meetings, breakfasts, mixers, and seminars to help people learn about the industry and network.

• <u>Writers Guild of America (WGA)</u>

8955 Beverly Blvd.
West Hollywood, CA 90048
(310) 550-1000

555 W. 57th St.
N.Y., N.Y. 10036
(212) 767-7800

CAMERA SPEED/TIME TABLES
(limited version)

The time it takes for film to pass through a camera or projector is useful to know when you are estimating how much film stock to buy and process. The figures below are for four of the most common speeds only: 16 frames per second (fps), 24 fps, 32 fps, and 64 fps. (24 fps is the speed for "normal" live action.) The range can go from 6 fps to 360 fps, but consult a book like the <u>ASC Manual</u> (American Society of Cinematographers) for the complete story. It costs in the $50 range, but it's loaded with information about shooting on film.

35mm film

Camera feet	16 fps	24 fps	32 fps	64 fps
50	:50	:33	:25	:13
100	1:40	1:07	:50	:27
200	3:20	2:13	1:40	:50
300	5:00	3:20	2:30	1:15
400	6:40	4:27	3:20	1:40
500	8:20	5:33	4:10	2:05
1000	16:40	11:07	8:20	4:10

16mm film

Camera feet	16 fps	24 fps	32 fps	64 fps
50	2:05	1:23	1:02	:31
100	4:10	2:47	2:05	1:02
200	8:20	5:20	4:10	1:23
300	12:30	8:20	6:15	3:07
400	16:40	11:07	8:20	4:10
500	20:50	13:53	10:25	5:13
1000	41:40	27:47	20:50	10:26
1200	50:00	33:20	25:00	12:30

COMMERCIAL BUDGET BIDFORMS

The Association of Independent Commercial Producers (AICP), and the Association of Independent Commercial Editors (AICE), have developed budget formats, called bidforms, that differ from those used in broadcast/cable television or feature films. We reprint blank bidforms below so you can see what they look like. For further information, contact either organization (see Appendix II - Trade Associations).

This bidform format reprinted courtesy of the The Association of Independent Commercial Producers (AICP).

ASSOCIATION
OF INDEPENDENT
COMMERCIAL
PRODUCERS

FILM PRODUCTION COST SUMMARY

Date May 27, 1993

Job No./Ref.	Job No./Ref.	
Director	Client	
Executive Producer	Product	
Producer	Art Director	
Director Photography	Writer	
	Executive Producer	
Set Designer	Producer	
Editor	Business Manager	
Pre-Light days	Commercial Title	
Pre-production days	1.	
Build/Strike days	2.	
Studio days	3.	
Location days	4.	
Location sites	5.	
	6.	

SUMMARY OF PRODUCTION COSTS		ESTIMATE			
1. Pre-production and wrap costs	Totals A & C				
2. Shooting crew labor	Total B				
3. Location and travel expenses	Total D				
4. Props, wardrobe, animals	Total E				
5. Studio & Set Construction Costs	Total F, G & H				
6. Equipment costs	Total I				
7. Film stock develop & print – No. ft. mm	Total J				
8. Miscellaneous	Total K				
9.					
10.	Sub-Total : Direct Costs				
11. Production Fee					
12. Insurance					
13. Director/Creative Fees	Total L				
14. Talent costs and expenses	Totals M & N				
15. Editorial and finishing	Totals O & P				
16.					
17.	GRAND TOTAL				
18. Contingency					

Comments

tm
Bidform

Page 1

	CREW	A: PRE-PRO/WRAP									B: SHOOT								
		ESTIMATE										ESTIMATE							
		Days	Rate	OTHrs	TOTAL	Days	Rate	OTHrs	TOTAL		Days	Rate	OTHrs	TOTAL	Days	Rate	OTHrs	TOTAL
1	Producer									51								
2	Asst. Director									52								
3	Dir. Photography									53								
4	Camera Operator									54								
5	Asst. Cameraman									55								
6	Outside Prop									56								
7										57								
8	Inside Prop									58								
9										59								
10										60								
11	Electrician									61								
12					'					62								
13										63								
14										64								
15										65								
16	Grip									66								
17										67								
18										68								
19										69								
20	Mixer									70								
21	Boom Man									71								
22	Recordist									72								
23	Playback									73								
24	Make Up									74								
25	Hair									75								
26	Stylist									76								
27	Wardrobe Attendant									77								
28	Script Clerk									78								
29	Home Economist									79								
30	Asst Home Economist									80								
31	VTR Man									81								
32	EFX Man									82								
33	Scenic									83								
34	Telepr. Operator									84								
35	Generator Man									85								
36	Still Man									86								
37	Loc. Contact/Scout									87								
38	P.A.									88								
39	2nd. A.D.									89								
40	Nurse									90								
41	Craft Service									91								
42	Fireman									92								
43	Policeman									93								
44	Wlfr./Tchr.									94								
45	Teamster									95								
46										96								
47										97								
48										98								
49										99								
50										100								

Sub-Total A
PT/P&W
TOTAL A

Sub-Total B
PT/P&W
TOTAL B

tm
Bidform

	PRE-PRO/WRAP MATERIALS & EXPENSES	ESTIMATE		
101	Auto Rentals			
102	Air Fares: No. of people ( ) x Amount per fare ( )			
103	Per Diems: No. of people ( ) x Amount per day ( )			
104	Still Camera Rental & Film			
105	Messengers			
106	Trucking			
107	Deliveries & Taxis			
108	Home Economist Supplies			
109	Telephone & Cable			
110	Casting: Call/Prep ⓐ Casting ⓐ CallBack ⓐ			
111	Casting Facilities			
112	Working Meals			
113				
	Sub Total C			

	LOCATION EXPENSES	ESTIMATE		
114	Location Fees			
115	Permits			
116	Car Rentals			
117	Bus Rentals			
118	Camper Dressing Room Vehicles			
119	Parking, Tolls & Gas			
120	Trucking			
121	Other Vehicles			
122	Other Vehicles			
123	Customs			
124	Air freight/Excess baggage			
125	Air Fares: No. of people ( ) x cost per fare ( )			
126	Per Diems: No. man/days ( ) x amount per day ( )			
127	Air Fares: No. of people ( ) x cost per fare ( )			
128	Per Diems: No. man/days ( ) x amount per day ( )			
129	Breakfast: No. man/days ( ) x amount per day ( )			
130	Lunch: No. man/days ( ) x amount per day ( )			
131	Dinner: No. man/days ( ) x amount per day ( )			
132	Guards			
133	Limousines (Celebrity Service)			
134	Cabs and Other Transportation			
135	Kit Rental			
136	Art Work			
137	Gratuities			
138				
139				
	Sub Total D			

	PROPS AND WARDROBE & ANIMALS	ESTIMATE		
140	Prop Rental			
141	Prop Purchase			
142	Wardrobe Rental			
143	Wardrobe Purchase			
144	Picture Vehicles			
145	Animals & Handlers			
146	Wigs & Mustaches			
147	Color Correction			
148				
149				
150				
	Sub Total E			

tm
BidForm

STUDIO RENTAL & EXPENSE - STAGE	No.	Rate	ESTIMATE	No.	Rate	
151 Rental for Build Days						
152 Rental for Build O.T. Hours						
153 Rental for Pre-Lite Days						
154 Rental for Pre-Lite O.T. Hours						
155 Rental for Shoot Days						
156 Rental for Shoot O.T. Hours						
157 Rental for Strike Days						
158 Rental for Strike O.T. Hours						
159 Generator & Operator						
160 Set Guards						
161 Total Power Charge & Bulbs						
162 Misc. Studio Charges (Cartage, Phone, Coffee)						
163 Meals for Crew & Talent (Lunch, Dinner)						
164						
165						
166						
167						
Sub Total F						

SET CONSTRUCTION CREW	ESTIMATE							
	Days	Rate	OTHrs	TOTAL	Days	Rate	OTHrs	TOTAL
168 Set Designer								
169 Carpenters								
170 Grips								
171 Outside Props								
172 Inside Props								
173 Scenics								
174 Electricians								
175 Teamsters								
176 Men for Strike								
177 P.A.s								
178								
179								
180								
Sub-Total G / PT/P&W / TOTAL G								

SET CONSTRUCTION MATERIALS	ESTIMATE		
181 Props (Set Dressing Purchase)			
182 Props (Set Dressing Rental)			
183 Lumber			
184 Paint			
185 Hardware			
186 Special Effects			
187 Special Outside Construction			
188 Trucking			
189 Messengers/Deliveries			
190 Kit Rental			
191			
192			
Sub Total H			

	EQUIPMENT RENTAL	ESTIMATE		
193	Camera Rental			
194	Sound Rental			
195	Lighting Rental			
196	Grip Rental			
197	Generator Rental			
198	Crane/Cherry Picker Rental			
199	VTR Rental: w/playback ( ) w/o playback ( )			
200	Walkie Talkies, Bull Horns			
201	Dolly Rental			
202	Camera Car			
203	Helicopter			
204	Production Supplies			
205	Teleprompter			
206				
207				
208				
209				
210				
	Sub Total I			

	FILM RAW STOCK DEVELOP AND PRINT	ESTIMATE					
		FOOTAGE	$/FT.	TOTAL	FOOTAGE	$/FT.	TOTAL
211	Purchase of stock						
212	Developing footage						
213	Printing footage						
214	Transfer to Mag.						
215	Sync/Screen Dailies						
216							
	Sub Total J						

	MISCELLANEOUS COSTS	ESTIMATE		
217	Petty Cash			
218	Air Shipping/Special Carriers			
219	Phones and Cables			
220	Accountable Cash Expenditures Under $15 Each			
221	External Billing Costs (Computer Accounting, etc.)			
222	Special Insurance			
223				
224				
225				
226				
	Sub Total K			

	DIRECTOR/CREATIVE FEES	ESTIMATE		
227	Prep			
228	Travel			
229	Shoot Days			
230	Post-Production			
231				
232				
233				
	Sub Total L			

TALENT	No.	Rate	Days	Tra-vel days	O/T hrs. 1½x	2x	ESTIMATE	No.	Rate	Days	Tra-vel days	O/T hrs. 1½x	2x	
234 O/C Principals														
235 O/C Principals														
236 O/C Principals														
237 O/C Principals														
238 O/C Principals														
239 O/C Principals														
240 O/C Principals														
241 O/C Principals														
242 O/C Principals														
243 O/C Principals														
244														
245														
246														
247 General Extras														
248 General Extras														
249 General Extras														
250 General Extras														
251 General Extras														
252 General Extras														
253														
254														
255														
256 Hand Model														
257														
258														
259 Voice Over														
260 Fitting Fees: S.A.G.														
261 Fitting Fees: S.E.G.														
262														
263 Audition Fees: S.A.G.														
264 Audition Fees: S.E.G.														
265														
Sub Total														
266 Payroll and P&W Taxes (%)														
267 Wardrobe														
268														
269 Other														
Sub Total														
270 Mark-up (%)														
Sub Total M														

TALENT EXPENSES	ESTIMATE		
271 Per diems: No. man/days ( ) x amount per day ( )			
272 Air Fares: No. people ( ) x amount per fare ( )			
273 Cabs and other transportation			
274			
275			
276 Mark-up			
Sub Total N			

434

	EDITORIAL COMPLETION	ESTIMATE		
277	Editing			
278	Asst. Editor			
279	Coding			
280	Projection			
281	Artwork for supers			
282	Shooting of artwork			
283	Stock footage			
284	Still photographs			
285	Opticals (incl. pre-optical)			
286	Animation			
287	Stock music			
288	Original music			
289	Sound effects			
290	Dubbing studio			
291	Studio for narration: No. hrs.( )			
292	Studio for mixing: No. hrs.( )			
293	Negative tracks			
294	Answer & corrected prints			
295	Contract items			
296	Film to tape transfer (incl. reprints & masters)			
297	Film to tape transfer (editorial fee)			
298				
299				
300				
	Sub Total O			

	VIDEOTAPE PRODUCTION & COMPLETION	ESTIMATE		
301	Basic crew: No. of men ( )			
302	Addl. crew: No. of men ( )			
303	Labor overtime			
304				
305				
306	VTR/Camera rental			
307	Addl. VTRs/Cameras			
308	Equipment overtime			
309	Special equipment:			
310	Special processes:			
311	Trucking			
312	Mobile unit			
313	Stock: rental( ) purchase( ) No. of hrs. ( )			
314	Screening			
315	On-line editing: No. VTR hrs. ( )			
316	Off-line editing: No. of hrs. ( )			
317	Videotape A/B roll preparation and stock			
318	Audio mix with VT projection			
319	Video air masters			
320	Video printing dupe			
321	3/4'' videocassette			
322	Tape to film transfer			
323	Markup			
	Sub Total P			

435

This bidform format reprinted courtesy of The Association of Independent Commercial Editors (AICE).

Association of Independent Commercial Editors Post Production Cost Summary

Bid Date:

Post Production Co.:	Agency:
Address:	Address:
Telephone:	Telephone:
Contact:	Client:
Editor:	Product:
Job #:	Agency Job #:
Production Co.:	Agency Producer:
Address:	Agency Business Manager:
Telephone:	Agency Creative Director:
Contact:	Agency Writer:
Director:	Agency Art Director:

COMMERCIAL IDENTIFICATION

Title: Length: Code #:

SCHEDULE

Shooting Date:
Dailies:
Edit Dates:
Due Date:
Material Required:

SUMMARY OF ESTIMATED POST PRODUCTION COSTS:

		ESTIMATE			ACTUAL
2000 Sound	Total				
3000 Opticals	Total				
4000 Laboratory	Total				
5000 Videotape	Total				
6000 Miscellaneous	Total				
7000 Labor (when applicable)	Total				
8100 SUB-TOTAL: DIRECT COST	SUB-TOTAL				
8200 Mark-up (%)					
8300 Creative Fee					
8000 TOTAL	TOTAL				
9100 Sales Tax					
9000 GRAND TOTAL	GRAND TOTAL				

Comments:

ASSOCIATION OF INDEPENDENT COMMERCIAL EDITORS · 150 EAST 74TH STREET · NEW YORK 10021 · 212 517 1777

Association of Independent Commercial Editors Post Production Cost Summary PAGE 1

2000	SOUND		ESTIMATE			ACTUAL	*TAX
2010	Narration Recording	(Hrs)					
2020	Dialog Replacement	(Hrs)					
2030	Music						
2040	Sound Effects	(Hrs)					
2041	Foley Studio	(Hrs)					
2042	Sampler/Synthesizer	(Hrs)					
2043	Digital Editing	(Hrs)					
2044	Sound Designer/Editor						
2050	Transfer & Stock						
2051	Visible Time Coded Cassettes	(#)					
2052	Prelay/Archiving	(Hrs)					
2060	Scratch Record/Mix	(Hrs)					
2070	Final Mix	(Hrs)					
2130	Audio Relay	(#)					
2131	Satellite/Digital Transmission	(Hrs)					
2140	Facility Overtime	(Hrs)					
2150							
		SUBTOTAL					

3000	FILM OPTICALS						
3010	Artwork						
3020	Projections	(#)					
3030	Title Prep & Photography						
3050	Color Stand Photography						
3070	Interpositive	(Ft)					
3080	Cynex/Wedges	(#)					
3090	Optical Testing						
3110	Optical Negative/Effects	(Ft)					
3120	Duping/Blow-ups	(Ft)					
3140							
		SUBTOTAL					

4000	LAB						
4001	Logging	(Hrs)					
4002	Trace Audio/Video EDLS	(Hrs)					
4010	Negative Prep & Management	(Scene)					
4011	Layout/EDL	(#)					
4020	Negative Develop + Print	(Ft)					
4030	Reprints	(Ft)					
4140	Video Dailies	(Ft)					
4150	Video Dailies Stock						
4160	Stock Footage Search + Fee						
4170	Pull Clips	(Hrs)					
4180							
		SUBTOTAL					

6000	MISC						
6010	Delivery + Messenger						
6020	Shipping						
6030	Editorial Supplies						
6040	Long Distance Telephone						
6041	Data Transmission Charge						
6050	Working Meals in Facilities						
6060	Air Fare						
6070	Per Diem	(Days)					
6080	Room/Equipment Rental	(Days)					
6081	Location Assistant	(Days)					
6090	Packing/Inventory	(Hrs)					
6100	Negative Insurance	(Weeks)					
6110							
		SUBTOTAL					

Association of Independent Commercial Editors Post Production Cost Summary

5000	VIDEO		ESTIMATE			ACTUAL	*TAX
5020	Film to Tape w/Color Correction: NTSC	(Hrs)					
5021	Film to Tape w/Color Correction: PAL	(Hrs)					
5030	Additional Machines	(#)					
5031	Frame Storer	(Hrs)					
5032	Steady Gate/EPR	(Hrs)					
5040	Ultimatte	(Hrs)					
5050	Time Compression	(Hrs)					
5060	Tape to Tape Transfers						
5100	Off-Line Edit Room	(Hrs)					
5101	Screen/Select	(Hrs)					
5102	Digitizing/Loading	(Hrs)					
5103	Off-Line Pre-Opticals	(Hrs)					
5104	Off-Line Conforms	(Hrs)					
5105	Off-Line Color Camera/Scanner	(Hrs)					
5106	Off-Line DVE	(Hrs)					
5107	Off-Line Graphics	(Hrs)					
5108	Graphics Designer	(Hrs)					
5110	Rough Cut Cassettes	(#)					
5111	Off-Line Work Material	(#)					
5112	Digital Media Storage	(Weeks)					
5130	On-Line Edit: NTSC	(Hrs)					
5131	On-Line Edit: PAL	(Hrs)					
5132	Interformat Edit	(Hrs)					
5133	Unsupervised Edit	(Hrs)					
5140	Additional Machines	(Hrs)					
5150	Digital Effects Equipment	(Hrs)					
5160	Digital Graphics/Paint	(Hrs)					
5161	Digital Graphics/Edit	(Hrs)					
5162	Digital Load/Unload	(Hrs)					
5163	Digital Graphics/CGI						
5180	Character Generator	(Hrs)					
5190	Color Camera/Animation Stand	(Hrs)					
5220	Tape Stock & Reels	(#)					
5230	Generic Master	(#)					
5240	Edited Master	(#)					
5250	Printing Dupe	(#)					
5260	Dubs	(#)					
5270	Finished Cassettes	(#)					
5280	Tape to Film Transfer						
5290	Videoprints	(#)					
5300	Standards Conversion						
5310	Satellite/Digital Transmission	(Hrs)					
5320	Facility Overtime	(Hrs)					
5330							
5340							
		SUBTOTAL					

7000	LABOR						
7010	Post-Production Management	(Hrs)					
7020	Editor	(Hrs)					
7030	Editor Overtime/Weekend	(Hrs)					
7040	Assistant Editor	(Hrs)					
7050	Assistant Editor Overtime/Weekend	(Hrs)					
7060	Travel Time	(Hrs)					
7100	Supervisory Labor	(Hrs)					
7110	Pre-Production						
7120							
		SUBTOTAL					

SERIES BUDGET

This section contains a sample budget, without commentary, of a thirteen episode series of half-hour programs. We include it because planning for a lot of production and post over a long haul, in this case seven months, requires serious thinking about resources and procedures.

This series has a magazine format with two eight to ten minute segments per episode. There is no studio. The host is on location in each segment, and does the intros and wraps from the field. A single video camera is used for most shooting.

SAMPLE BUDGET

13 - Episodes
24 - Segments
13 Wraps
61 - VTR Days
39 weeks of reruns

Production Period
7 months / 30 weeks

Acct #	Category Title	Page			Total
100	STORY RIGHTS/SCREENPLAY				0
101	PRODUCERS UNIT	1			227,020
102	DIRECTORS UNIT	1			163,586
103	CAST	1			153,698
	TOTAL ABOVE-THE-LINE				544,304
200	PRODUCTION STAFF	2			273,432
201	PROPERTY	2			4,000
202	SET OPERATIONS	3			13,725
203	WARDROBE	3			5,000
204	MAKE-UP/HAIR				0
205	VIDEO PRODUCTION	3			131,800
206	LOCATIONS	3			19,150
207	TAPE STOCK	3			23,600
208	PRESENTATION				0
209	TRANSPORTATION	4			8,040
210	TRAVEL, LODGING, PER DIEMS	4			126,900
	TOTAL PRODUCTION				605,647
300	GRAPHICS	4			35,000
301	POST PRODUCTION VIDEO	4			205,685
302	POST PRODUCTION SOUND	5			17,550
305	MUSIC	5			23,450
306	VISUAL RIGHTS				0
	TOTAL POST PRODUCTION				281,685
400	INSURANCE	5			26,000
401	LEGAL	5			15,000
402	GENERAL & ADMINISTRATIVE	5			113,810
403	PUBLIC RELATIONS				0
500	RESIDUALS	6			84,844
	Total Other				239,654
	Total Below-the-line				1,126,986
	Total Above & Below-the-line				1,671,290
	Grand Total				1,671,290

441

FILM & VIDEO BUDGETS / WIESE AND SIMON

SAMPLE BUDGET

13 - Episodes
24 - Segments
13 Wraps
61 - VTR Days
39 weeks of reruns

Production Period
7 months / 30 weeks

Acct #	Description	Amount	Units	X	Rate	Subtotal	Total
101	PRODUCERS UNIT						
101-01	EXECUTIVE PRODUCER						
			Allow		100,000	100,000	100,000
101-03	PRODUCER						
		30	Weeks		2,000	60,000	60,000
101-04	ASSOCIATE PRODUCER						
		30	Weeks		1,650	49,500	49,500
10-99	Total Fringes						
	Payroll Tax	16%			109,500	17,520	17,520
						Total For 101	227,020
102	DIRECTORS UNIT						
102-01	DIRECTOR						
	Show Director	13	Episodes		1,928	25,064	25,064
102-02	SEGMENT DIRECTOR						
	Segment Director	24	Segments	2	2,130	102,240	102,240
102-99	Total Fringes						
	Payroll Tax	16%			127,304	20,369	
	DGA	12.50%			127,304	15,913	36,282
						Total For 102	163,586
103	CAST						
103-01	HOST	13	Episodes		7,500	97,500	97,500
103-02	CELEBRITY GUESTS						
	Celebrity Guests	12	Segments		484	5,808	5,808
103-06	TALENT AIRFARE						
	Celebrity Guest	8	Segments		1,500	12,000	12,000
103-07	TALENT HOTEL						
	Celebrity Guest	8	Segments	2	150	2,400	2,400
103-08	TALENT GRND TRANSPORTATION						
	Host	12	Segments		150	1,800	
	Celebrity Guests	8	Segments		150	1,200	3,000
103-09	TALENT PER DIEM						
	Host	12	Segments	4	50	2,400	
	Celebrity Guest	8	Segments	4	50	1,600	4,000
103-99	Total Fringes						

APPENDIX

SAMPLE BUDGET   Page 2

Acct #	Description	Amount	Units	X	Rate	Subtotal	Total
103	CAST (CONT'D)						
	Payroll Tax	16%			103,308	16,529	
	Agent Fee	10%			5,808	581	
	AFTRA	11.50%			103,308	11,880	28,990
						Total For 103	153,698
	TOTAL ABOVE-THE-LINE						544,304
200	PRODUCTION STAFF						
200-03	PRODUCTION MANAGER						
		20	Weeks		1,000	20,000	20,000
200-04	SEGMENT PRODUCER #1						
		16	Weeks		1,250	20,000	20,000
200-05	SEGMENT PRODUCER #2						
		16	Weeks		1,000	16,000	16,000
200-06	FIELD PRODUCER #1						
		14	Weeks		1,000	14,000	14,000
200-07	FIELD PRODUCER #2						
		14	Weeks		1,000	14,000	14,000
200-08	RESEARCHERS						
	Researcher	12	Weeks	4	650	31,200	31,200
200-10	SECRETARY						
	Assistant to Producer	30	Weeks		500	15,000	15,000
200-11	RECEPTIONIST						
		30	Weeks		350	10,500	10,500
200-12	ASSISTANT TO EXECUTIVE PRODUCER						
		30	Weeks		600	18,000	18,000
200-13	RUNNER						
	PA #1	30	Weeks		350	10,500	
	PA #2	20	Weeks		350	7,000	17,500
200-14	LOCATION PA	12	Segments	2	125	3,000	3,000
200-16	POST PRODUCTION COORDINATOR	26	Weeks		1,000	26,000	26,000
200-17	TRANSCRIBING						
		24	Segments		750	18,000	18,000
200-18	TALENT COORDINATOR						
	Talent Booker	12	Weeks		1,250	15,000	15,000
200-99	Total Fringes						
	Payroll Tax	16%			220,200	35,232	35,232
						Total For 200	273,432

443

Acct #	Description	Amount	Units	X	Rate	Subtotal	Total
201	PROPERTY						
201-01	PROPERTY PURCHASE/RENTALS						
			Allow		4,000	4,000	4,000
						Total For 201	4,000
202	SET OPERATIONS						
202-01	CATERING	61	Days		125	7,625	7,625
202-02	CRAFT SERVICES	61	Days		100	6,100	6,100
						Total For 202	13,725
203	WARDROBE						
203-01	WARDROBE PURCHASE		Allow		3,500	3,500	3,500
203-02	WARDROBE RENTALS		Allow		1,500	1,500	1,500
						Total For 203	5,000
205	VIDEO PRODUCTION						
205-01	REMOTE FACILITIES						
	Equipment & Crew Package	61	Days		1,400	85,400	
	2 man Crew travel days	12	Segments		1,000	12,000	97,400
205-02	EXTRA TECH EQUIPMENT	61	Days		400	24,400	24,400
205-03	LIGHTING PACKAGE						
	Lighting Equipment/Labor	10	Days		1,000	10,000	10,000
						Total For 205	131,800
206	LOCATIONS						
206-01	LOCATION FEES	24	Segments		500	12,000	12,000
206-02	PERMITS/SECURITY						
			13	Episodes		550	7,150	7,150
						Total For 206	19,150
207	TAPE STOCK						
207-02	3/4" TAPE STOCK		Allow		750	750	750
207-03	BETA CAM STOCK						
	VTR – Segments	24	Segments	15	25	9,000	
	VTR – Wraps	13	Wraps	3	25	975	
	Editing		Allow		750	750	10,725
207-04	D-2						
	Stock Segments	24	Segments		200	4,800	
	Stock Masters	13	Episodes		200	2,600	
	Stock Final	13	Episodes		200	2,600	10,000
207-05	VHS STOCK		Allow		500	500	500

SAMPLE BUDGET   Page 4

Acct #	Description	Amount	Units	X	Rate	Subtotal	Total
207	TAPE STOCK (CONT'D)						
207-06	AUDIO STOCK						
		13	Episodes		125	1,625	1,625
					Total For	207	23,600
209	TRANSPORTATION						
209-01	GROUND TRANSPORTATION						
	Van rentals	12	Segments	6	70	5,040	
	Gas	12	Segments		25	300	5,340
209-02	EXCESS BAGGAGE	12	Segments		225	2,700	2,700
					Total For	209	8,040
210	TRAVEL, LODGING, PER DIEMS						
210-01	AIR FARES						
	Staff	12	Segments	3	1,800	64,800	
	Crew	12	Segment	2	1,100	26,400	91,200
210-02	HOTEL						
	5 Rooms x 3 nights per segment	12	Segments	15	125	22,500	22,500
210-03	PER DIEM						
	5 people x 50. per day	12	Segments	4	250	12,000	12,000
210-04	TOLLS, CABS, TIPS, ETC.						
		12	Segments		100	1,200	1,200
					Total For	210	126,900
	TOTAL PRODUCTION						605,647
300	GRAPHICS						
300-01	OPENING, CLOSE, BUMPER, ETC.						
	Opening Titles/Bumpers		Allow		20,000	20,000	
	Graphics		Allow		15,000	15,000	35,000
					Total For	300	35,000
301	POST PRODUCTION VIDEO						
301-01	SEGMENT EDITING						
	Off-line segment editing	24	Hours	24	110	63,360	
	On-line segment editing	16	Hours	24	250	96,000	159,360
301-02	COMPOSITE EDITING	13	Episodes	10	275	35,750	35,750
301-03	VIDEOTAPE TRANSFER/DUBS						
	Video Transfers	13	Weeks		350	4,550	
	Dubs Segments	150	Hours		25	3,750	
	Dubs Masters	13	Episodes		175	2,275	10,575

FILM & VIDEO BUDGETS / WIESE AND SIMON

SAMPLE BUDGET   Page 5

Acct #	Description	Amount	Units	X	Rate	Subtotal	Total
301	POST PRODUCTION VIDEO (CONT'D)						
						Total For 301	205,685
302	POST PRODUCTION SOUND						
302-03	SWEENTENING						
	Mixing	6	Hours	13	225	17,550	17,550
						Total For 302	17,550
305	MUSIC						
305-01	MUSIC LIBRARY						
	Music Library	13	Episodes		650	8,450	8,450
305-06	ORIGINAL ARTIST PACKAGE						
	Original Music		Allow		15,000	15,000	15,000
						Total For 305	23,450
	TOTAL POST PRODUCTION						281,685
400	INSURANCE						
400-01	INSURANCE		Allow		26,000	26,000	26,000
						Total For 400	26,000
401	LEGAL						
401-01	LEGAL		Allow		15,000	15,000	15,000
						Total For 401	15,000
402	GENERAL & ADMINISTRATIVE						
402-01	OFFICE SPACE						
	Office Rental	7	Months		6,000	42,000	
	Parking	7	Months	12	50	4,200	46,200
402-03	PRODUCTION RESEARCH						
	Research Costs		Allow		2,000	2,000	2,000
402-07	STATIONARY & PRINTING		Allow		2,500	2,500	2,500
402-08	OFFICE SUPPLIES	7	Months		800	5,600	5,600
402-09	TELEPHONE & FAX						
	Usage	7	Months		1,800	12,600	
	Installation		Allow		1,250	1,250	13,850
402-10	OFFICE EQUIPMENT/COMPUTERS						
	Office Pagers	7	Months	4	20	560	
	Office Computer Rentals	7	Months	10	200	14,000	
	Xerox	7	Months		800	5,600	20,160
402-11	POSTAGE	7	Months		150	1,050	1,050

SAMPLE BUDGET   Page 6

Acct #	Description	Amount	Units	X	Rate	Subtotal	Total
402	GENERAL & ADMINISTRATIVE (CONT'D)						
402-12	MESSENGER/MILEAGE						
	Mileage	7	Months	2	200	2,800	
	Messenger	7	Months		150	1,050	3,850
402-13	FED EX/UPS/FREIGHT	7	Months		750	5,250	5,250
402-14	VIEWING EQUIPMENT						
		7	Months		700	4,900	4,900
402-15	GIFTS & GRATUITIES		Allow		750	750	750
402-16	ENTERTAINMENT	7	Months		500	3,500	3,500
402-17	WORKING MEALS	7	Months		400	2,800	2,800
402-18	OFFICE FOOD & REFRESHMENTS	7	Months		200	1,400	1,400
						Total For 402	113,810
500	RESIDUALS						
500-01	DIRECTOR						
	Run #2	13	Episodes		964	12,532	
	Run #3	13	Episodes		771	10,023	
	Run #4	13	Episodes		482	6,266	28,821
500-02	SEGMENT DIRECTOR						
	Run #2	13	Shows	2	278	7,228	
	Run #3	13	Shows	2	222	5,772	
	Run #4	13	Shows	2	139	3,614	16,614
500-03	HOST						
	Host Runs #2 & #3	26	Episodes		353	9,178	
	Host Run #4	13	Episodes		235	3,055	12,233
500-04	GUEST HOST						
	Celebrity Guest Runs #2 & #3	26	Episodes		353	9,178	
	Celebrity Guest Runs #4	13	Episodes		235	3,055	12,233
500-99	Total Fringes						
	Payroll Tax	16%			53,287	8,526	
	DGA	12.50%			28,821	3,603	
	AFTRA	11.50%			24,466	2,814	14,943
						Total For 500	84,844
	Total Other						239,654
	Total Below-the-line						1,126,986
	Total Above & Below-the-line						1,671,290
	Grand Total						1,671,290

447

BUDGETS FOR GRANTS AND DONATIONS:
The Top Ten Do's and Don'ts

By Morrie Warshawski

Funders of non-commercial grant supported films and videos have a very different mind-set than investors. A savvy funder will read your budget like a book, hoping to find a romance novel and not a mystery nor a comedy. Keep in mind that most funders only rarely review film budgets. Their time is spent primarily on budgets from other types of endeavors in the arts and social services - ballet concerts, capital campaigns, programs for the elderly, etc. Begin with your generic production budget and then go through carefully to adjust for the following before submitting a grant proposal.

1. YOUR SALARY. Be sure to include some payment for yourself. Funders are suspicious when you either do not pay yourself, or underpay yourself. To compute your fee (and those of all other participants) use an amount that is fair and comparable for: a) the role you will play in the film; b) your level of expertise in that role; c) your region of the country.

2. CONTINGENCY. Most funders do not understand the concept of "contingency." Only include contingency with funders who have had extensive experience with film, or who specifically put contingency as a line item in their budget formats. Otherwise, just build in a fair contingency amount throughout your budget in all the line items.

3. TALENT. Do not use this word in a grant proposal. Funders equate talent with high budget Hollywood movies. List all people under a "PERSONNEL" heading and then specifically label the roles they fulfill (e.g. "actors," "director," etc.).

4. DISTRIBUTION. For a non-commercial project you must include at least some start-up costs to get distribution launched. I recommend allocating funds for: package design and production, VHS screening copies, press kits, production stills, and festival entry fees.

5. IN-KIND. This term refers to any goods or services that are donated to your project and for which you will not have to pay cash. Reflect these items in your budget to give funders a sense of the community support you have engendered. These items can include: free lunches for your crew, a 50% discount on editing rates, donation of a box of videotape cassettes, etc. Again, use the concepts of "fair and comparable" to decide how much these items are worth.

6. EQUIPMENT PURCHASE. Never! It is the rare funder that will let money go towards the purchase of equipment. Always show your equipment as being leased or rented - even if it costs more in the long run than outright purchase.

7. RED FLAG NOTES. Because many funders are unfamiliar with films, it is doubly important that you go through your budget item-by-item and look for anything that might call undue attention to itself. Some examples could include: a higher than normal shooting ratio, extensive travel costs, transfer from tape to film if there is no theatrical distribution in your narrative, etc. Mark each and every questionable budget item with a number or asterisk, and then explain them fully in a BUDGET NOTES section at the end of the budget.

8. STUDY GUIDES. Any program intended for non-theatrical educational distribution should build in a fee for creating at least a modest study guide.

9. FISCAL SPONSOR FEES. Non-commercial projects must use the non-profit status of a fiscal sponsor in order to receive tax-deductible grants and donations (unless the filmmaker has obtained his or her own non-profit status). Be sure to include at the end of your budget the fee that your fiscal sponsor charges. Currently, anything under 10% is considered a fair fee. Anything higher than that should get an explanatory note.

10. INCOME. Since most funders will provide only partial funding for your project, you must demonstrate how the rest of your budget will be raised. Create an "INCOME" section divided between these two categories: "Actual To-Date" and "Projected."

Within these categories you can list the actual and potential sources for funding your project (e.g. Foundations, Corporations, Individuals, Special Events, etc.). If you have given money out of your own pocket to produce the film then do not list yourself as a donor. Instead, lump your money under "Miscellaneous Individual Donations."

MORRIE WARSHAWSKI is a consultant and writer whose clients include film and video producers, arts organizations and foundations. He is the author of SHAKING THE MONEY TREE: HOW TO GET GRANTS AND DONATIONS FOR FILM AND VIDEO (also available from Michael Wiese Productions). Clients interested in working with Mr. Warshawski can contact him directly at:

Morrie Warshawski
6364 Forsyth Blvd.
St. Louis, MO 63105
Tele: 314.727.7880. Fax: 314.727.8122
E-Mail: MorrieWar@AOL.COM.

AUTHORS' PAGE

MICHAEL WIESE is a producer, director, and consultant with more than 26 years of experience in film, television, pay TV, and home video. He has executive-produced, acquired, developed, and/or marketed more than 300 video programs. His credits include *The Beach Boys: An American Band, Hardware Wars, Shirley MacLaine's Inner Workout,* and *Diet for a New America.* He is the author of six best-selling books.

DEKE SIMON is an award-winning writer and producer of informational, children's, and documentary programming for television and home video. His credits include *Help Save Planet Earth* and *Harley-Davidson: The American Motorcycle* plus specials for Fox, Paramount, ESPN, and PBS. He has received numerous awards, including two Emmy Awards.

INDEX

Narration Record, 80, 180, 277, 366
Narrator, 5, 25, 51, 68, 84, 94, 180-182, 269-270, 340, 364, 366, 412, 414
Negative, 54-56, 76, 78-80, 123, 143, 145-146, 150, 152, 158, 164-168,
    184, 251, 254-257, 259, 320, 322, 324-326, 328-329, 386, 406
Off-Line Editing, 53-54, 78, 144, 156, 158, 163, 180, 194, 268-270, 274-275, 277-
    278, 304, 306, 322, 324, 326-327, 338, 342, 356, 364, 366, 380,   386,
    388, 406, 414
Office, 12, 18, 24, 56, 58, 70, 74, 80, 106, 114, 138, 140, 153, 175, 192, 194, 196,
    229, 248, 250, 260, 270, 276, 278, 296, 304, 322, 330, 344, 362, 408
On-Line Editing, 54, 156, 158, 160, 270, 380, 388
Optical Effects, 33, 79, 152, 164, 166, 254-255, 326
Options, 15, 23-25, 36, 66, 82-83, 124, 411
Parking, 59, 71, 76, 80, 106, 136-137, 196, 249, 271, 302, 362
Payroll Service, 14, 16, 18, 37, 40, 44-48, 70, 78, 98, 150, 170, 172, 174,
    192, 295, 307, 382, 388, 425
Payroll Taxes, 18, 42, 44, 49, 70, 78, 92, 98, 231
Per Diem, 42, 44, 68, 78, 96, 98, 148-149, 234, 252
Permits, 57-58, 60, 76, 104, 137-138, 140, 248, 260, 342, 377, 382, 386, 404
Police, 60, 76, 88, 137-138, 140, 236, 248, 402
Polish Script, 67, 229
Post-Production, 5, 33, 50, 52, 54, 60, 78, 88, 126, 132, 135, 142, 144, 146, 152,
    154, 156, 162, 170, 176, 186, 188, 192, 194, 230, 254, 260, 268, 292,306,
    316, 322, 323, 324, 325, 326, 366, 400, 406, 414, 416
Power, 70, 106, 110, 112, 120, 271, 273, 302, 384
Pre-Dub, 80, 182-184, 258
Pre-Lay, 80, 152, 178, 180, 182, 186
Printmaster, 80, 184, 259
Processing, 55, 57, 59, 77, 81, 124, 142, 167, 318, 364, 387, 406, 414
Producer, 8, 13, 15, 17, 26-29, 32-33, 37, 40-41, 43-46, 50-52, 56, 58, 60,
Producer, 62-63, 66, 68, 80, 82, 86, 88-89, 94, 96, 98, 100, 104, 110, 123-124,
    146, 148, 152, 154-155, 157, 171, 174, 176, 178, 180, 182, 184, 189-190,
    192, 194, 196-198, 202, 228-232, 234, 236, 238, 240, 242, 244, 246, 248-
    249, 252, 254, 256, 258, 260, 268, 270, 272-278, 292, 294, 296, 298,
    302-304, 306, 316, 318-320, 322, 324-330, 338, 340, 342,354, 356, 358,
    360, 362, 364, 366-368, 378-380, 400-401, 404, 406, 408, 410, 412, 414,
    428
Producer's Unit, 32, 68, 86, 230
Production Assistants, 70, 103, 131, 194, 196
Production Coordinator, 40, 70, 102, 139, 194, 235, 253, 318, 400
Production Design, 32, 36, 44, 60, 70, 96, 106, 237-238, 240, 242, 252, 298, 340,
    356, 400, 402-403
Production Designer, 108, 114, 148-149, 247, 252, 294, 296, 298, 304, 400
Production Fee, 81, 100-102, 196, 234, 296-297, 378, 380-388
Production Office, 70, 102, 106, 194, 196, 248, 250, 260, 278
Production Staff, 32, 70, 88, 100, 192, 234, 270, 296, 318, 340, 356, 400
Projection, 77, 178, 180, 252, 414
Property Master, 73, 114, 241, 253, 402
Props, 31, 57, 61, 75, 80, 100, 110, 114, 121, 123-124, 240-241, 246, 252,
    382, 398, 400, 402
Publicity, 81, 123-124, 196, 279, 302, 318
Purchases, 61, 70-72, 74, 78, 102, 108, 114, 117, 239, 241, 244, 358, 382, 402
Radio Mics & Head Sets, 74
Rail, 68-69, 78
Raw Stock, 63, 78, 142, 144, 250, 320, 364, 386, 404, 406
Release Prints, 26, 54, 78, 164, 166-167, 186, 193, 254, 256, 258, 324
Research, 36, 66, 70, 82, 108, 190, 192, 198, 229, 269-270, 340, 356
Residuals, 17-18, 24, 28, 32, 68, 94, 98, 173-174

FROM
MICHAEL
WIESE
PRODUCTIONS

THE DIGITAL VIDEOMAKER'S GUIDE
by Kathryn Shaw Whitver

Digital video is a hot topic. The jargon is new and it's difficult to sort out what's real, what's likely to be achieved, and what's just hype.

Digital video (including Video CD) is expected to revolutionize the film and video industry in the same ways that audio CDs changed the face of the recording industry. Understanding digital video technology and taking advantage of its uniqueness is the foundation on which success in this industry will be defined.

The Digital Videomaker's Guide explores the creation of digital videos from concept to finished product.

Contents include:

- An overview of the digital video market including movies, music videos, educational products, and training videos.
- Explanations of the various platforms for digital video including CD-i, Video CD, CD-ROM, CD-based game machines, and interactive TV.
- The digital video studio.
- How to build a production team.
- The design, production, and manufacturing process.
- Information about marketing a finished title.
- How to copyright, duplicate, and distribute your title
.• Complete Bibliography and Resource Guide and more.

Kathryn Shaw Whitver is an award-winning technical writer specializing in digital technologies. She currently works for OptImage, a leading multimedia and software design company.

$24.95, ISBN 0-941188-21-3, Approx 300 pages, 5 1/2 x 8 1/4

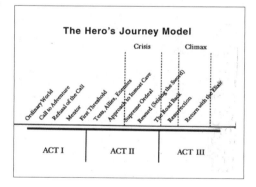

SOFTWARE

MovieMagic: Budgeting
Regular Price: ~~$595~~
MWP Price: $385

MovieMagic represents a major leap forward in budgeting software. Fast and flexible, Movie Magic: Budgeting has become the industry standard for producers, production managers, and estimators and other film professionals. Features include: "What-if" Functions, Database of rates, Globals for speedy entry, instant recalculation, chart of accounts, etc.

Requires:
Macintosh
•MacPlus or better including Classic, Classic II, SE, SE30, II, IIILC, IIX, IICX, IISI, IIci, IIfx, Quadras, Performas, Notebooks, etc.
•Minimum 512K RAM memory, 4 Megabytes (or more) recommended for use with System 7.
•Minimum system 6.0.5 or higher. System 7-friendly.
•Two disk drives; one may be a hard disk. •Any Macintosh compatible printer & most serial printers.
IBM
•Any IBM compatible with 384K RAM memory •DOS 3.1 or higher; DOS 5.0 recommended.
•Two disk drives; one may be a hard disk.
•A printer; it can be a dot matrix, daisy-wheel or laser printer. The printer must be able to print condensed fonts (15 to 17 characters per inch) or elite fonts (12 characters per inch).

FilmProfit
MWP PRICE: $99

Created by the former CFO of Lucasfilm, FilmProfit is a dynamic new spreadsheet program for the MAC or PC which enables you to track cash flow through all phases of distribution and generate reports for business plans and investor presentations. Features include: Income Revenue Projections for film, TV, home video, and foreign markets, "What If" Scenarios, Calculation of Distribution Fees, Producer's Financial Reports, etc. Great for business plans and projections!

Special Bonus! Includes a _free_ 100 page book titled, *The User's Guide to Film Distribution.*

Requires:
Macintosh •Hard disk • Microsoft Excel 3.0 or higher
PC •500K hard disk •DOS version 2.1 or higher

FREE BOOK CATALOG
CALL 1-800-379-8808

ORDER FORM

To order these products please call 1-800-379-8808 or fax (818) 986-3408 or mail this order form to:

MICHAEL WIESE PRODUCTIONS
4354 Laurel Canyon Blvd., Suite 234
Studio City, CA 91604
1-800-379-8808

BOOKS:

_____
_____
_____

_____

CREDIT CARD ORDERS

CALL 1-800-379-8808

OR **FAX YOUR ORDER**

818 986-3408

Subtotal $_____
Shipping $_____
8.25% Sales Tax (Ca Only) $_____

TOTAL ENCLOSED_____

Please make check or money order payable to
Michael Wiese Productions

(Check one) ____ Master Card ____Visa _____Amex

Company PO#_____

Credit Card Number_____
Expiration Date_____
Cardholder's Name_____
Cardholder's Signature_____

SHIP TO:

Name_____
Address_____
City_____State_____Zip_____
Country_____Telephone_____

SHIPPING

1ST CLASS MAIL
One Book - $5.00
Two Books - $7.00
For each additional
book, add $1.00.

AIRBORNE EXPRESS
2nd Day Delivery
Add an additional
$11.00 per order.

OVERSEAS (PREPAID)
Surface - $7.00 ea.
book
Airmail - $15.00 ea. book

Please inquire about discounts for organizations and groups. Special prices for professors and classroom adoptions.

Please allow 2-3 weeks for delivery.

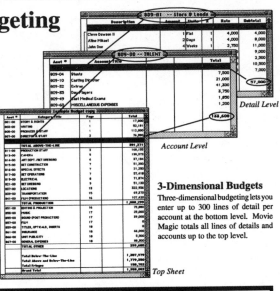
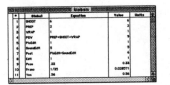

ABC Home Video announced that it has changed its name to **Audio Video Color Corporation**. The name change came as a result of the process of adding services to create a **"one-stop shop"**. AVC is now licensed by **JVC** and **Macrovision** (anti-copying process). In addition to pre-press electronic and design services, Audio Video Color has added a sound studio to assist clients in translating and dubbing domestic shows to foreign languages for the international market. The design department has been

After nine months of development, AVC has completed a customer service computer program based on management. The uniqueness of the program is that all clients will be able to connect to the computer system via modem and update their records on a daily basis, which will eliminate the need for a report. An additional 40,000 square foot warehouse space has been added to accommodate increased fulfillment services. With the addition of a sound studio, international dubbing ser-

Audio & Video Duplication
Fulfillment & Customer Service
Design & Packaging
Digital Color & Printing
Sound Studio

expanded to include ten computer stations equipped with Power PCs, Quadras, and Scitex-Prisma's in order to help clients bring their idea from the concept stage to finished product and mock-ups. AVC has also created a partnership with Specialty Box, a vinyl manufacturer, to attain more control of production of vinyl albums and to offer better

vices, customer service, expanded design services and the partnership with a vinyl manufacturer added to the existing divisions of video duplication, audio duplication, packaging and mock-ups, fulfillment, pre-press electronic and printing services, AVC is now a complete full service facility under one roof.

7045 RADFORD AVE
N. HOLLYWOOD, CA 91605
TEL. (818) 982-6800
FAX. (818) 982-0440

MACROVISION
Protecting your image

YES! THIS IS IT!

This tiny floppy disk can save you hundreds of hours in preparing all the budgets you'll ever what to make. The diskette contains all the budget formats found in the FILM & VIDEO ıUDGETS — 2nd EDITION book.

FILM & VIDEO BUDGETS – FORMATS DISKETTE

MWP PRICE: $25

Here it is. All in one place! All the budgets (including feature films, music videos, documentary, etc.) found in our FILM & VIDEO BUDGETS book, formatted on the Mac on Microsoft Excel®3.0 or 4.0 and ready to use for your projects. Save countless hours inputting! Only $25 for the diskette or, bundled with the book, $49.